"I do not know whether you know all
that is to be known concerning small
mirrors : but of this, silence."

Arthur Machen, in a letter to
James Branch Cabell. 17 Feb. 1918

"Writers are liars."

Erasmus Fry, in conversation, 6 May 1986

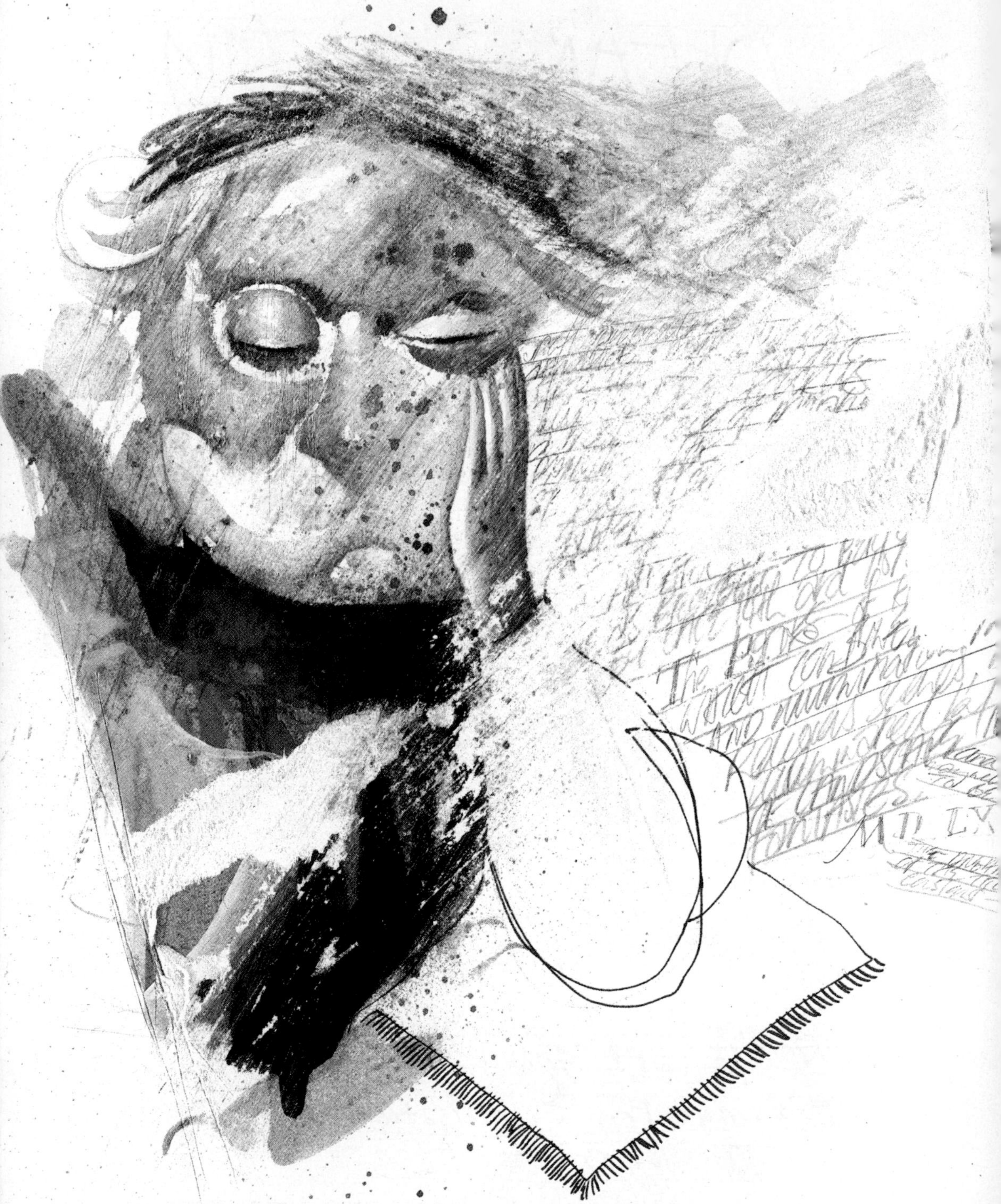

The SANDMAN™

DREAM COUNTRY

WRITTEN by NEIL GAIMAN

1.
calliope
ILLUSTRATED by
KELLEY JONES & MALCOLM JONES III

2.
a Dream of a Thousand Cats
ILLUSTRATED by
KELLEY JONES & MALCOLM JONES III

3.
a Midsummer Night's Dream
ILLUSTRATED by
CHARLES VESS

4.
FAÇADE
ILLUSTRATED by
COLLEEN DORAN & MALCOLM JONES III

ORIGINAL SCRIPT of CALLIOPE
by NEIL GAIMAN

FEATURING CHARACTERS
CREATED by
NEIL GAIMAN, SAM KIETH & MIKE DRINGENBERG

THE SANDMAN: DREAM COUNTRY

Published by DC Comics. Cover and compilation
Copyright © 2010 DC Comics. All Rights Reserved.
Introduction Copyright © 1991 DC Comics. All Rights Reserved.

Originally published in single magazine form as THE SANDMAN
17-20. Copyright © 1990 DC Comics. All Rights Reserved.
All characters, their distinctive likenesses and related elements
featured in this publication are trademarks of DC Comics.
The stories, characters, and incidents featured in this publication
are entirely fictional. DC Comics does not read or accept
unsolicited submissions of ideas, stories, or artwork.

DC Comics, 2900 W. Alameda Avenue, Burbank, CA 91505
Printed by RR Donnelley, Salem, VA, USA. Seventh Printing.
ISBN: 978-1-4012-2935-1

Cover art, interior illustrations and
publication design by Dave McKean.

PEFC Certified

Printed on paper from
sustainably managed
forests and controlled
sources

PEFC/29-31-75   www.pefc.org

DREAM COUNTRY

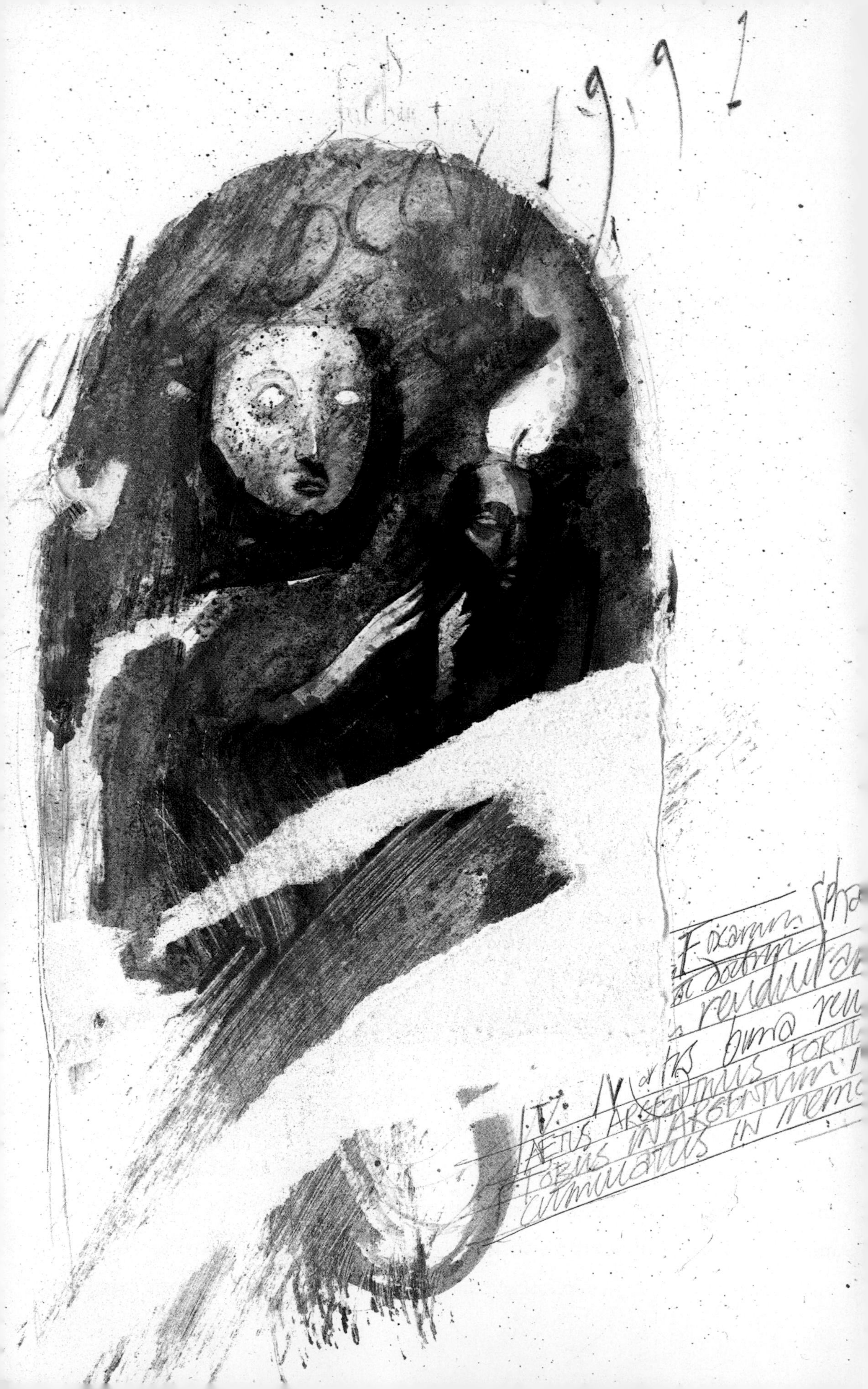

1991
AETUS ARGENTINUS
OBUS IN ARGENTUM
CUMULATUS IN

INTRODUCTION
by STEVE ERICKSON

My father died last year. He'd been sick for some time. Two weeks after his death I had a dream about him. I was walking through the rooms of a very nice rest home; the windows were open, and outside the sky was and trees were swaying in the breeze. There was no one else in this home, no one but my father. He was sitting up in his bed and looked fine; he was tranquil and happy. He greeted me. Oh, I said, this is a dream.

This is not a dream, he answered.

We sat there for some time discussing this. On his lap he held a small plate and on the plate was a small pastry. He gave the pastry to me and said, Here, taste this; and I did. He said, You can taste it, can't you? and I could. He said, You can taste it because this isn't a dream. But I wouldn't believe him, and then I woke up. Except I didn't wake into consciousness but rather into *another* dream.

I've told a number of people about this since it happened, and every one of them has said the same thing. Every one of them has said that my father was right.

I'm writing this in the morning now. I'm writing this on the fine edge of that blade that's consciousness on one side and dream on the other, that thin silver horizon where you hover right before falling asleep, and right before completely waking. Neil Gaiman lives here all the damn time. He scribbles his stories and sends them out from the thin silver horizon whose bridge the rest of us traverse just twice a day. Gaiman is the troll who lives beneath the bridge; he exhales into word balloons the visions that flash only fleetingly across our gaze and then are gone with the next memory. Dreams of what we've loved and lost, dreams that are more vivid than our lives, dreams that tell you they aren't dreams, from which come the questions that trouble and enthrall and finally free our spirits, if we're brave enough for the answers. Gaiman's ideas, in other words, of a good time.

If I say that he writes circles around everyone else in comics, it's not simply to put him in a rare class with Gilbert Hernandez and Art Spiegelman and fellow Briton Alan Moore, but to speak literally: for Neil Gaiman's stories in *The Sandman* descend concentrically through a narrative maze to a room at the center, where you expect to find a confessional and instead step into a veldt that stretches as far as the eye can see.

In the same fashion the character called Dream or Morpheus or Sandman lurks at the center of every story in this collection by inhabiting the outer passages. In "Calliope," a once successful novelist who's become so impotent in his art he can no longer write makes a bargain to enslave his muse, devouring her for his inspiration when he isn't ravaging her for his pleasure. In "A Dream of a Thousand Cats" a pilgrimage of cats, their world dominated by people who snatch their kittens, stuff them in bags and hurl them to oblivion, find they can transform their destiny through a memory dreamt in common. "A Midsummer-Night's Dream" follows a wandering sixteenth-century theatrical troupe into a performance where everything will change mid-play; when the masks are lifted at the end, the actors revealed aren't the same as the ones who put the masks on. And an old comic book character, unnamed here to those of us who don't ordinarily spend a lot of time in comicbookland, runs out of masks of her own in "Façade." She can transform every element of her existence but the one that matters, because the equation of the soul is written in a physics both far simpler and more complicated than any that men have devised. Only the foxiest little incarnation of Death you ever saw can comfort her desolation; in the final blast of sunlight, when the thin silver horizon bathes her in its furious glory, Element Girl is delivered from her mortal chemistry to something that defies decomposition. Then the eternal face of the heart gazes with pity on the ravaged face of the psyche.

Dream Country follows the previous Sandman novel, *The Doll's House*, published last year. I'd say that *The Doll's House* is Gaiman's masterpiece because at the time he wrote it, it was; but then he went and complicated matters by writing *A Season of Mists* in *Sandman* issues #21-28, which was better, confronting the Dreambearer with the necessity of his own redemption. In some ways, however, it may be *Dream Country*, the interlude between these two novels, that best defines what *Sandman* has been about. As rendered by the splendid art of Kelley Jones, Charles Vess, Colleen Doran, and Malcolm Jones, it holds the dark mirror of Gaiman's efforts up to the variety of cracked lives listed above, any one of which we're bound to bear some resemblance to. This, then, is the Sandman of your particular bridge, the bridge you came across this morning, the one you will return across tonight. Don't pay too much attention to the troll underneath, cheeky bastard that he

is. He isn't going anywhere.
He'll still be there tomorrow,
and the day after; hear,
rather, those other voices in
the Neil Gaiman night. They're
feline and Shakespearean,
nakedly ambitious and
heartbreakingly alone.

It's a dream, you say.

It's not a dream, they answer.

Steve Erickson

Los Angeles, July 1991

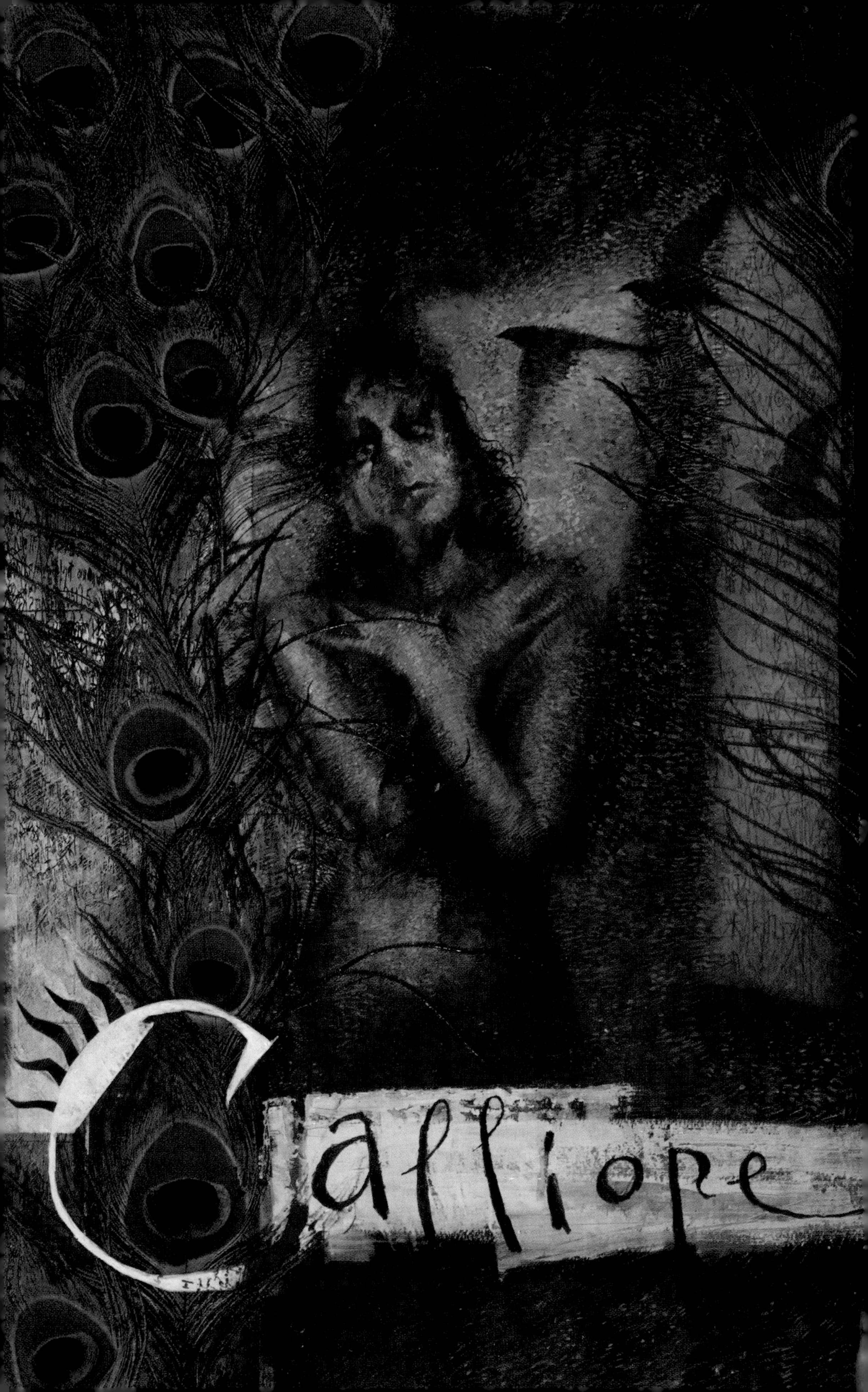
Calliope

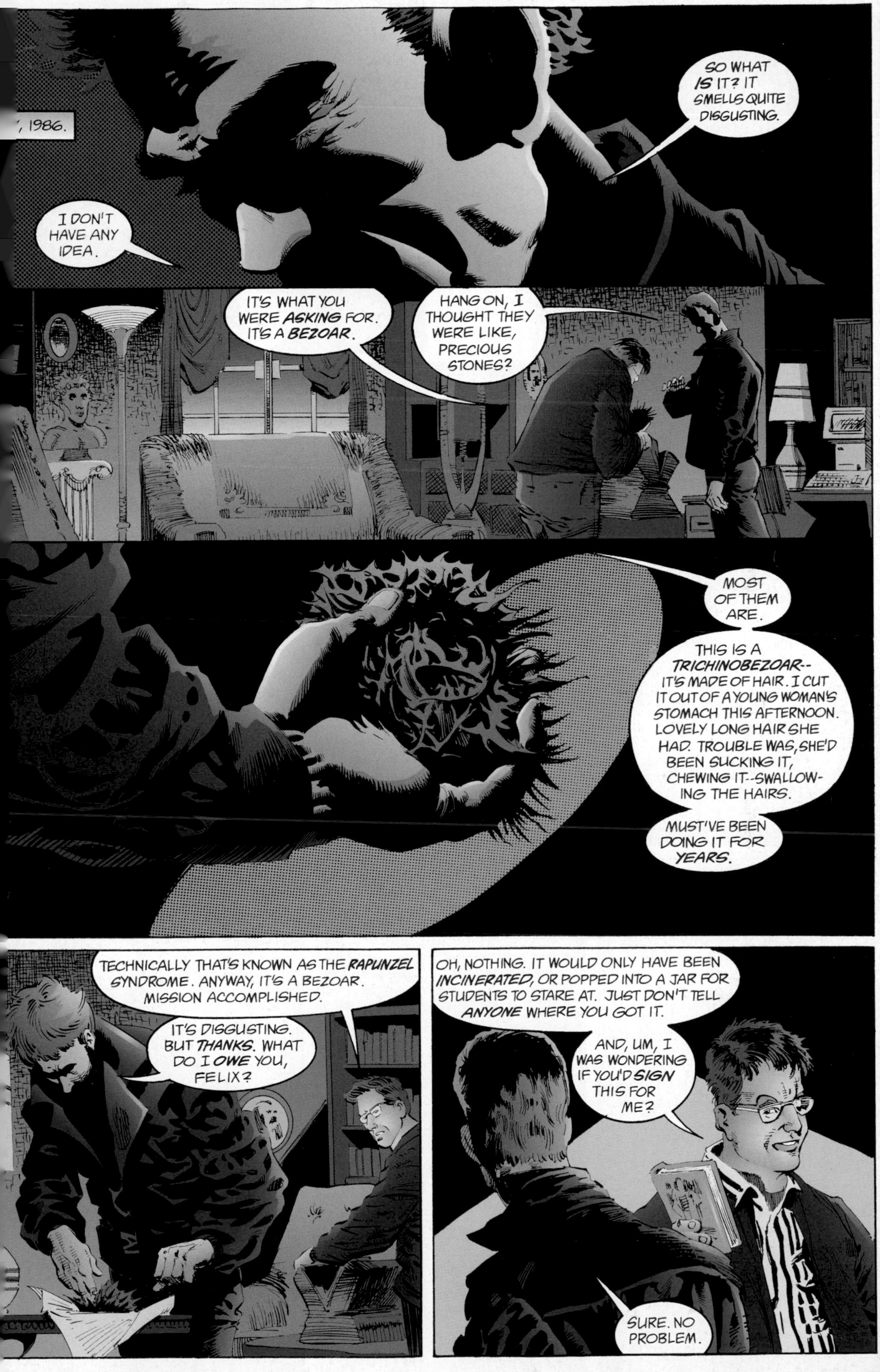
, 1986.
SO WHAT *IS* IT? IT SMELLS QUITE DISGUSTING.
I DON'T HAVE ANY IDEA.
IT'S WHAT YOU WERE *ASKING* FOR. IT'S A *BEZOAR*.
HANG ON, *I* THOUGHT THEY WERE LIKE, PRECIOUS STONES?
MOST OF THEM ARE.
THIS IS A *TRICHINOBEZOAR*-- IT'S MADE OF HAIR. I CUT IT OUT OF A YOUNG WOMAN'S STOMACH THIS AFTERNOON. LOVELY LONG HAIR SHE HAD. TROUBLE WAS, SHE'D BEEN SUCKING IT, CHEWING IT--SWALLOWING THE HAIRS.
MUST'VE BEEN DOING IT FOR *YEARS*.
TECHNICALLY THAT'S KNOWN AS THE *RAPUNZEL SYNDROME*. ANYWAY, IT'S A BEZOAR. MISSION ACCOMPLISHED.
IT'S DISGUSTING. BUT *THANKS*. WHAT DO I *OWE* YOU, FELIX?
OH, NOTHING. IT WOULD ONLY HAVE BEEN *INCINERATED*, OR POPPED INTO A JAR FOR STUDENTS TO STARE AT. JUST DON'T TELL *ANYONE* WHERE YOU GOT IT.
AND, UM, I WAS WONDERING IF YOU'D *SIGN* THIS FOR ME?
SURE. NO PROBLEM.

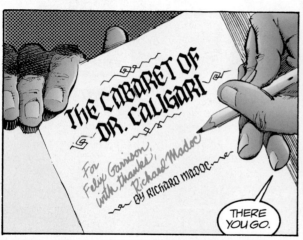

THE CABARET OF DR. CALIGARI

For Felix Garrison, with thanks, Richard Madoc
~ BY RICHARD MADOC ~

THERE YOU GO.

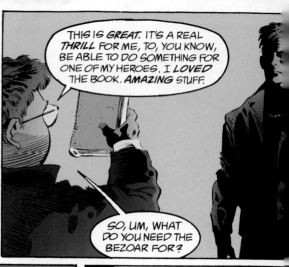

THIS IS *GREAT*. IT'S A REAL *THRILL* FOR ME, TO, YOU KNOW, BE ABLE TO DO SOMETHING FOR ONE OF MY HEROES. I *LOVED* THE BOOK. *AMAZING* STUFF.

SO, UM, WHAT DO YOU NEED THE BEZOAR FOR?

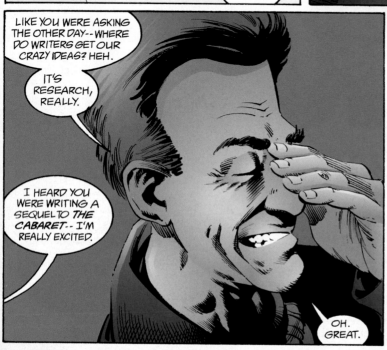

LIKE YOU WERE ASKING THE OTHER DAY-- WHERE DO WRITERS GET OUR CRAZY IDEAS? HEH.

IT'S RESEARCH, REALLY.

I HEARD YOU WERE WRITING A SEQUEL TO *THE CABARET*-- I'M REALLY EXCITED.

OH. GREAT.

UH, THAT'S THE PHONE. LISTEN, THANKS AGAIN FOR THE THING.

NO PROBLEM. I KNOW HOW *BUSY* YOU ARE. I'LL JUST LET MYSELF OUT, THEN. 'BYE.

BREEP BREEP

HELLO? RICHARD MADOC SPEAKING.

OH. HI, HARRY.

RICK? IT'S HARRY. LISTEN, WE HAVE TO *TALK*. YOUR PUBLISHERS WERE ONTO ME AGAIN TODAY.

LISTEN, THE NOVEL'S ALMOST NINE MONTHS OVERDUE, AND THEY'RE THREATENING TO CAUSE TROUBLE. YOU'RE IN BREACH OF CONTRACT, RICK. IS IT FINISHED *YET*?

NEARLY FINISHED.

WELL, *HOW* MUCH HAVE YOU GOT TO GO?

IT'S *ALMOST* FINISHED, HARRY. YOU CAN RUSH THESE THINGS. ANOTHER COUPLE OF WEEKS, MAYBE, OKAY?

LISTEN, I'M *REALLY* BUSY. I'LL GET BACK TO YOU. OKAY?

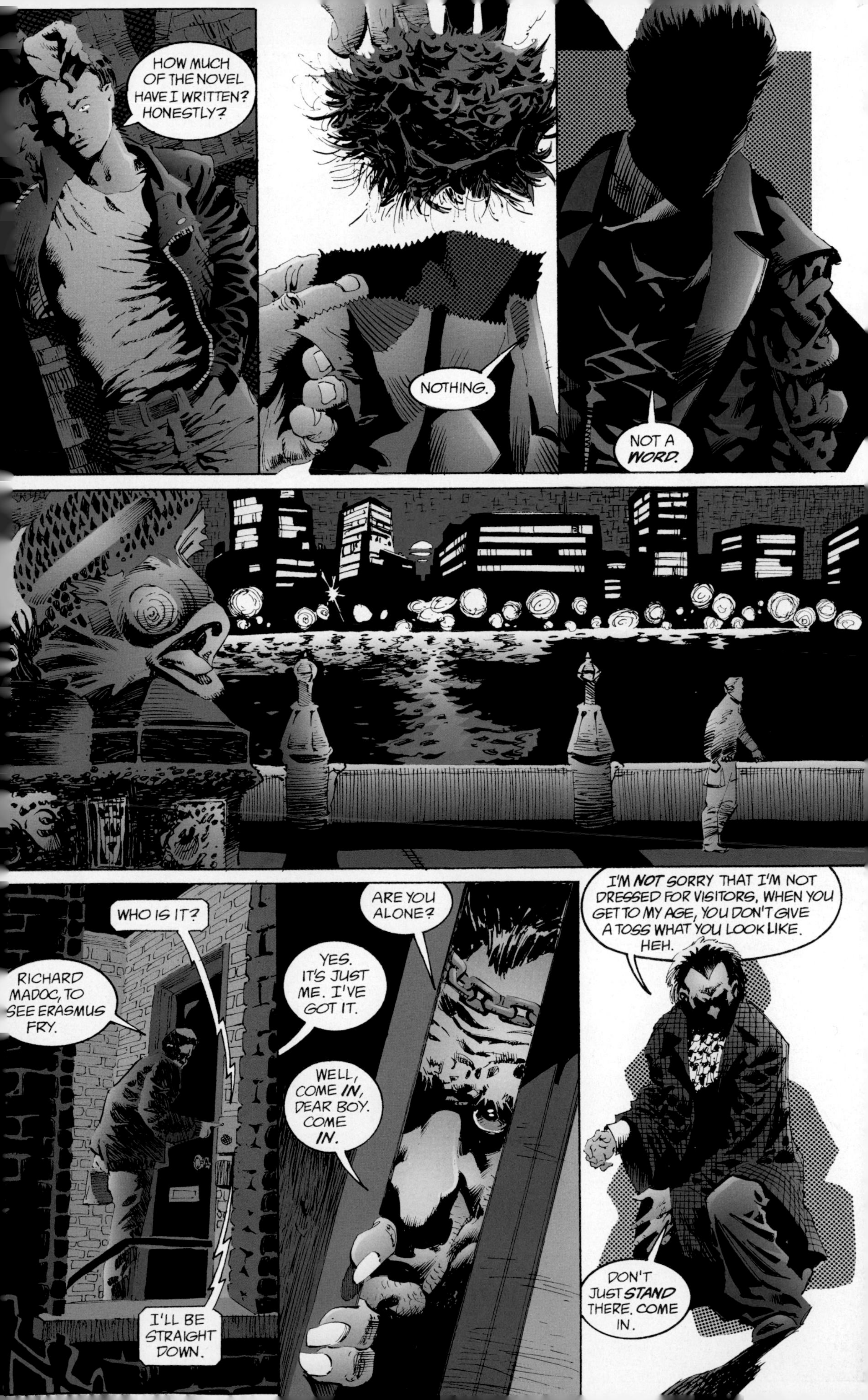
HOW MUCH OF THE NOVEL HAVE I WRITTEN? HONESTLY?
NOTHING.
NOT A WORD.
WHO IS IT?
RICHARD MADOC, TO SEE ERASMUS FRY.
I'LL BE STRAIGHT DOWN.
ARE YOU ALONE?
YES. IT'S JUST ME. I'VE GOT IT.
WELL, COME IN, DEAR BOY. COME IN.
I'M NOT SORRY THAT I'M NOT DRESSED FOR VISITORS. WHEN YOU GET TO MY AGE, YOU DON'T GIVE A TOSS WHAT YOU LOOK LIKE. HEH.
DON'T JUST STAND THERE. COME IN.

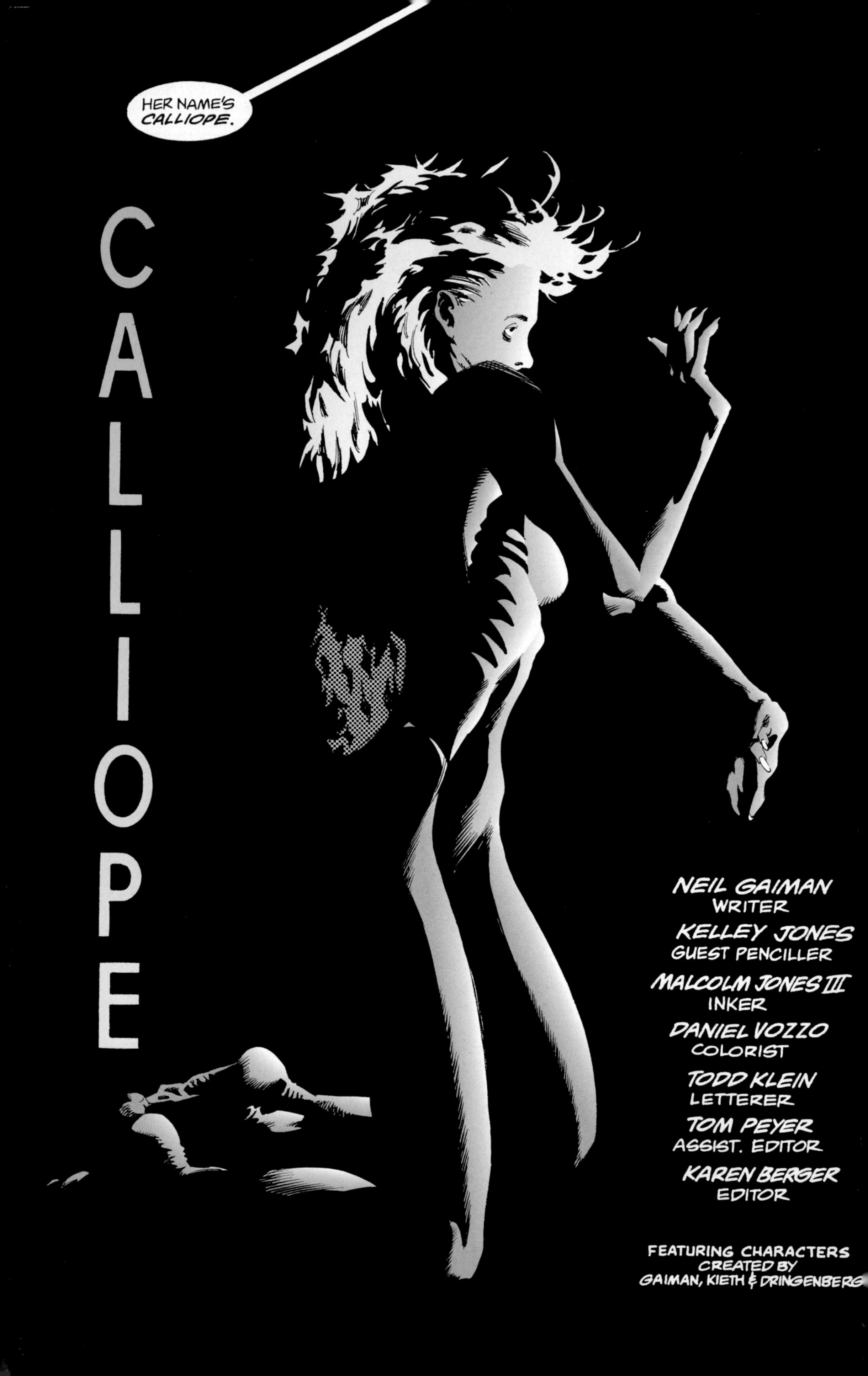
HER NAME'S CALLIOPE.
CALLIOPE
NEIL GAIMAN WRITER
KELLEY JONES GUEST PENCILLER
MALCOLM JONES III INKER
DANIEL VOZZO COLORIST
TODD KLEIN LETTERER
TOM PEYER ASSIST. EDITOR
KAREN BERGER EDITOR
FEATURING CHARACTERS CREATED BY GAIMAN, KIETH & DRINGENBERG

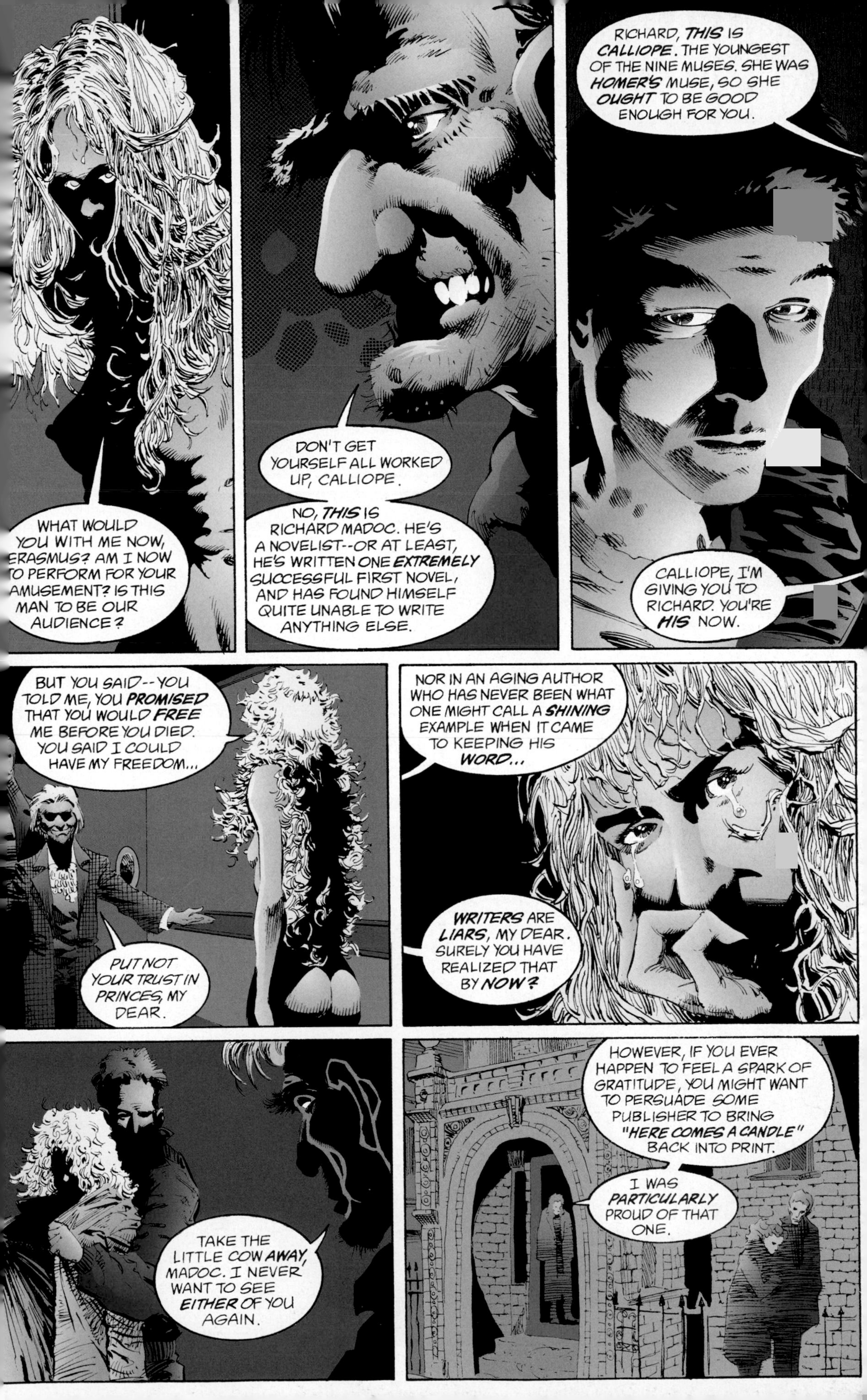

WHAT WOULD YOU WITH ME NOW, ERASMUS? AM I NOW TO PERFORM FOR YOUR AMUSEMENT? IS THIS MAN TO BE OUR AUDIENCE?
DON'T GET YOURSELF ALL WORKED UP, CALLIOPE.
NO, **THIS** IS RICHARD MADOC. HE'S A NOVELIST--OR AT LEAST, HE'S WRITTEN ONE **EXTREMELY** SUCCESSFUL FIRST NOVEL, AND HAS FOUND HIMSELF QUITE UNABLE TO WRITE ANYTHING ELSE.
RICHARD, **THIS** IS **CALLIOPE**. THE YOUNGEST OF THE NINE MUSES. SHE WAS **HOMER'S** MUSE, SO SHE **OUGHT** TO BE GOOD ENOUGH FOR YOU.
CALLIOPE, I'M GIVING YOU TO RICHARD. YOU'RE **HIS** NOW.
BUT YOU SAID--YOU TOLD ME, YOU **PROMISED** THAT YOU WOULD **FREE** ME BEFORE YOU DIED. YOU SAID I COULD HAVE MY FREEDOM...
PUT NOT YOUR TRUST IN PRINCES, MY DEAR.
NOR IN AN AGING AUTHOR WHO HAS NEVER BEEN WHAT ONE MIGHT CALL A **SHINING** EXAMPLE WHEN IT CAME TO KEEPING HIS **WORD...**
WRITERS ARE **LIARS**, MY DEAR. SURELY YOU HAVE REALIZED THAT BY **NOW?**
TAKE THE LITTLE COW **AWAY**, MADOC. I NEVER WANT TO SEE **EITHER** OF YOU AGAIN.
HOWEVER, IF YOU EVER HAPPEN TO FEEL A SPARK OF GRATITUDE, YOU MIGHT WANT TO PERSUADE SOME PUBLISHER TO BRING **"HERE COMES A CANDLE"** BACK INTO PRINT.
I WAS **PARTICULARLY** PROUD OF THAT ONE.

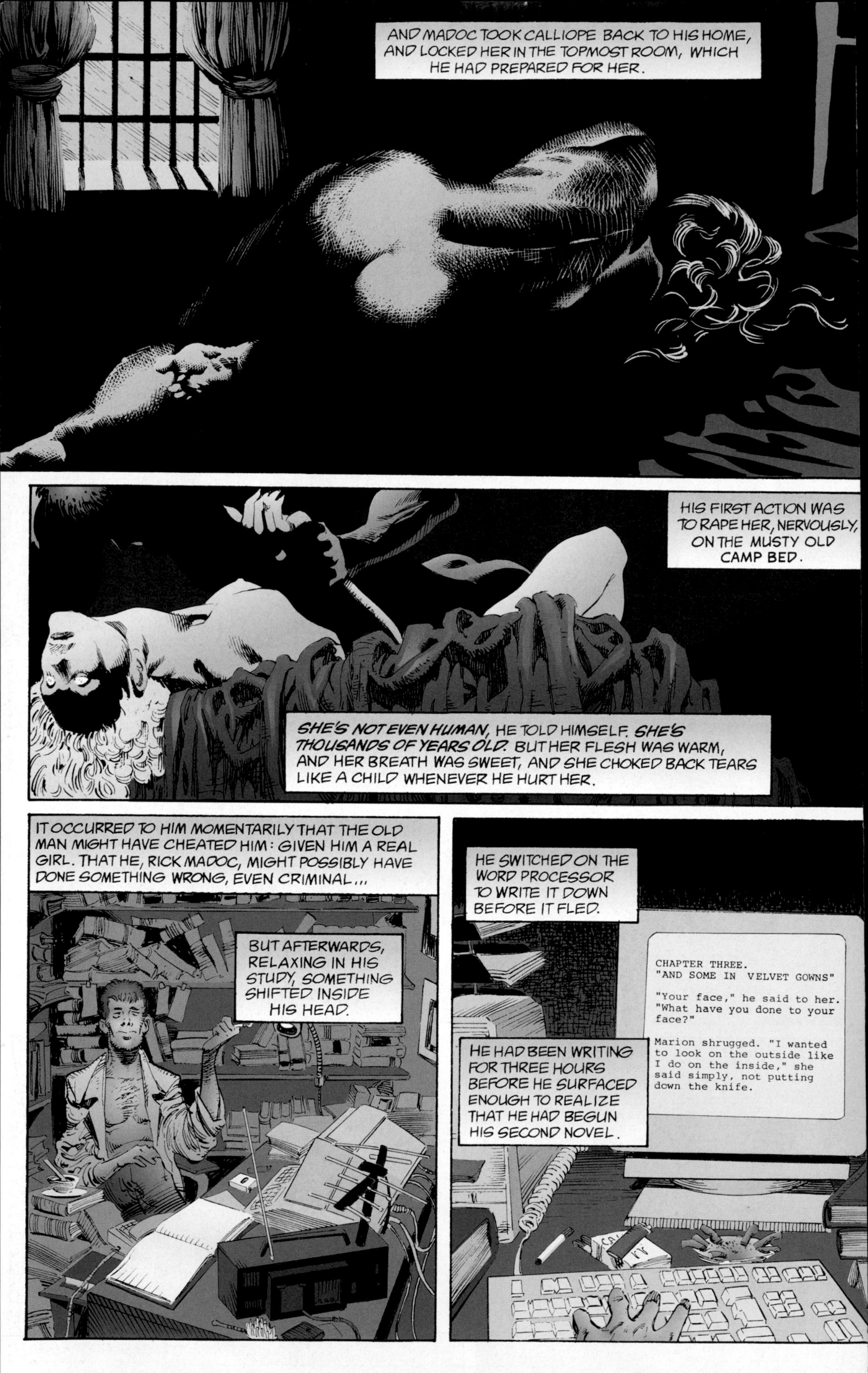
AND MADOC TOOK CALLIOPE BACK TO HIS HOME, AND LOCKED HER IN THE TOPMOST ROOM, WHICH HE HAD PREPARED FOR HER.
HIS FIRST ACTION WAS TO RAPE HER, NERVOUSLY, ON THE MUSTY OLD CAMP BED.
SHE'S NOT EVEN HUMAN, HE TOLD HIMSELF. SHE'S THOUSANDS OF YEARS OLD. BUT HER FLESH WAS WARM, AND HER BREATH WAS SWEET, AND SHE CHOKED BACK TEARS LIKE A CHILD WHENEVER HE HURT HER.
IT OCCURRED TO HIM MOMENTARILY THAT THE OLD MAN MIGHT HAVE CHEATED HIM: GIVEN HIM A REAL GIRL. THAT HE, RICK MADOC, MIGHT POSSIBLY HAVE DONE SOMETHING WRONG, EVEN CRIMINAL...
BUT AFTERWARDS, RELAXING IN HIS STUDY, SOMETHING SHIFTED INSIDE HIS HEAD.
HE SWITCHED ON THE WORD PROCESSOR TO WRITE IT DOWN BEFORE IT FLED.
CHAPTER THREE.
"AND SOME IN VELVET GOWNS"
"Your face," he said to her. "What have you done to your face?"
Marion shrugged. "I wanted to look on the outside like I do on the inside," she said simply, not putting down the knife.
HE HAD BEEN WRITING FOR THREE HOURS BEFORE HE SURFACED ENOUGH TO REALIZE THAT HE HAD BEGUN HIS SECOND NOVEL.

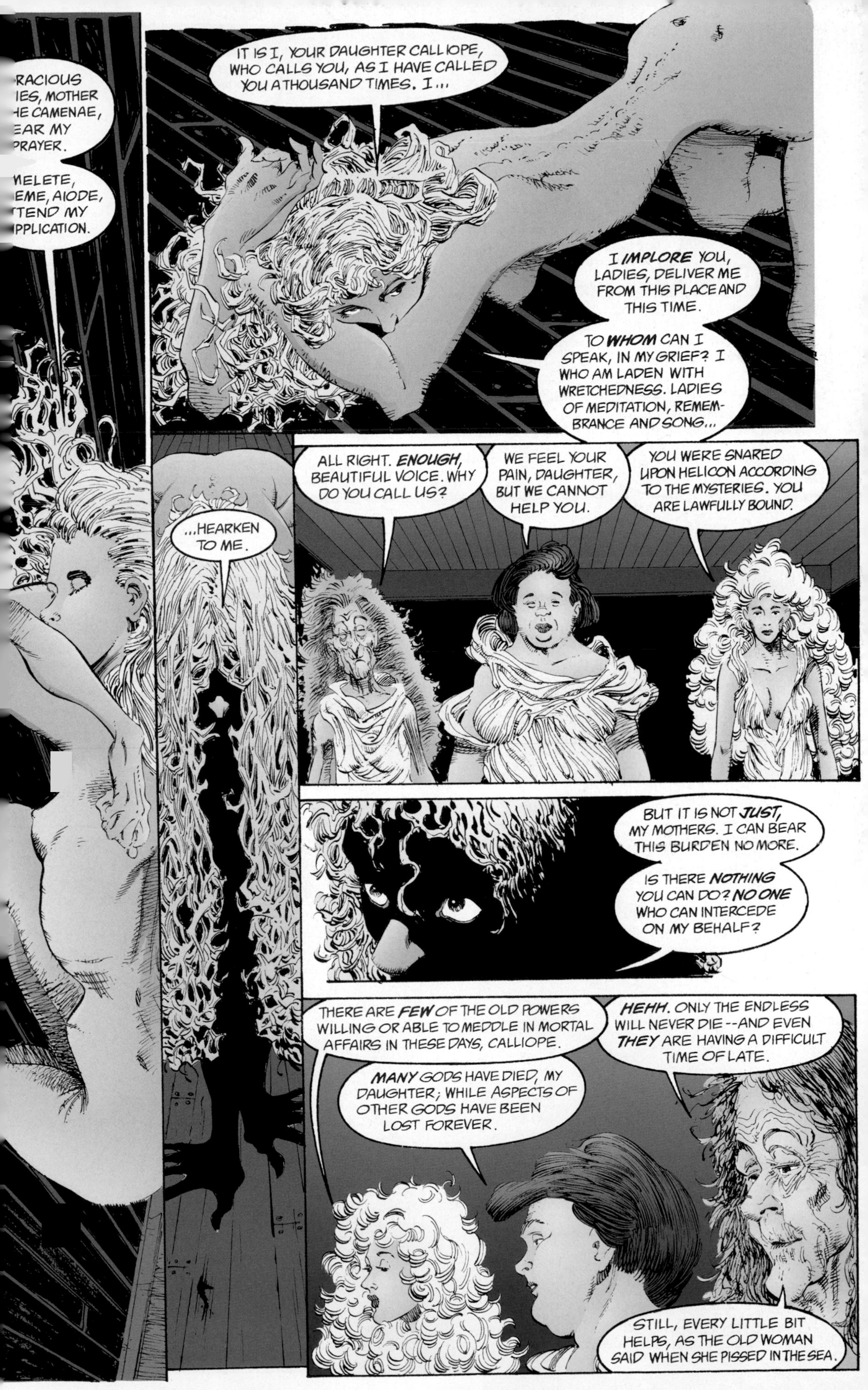
RACIOUS IES, MOTHER HE CAMENAE, EAR MY PRAYER.
MELETE, EME, AIODE, TTEND MY PPLICATION.
IT IS I, YOUR DAUGHTER CALLIOPE, WHO CALLS YOU, AS I HAVE CALLED YOU A THOUSAND TIMES. I...
I IMPLORE YOU, LADIES, DELIVER ME FROM THIS PLACE AND THIS TIME.
TO WHOM CAN I SPEAK, IN MY GRIEF? I WHO AM LADEN WITH WRETCHEDNESS. LADIES OF MEDITATION, REMEMBRANCE AND SONG...
...HEARKEN TO ME.
ALL RIGHT. ENOUGH, BEAUTIFUL VOICE. WHY DO YOU CALL US?
WE FEEL YOUR PAIN, DAUGHTER, BUT WE CANNOT HELP YOU.
YOU WERE SNARED UPON HELICON ACCORDING TO THE MYSTERIES. YOU ARE LAWFULLY BOUND.
BUT IT IS NOT JUST, MY MOTHERS. I CAN BEAR THIS BURDEN NO MORE.
IS THERE NOTHING YOU CAN DO? NO ONE WHO CAN INTERCEDE ON MY BEHALF?
THERE ARE FEW OF THE OLD POWERS WILLING OR ABLE TO MEDDLE IN MORTAL AFFAIRS IN THESE DAYS, CALLIOPE.
MANY GODS HAVE DIED, MY DAUGHTER; WHILE ASPECTS OF OTHER GODS HAVE BEEN LOST FOREVER.
HEHH. ONLY THE ENDLESS WILL NEVER DIE--AND EVEN THEY ARE HAVING A DIFFICULT TIME OF LATE.
STILL, EVERY LITTLE BIT HELPS, AS THE OLD WOMAN SAID WHEN SHE PISSED IN THE SEA.

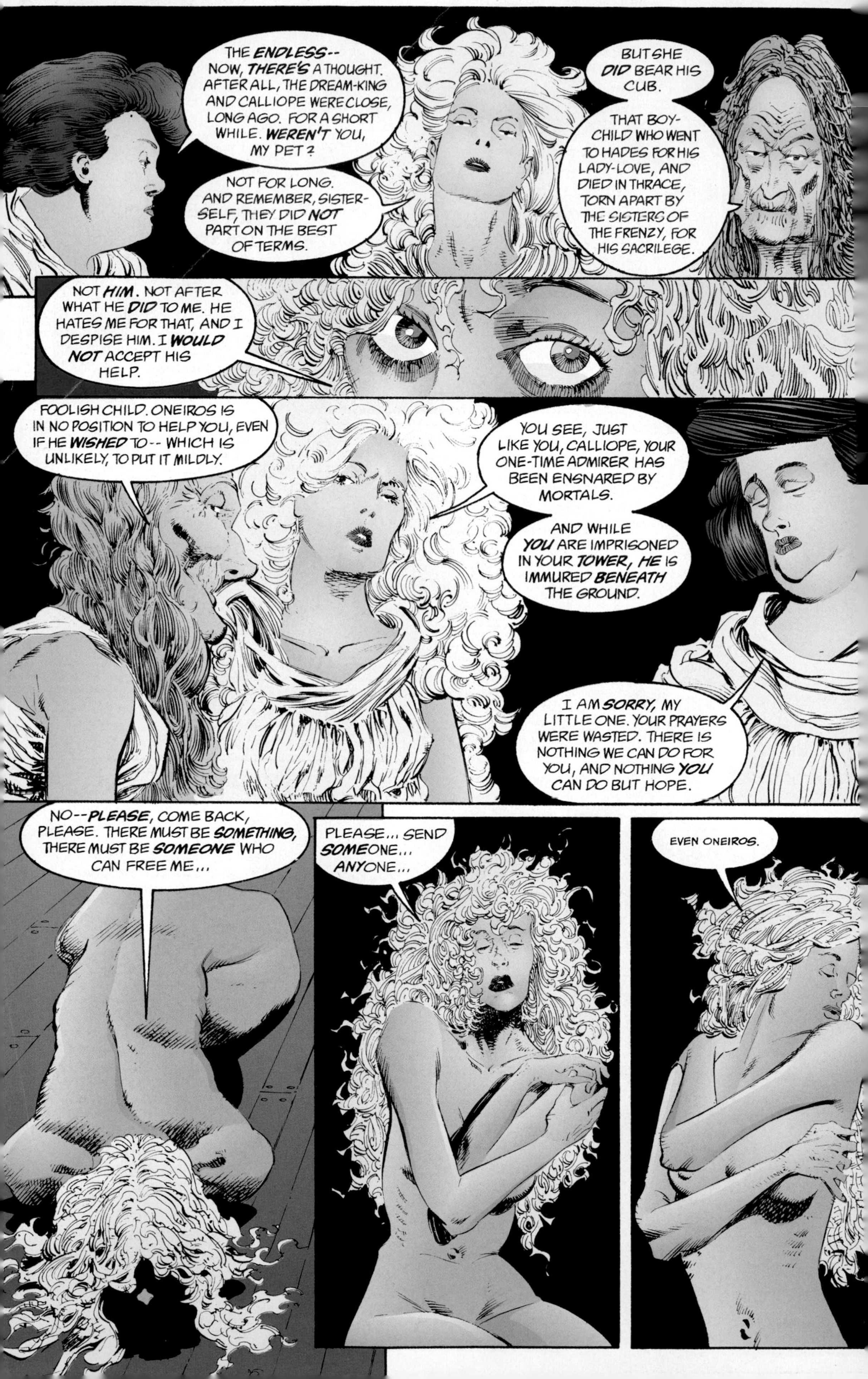
THE ENDLESS-- NOW, THERE'S A THOUGHT. AFTER ALL, THE DREAM-KING AND CALLIOPE WERE CLOSE, LONG AGO. FOR A SHORT WHILE. WEREN'T YOU, MY PET?
NOT FOR LONG. AND REMEMBER, SISTER-SELF, THEY DID NOT PART ON THE BEST OF TERMS.
BUT SHE DID BEAR HIS CUB.
THAT BOY-CHILD WHO WENT TO HADES FOR HIS LADY-LOVE, AND DIED IN THRACE, TORN APART BY THE SISTERS OF THE FRENZY, FOR HIS SACRILEGE.
NOT HIM. NOT AFTER WHAT HE DID TO ME. HE HATES ME FOR THAT, AND I DESPISE HIM. I WOULD NOT ACCEPT HIS HELP.
FOOLISH CHILD. ONEIROS IS IN NO POSITION TO HELP YOU, EVEN IF HE WISHED TO-- WHICH IS UNLIKELY, TO PUT IT MILDLY.
YOU SEE, JUST LIKE YOU, CALLIOPE, YOUR ONE-TIME ADMIRER HAS BEEN ENSNARED BY MORTALS.
AND WHILE YOU ARE IMPRISONED IN YOUR TOWER, HE IS IMMURED BENEATH THE GROUND.
I AM SORRY, MY LITTLE ONE. YOUR PRAYERS WERE WASTED. THERE IS NOTHING WE CAN DO FOR YOU, AND NOTHING YOU CAN DO BUT HOPE.
NO--PLEASE, COME BACK, PLEASE. THERE MUST BE SOMETHING, THERE MUST BE SOMEONE WHO CAN FREE ME...
PLEASE... SEND SOMEONE... ANYONE...
EVEN ONEIROS.

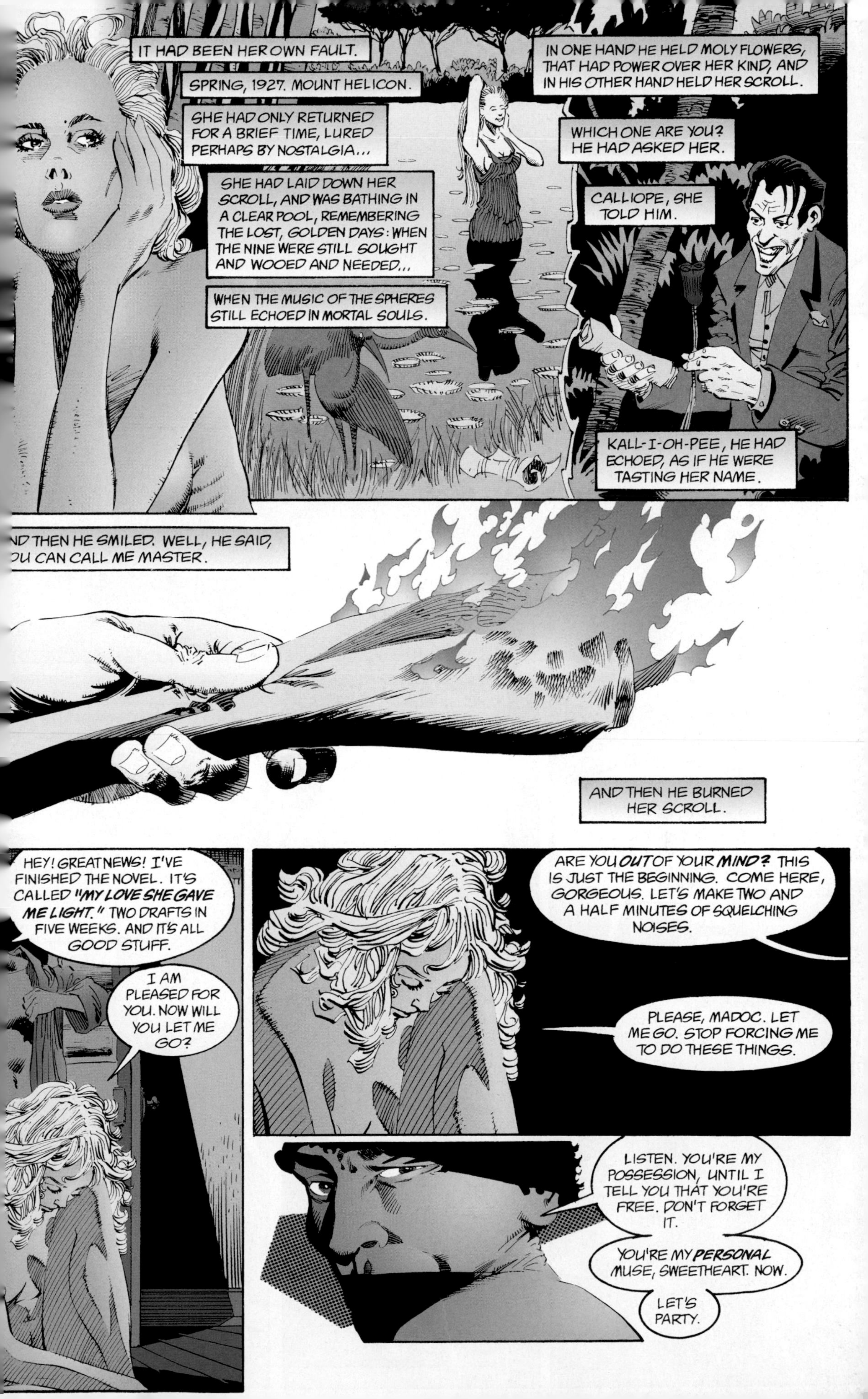
IT HAD BEEN HER OWN FAULT.
SPRING, 1927. MOUNT HELICON.
SHE HAD ONLY RETURNED FOR A BRIEF TIME, LURED PERHAPS BY NOSTALGIA...
SHE HAD LAID DOWN HER SCROLL, AND WAS BATHING IN A CLEAR POOL, REMEMBERING THE LOST, GOLDEN DAYS: WHEN THE NINE WERE STILL SOUGHT AND WOOED AND NEEDED...
WHEN THE MUSIC OF THE SPHERES STILL ECHOED IN MORTAL SOULS.
IN ONE HAND HE HELD MOLY FLOWERS, THAT HAD POWER OVER HER KIND, AND IN HIS OTHER HAND HELD HER SCROLL.
WHICH ONE ARE YOU? HE HAD ASKED HER.
CALLIOPE, SHE TOLD HIM.
KALL-I-OH-PEE, HE HAD ECHOED, AS IF HE WERE TASTING HER NAME.
ND THEN HE SMILED. WELL, HE SAID, OU CAN CALL ME MASTER.
AND THEN HE BURNED HER SCROLL.
HEY! GREAT NEWS! I'VE FINISHED THE NOVEL. IT'S CALLED **"MY LOVE SHE GAVE ME LIGHT."** TWO DRAFTS IN FIVE WEEKS. AND IT'S ALL GOOD STUFF.
I AM PLEASED FOR YOU. NOW WILL YOU LET ME GO?
ARE YOU **OUT** OF YOUR **MIND?** THIS IS JUST THE BEGINNING. COME HERE, GORGEOUS. LET'S MAKE TWO AND A HALF MINUTES OF SQUELCHING NOISES.
PLEASE, MADOC. LET ME GO. STOP FORCING ME TO DO THESE THINGS.
LISTEN. YOU'RE MY POSSESSION, UNTIL I TELL YOU THAT YOU'RE FREE. DON'T FORGET IT.
YOU'RE MY **PERSONAL** MUSE, SWEETHEART. NOW.
LET'S PARTY.

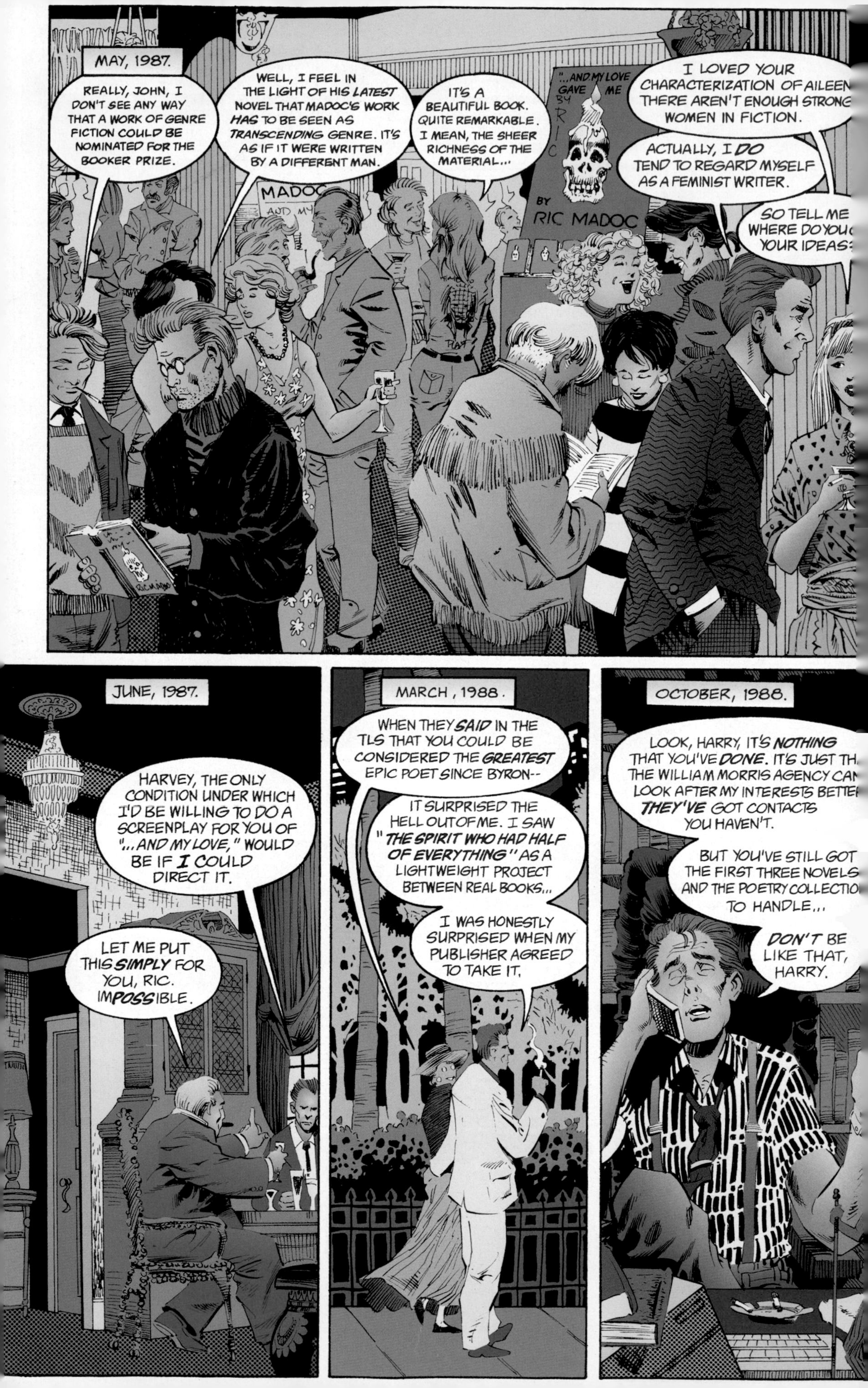
MAY, 1987.
REALLY, JOHN, I DON'T SEE ANY WAY THAT A WORK OF GENRE FICTION COULD BE NOMINATED FOR THE BOOKER PRIZE.
WELL, I FEEL IN THE LIGHT OF HIS *LATEST* NOVEL THAT MADOC'S WORK *HAS* TO BE SEEN AS *TRANSCENDING* GENRE. IT'S AS IF IT WERE WRITTEN BY A DIFFERENT MAN.
IT'S A BEAUTIFUL BOOK. QUITE REMARKABLE. I MEAN, THE SHEER RICHNESS OF THE MATERIAL...
"...AND MY LOVE GAVE ME
BY RIC MADOC
I LOVED YOUR CHARACTERIZATION OF AILEEN THERE AREN'T ENOUGH STRONG WOMEN IN FICTION.
ACTUALLY, I *DO* TEND TO REGARD MYSELF AS A FEMINIST WRITER.
SO TELL ME WHERE DO YOU G YOUR IDEAS?
MADOC
JUNE, 1987.
HARVEY, THE ONLY CONDITION UNDER WHICH I'D BE WILLING TO DO A SCREENPLAY FOR YOU OF "...AND MY LOVE," WOULD BE IF *I* COULD DIRECT IT.
LET ME PUT THIS *SIMPLY* FOR YOU, RIC. IM*POSS*IBLE.
MARCH, 1988.
WHEN THEY *SAID* IN THE TLS THAT YOU COULD BE CONSIDERED THE *GREATEST* EPIC POET SINCE BYRON--
IT SURPRISED THE HELL OUT OF ME. I SAW "*THE SPIRIT WHO HAD HALF OF EVERYTHING*" AS A LIGHTWEIGHT PROJECT BETWEEN REAL BOOKS...
I WAS HONESTLY SURPRISED WHEN MY PUBLISHER AGREED TO TAKE IT.
OCTOBER, 1988.
LOOK, HARRY, IT'S *NOTHING* THAT YOU'VE *DONE*. IT'S JUST TH THE WILLIAM MORRIS AGENCY CAN LOOK AFTER MY INTERESTS BETTER *THEY'VE* GOT CONTACTS YOU HAVEN'T.
BUT YOU'VE STILL GOT THE FIRST THREE NOVELS AND THE POETRY COLLECTIO TO HANDLE...
DON'T BE LIKE THAT, HARRY.

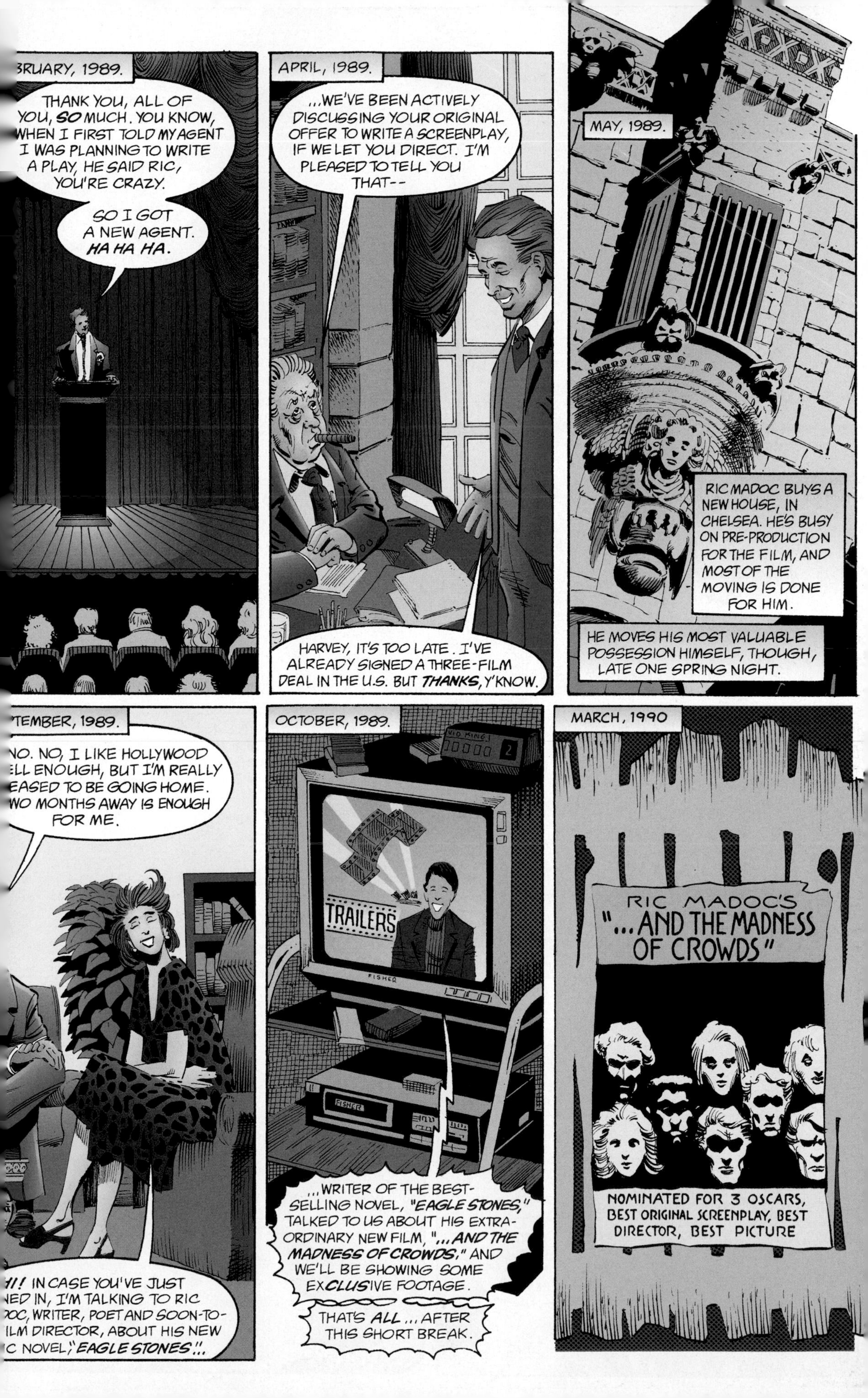
BRUARY, 1989.
THANK YOU, ALL OF YOU, SO MUCH. YOU KNOW, WHEN I FIRST TOLD MY AGENT I WAS PLANNING TO WRITE A PLAY, HE SAID RIC, YOU'RE CRAZY.
SO I GOT A NEW AGENT. HA HA HA.
APRIL, 1989.
...WE'VE BEEN ACTIVELY DISCUSSING YOUR ORIGINAL OFFER TO WRITE A SCREENPLAY, IF WE LET YOU DIRECT. I'M PLEASED TO TELL YOU THAT--
HARVEY, IT'S TOO LATE. I'VE ALREADY SIGNED A THREE-FILM DEAL IN THE U.S. BUT THANKS, Y'KNOW.
MAY, 1989.
RIC MADOC BUYS A NEW HOUSE, IN CHELSEA. HE'S BUSY ON PRE-PRODUCTION FOR THE FILM, AND MOST OF THE MOVING IS DONE FOR HIM.
HE MOVES HIS MOST VALUABLE POSSESSION HIMSELF, THOUGH, LATE ONE SPRING NIGHT.
PTEMBER, 1989.
NO. NO, I LIKE HOLLYWOOD ELL ENOUGH, BUT I'M REALLY EASED TO BE GOING HOME. WO MONTHS AWAY IS ENOUGH FOR ME.
HI! IN CASE YOU'VE JUST NED IN, I'M TALKING TO RIC DOC, WRITER, POET AND SOON-TO- ILM DIRECTOR, ABOUT HIS NEW C NOVEL, "EAGLE STONES"!.
OCTOBER, 1989.
VID KING
TRAILERS
FISHER
...WRITER OF THE BEST-SELLING NOVEL, "EAGLE STONES," TALKED TO US ABOUT HIS EXTRA-ORDINARY NEW FILM, "...AND THE MADNESS OF CROWDS," AND WE'LL BE SHOWING SOME EXCLUSIVE FOOTAGE.
THAT'S ALL ... AFTER THIS SHORT BREAK.
MARCH, 1990
RIC MADOC'S "...AND THE MADNESS OF CROWDS"
NOMINATED FOR 3 OSCARS, BEST ORIGINAL SCREENPLAY, BEST DIRECTOR, BEST PICTURE

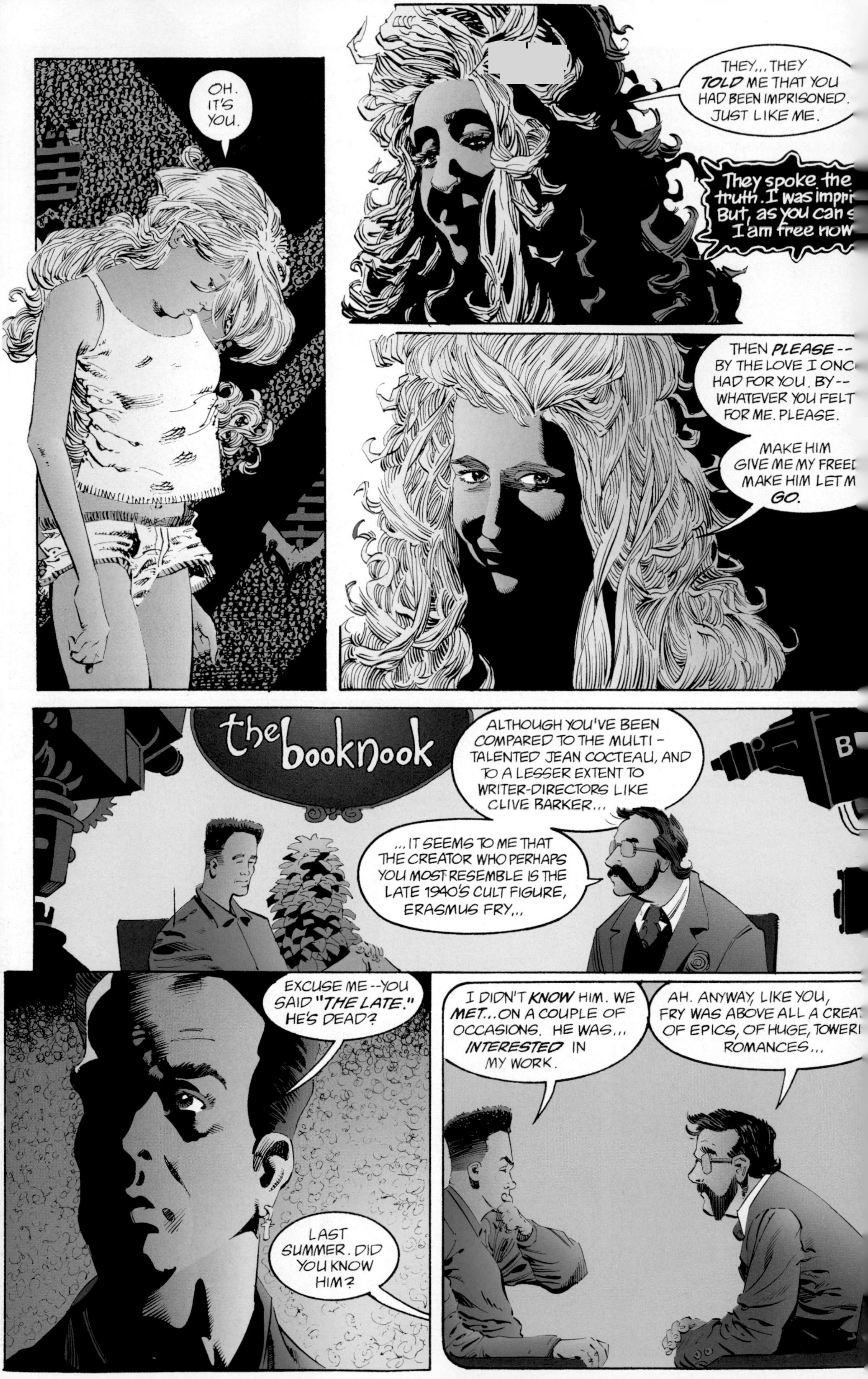

OH. IT'S YOU.
THEY... THEY *TOLD* ME THAT YOU HAD BEEN IMPRISONED. JUST LIKE ME.
They spoke the truth. I was impri But, as you can s I am free now
THEN *PLEASE* -- BY THE LOVE I ONC HAD FOR YOU. BY-- WHATEVER YOU FELT FOR ME. PLEASE.
MAKE HIM GIVE ME MY FREED MAKE HIM LET M *GO.*
the booknook
ALTHOUGH YOU'VE BEEN COMPARED TO THE MULTI-TALENTED JEAN COCTEAU, AND TO A LESSER EXTENT TO WRITER-DIRECTORS LIKE CLIVE BARKER...
...IT SEEMS TO ME THAT THE CREATOR WHO PERHAPS YOU MOST RESEMBLE IS THE LATE 1940'S CULT FIGURE, ERASMUS FRY...
EXCUSE ME --YOU SAID "*THE LATE.*" HE'S DEAD?
LAST SUMMER. DID YOU KNOW HIM?
I DIDN'T *KNOW* HIM. WE *MET*...ON A COUPLE OF OCCASIONS. HE WAS... *INTERESTED* IN MY WORK.
AH. ANYWAY, LIKE YOU, FRY WAS ABOVE ALL A CREAT OF EPICS, OF HUGE, TOWERI ROMANCES...

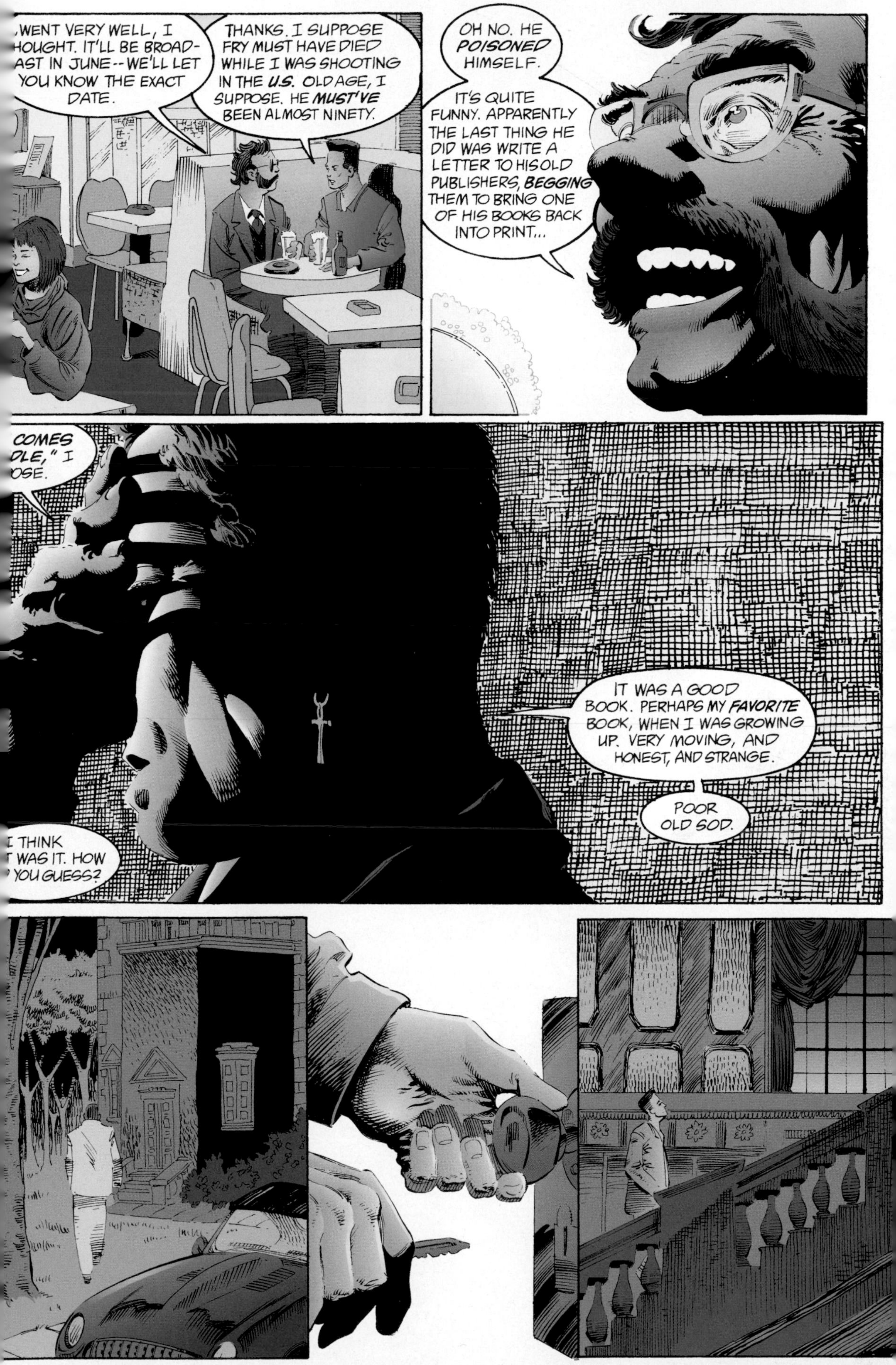
WENT VERY WELL, I
HOUGHT. IT'LL BE BROAD-
AST IN JUNE--WE'LL LET
YOU KNOW THE EXACT
DATE.
THANKS. I SUPPOSE FRY MUST HAVE DIED WHILE I WAS SHOOTING IN THE U.S. OLD AGE, I SUPPOSE. HE MUST'VE BEEN ALMOST NINETY.
OH NO. HE POISONED HIMSELF.
IT'S QUITE FUNNY. APPARENTLY THE LAST THING HE DID WAS WRITE A LETTER TO HIS OLD PUBLISHERS, BEGGING THEM TO BRING ONE OF HIS BOOKS BACK INTO PRINT...
COMES
DLE," I
OSE.
IT WAS A GOOD BOOK. PERHAPS MY FAVORITE BOOK, WHEN I WAS GROWING UP. VERY MOVING, AND HONEST, AND STRANGE.
POOR OLD SOD.
I THINK
T WAS IT. HOW
YOU GUESS?

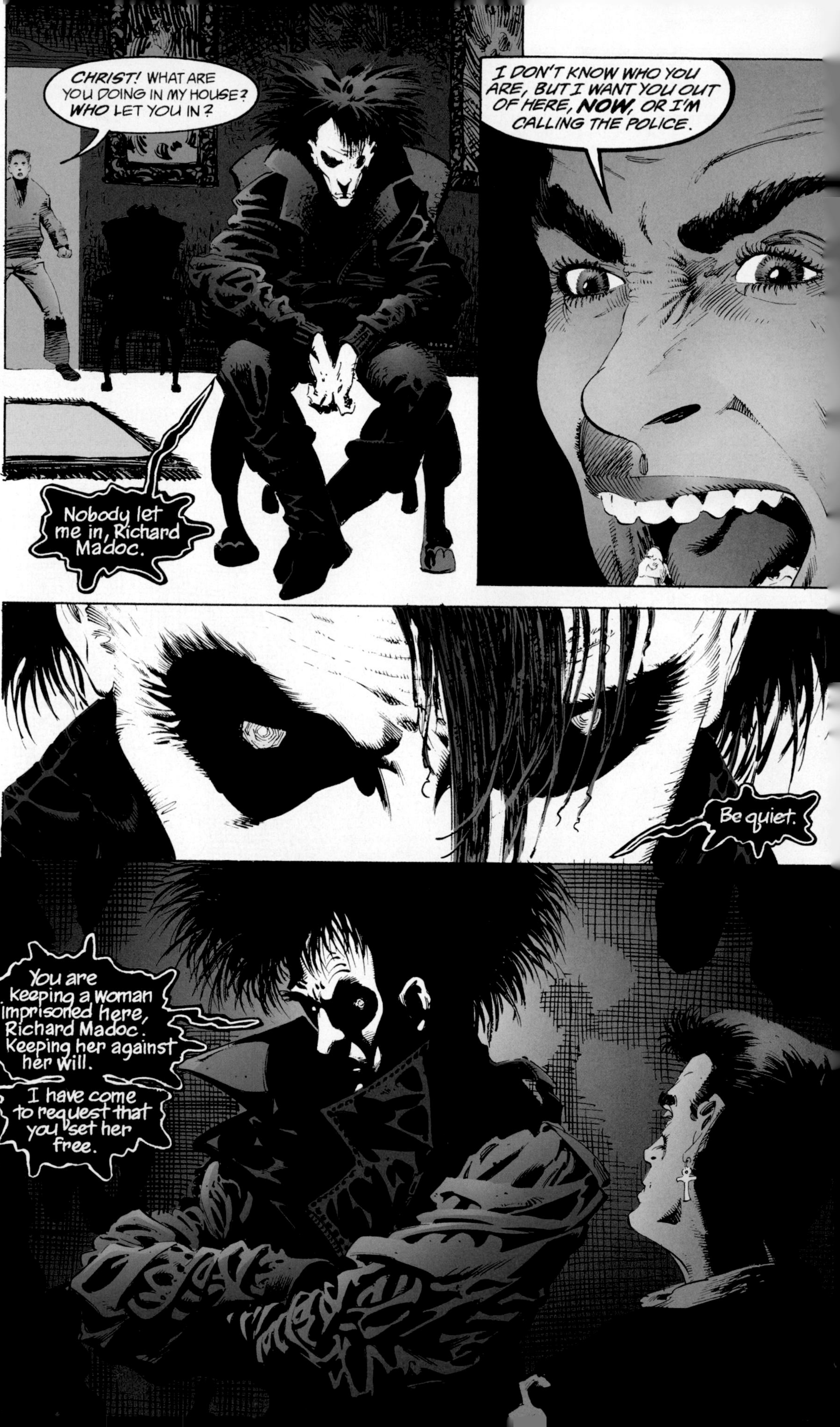
CHRIST! WHAT ARE YOU DOING IN MY HOUSE? WHO LET YOU IN?
Nobody let me in, Richard Madoc.
I DON'T KNOW WHO YOU ARE, BUT I WANT YOU OUT OF HERE, NOW, OR I'M CALLING THE POLICE.
Be quiet.
You are keeping a woman imprisoned here, Richard Madoc. Keeping her against her will.
I have come to request that you set her free.

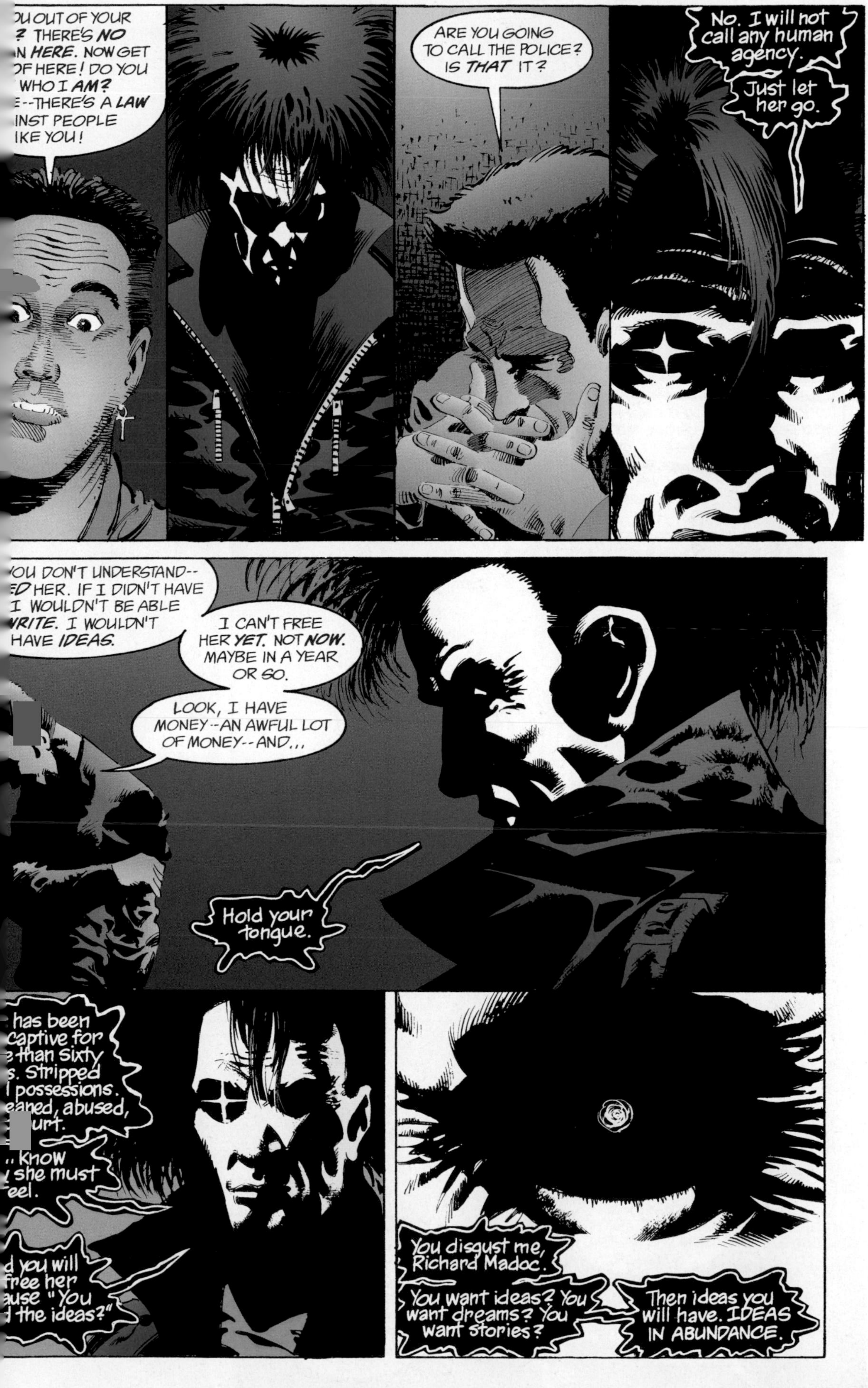

OU OUT OF YOUR ? THERE'S NO N HERE. NOW GET OF HERE! DO YOU WHO I AM? E--THERE'S A LAW INST PEOPLE IKE YOU!
ARE YOU GOING TO CALL THE POLICE? IS THAT IT?
No. I will not call any human agency.
Just let her go.
OU DON'T UNDERSTAND-- D HER. IF I DIDN'T HAVE I WOULDN'T BE ABLE WRITE. I WOULDN'T HAVE IDEAS.
I CAN'T FREE HER YET. NOT NOW. MAYBE IN A YEAR OR SO.
LOOK, I HAVE MONEY--AN AWFUL LOT OF MONEY--AND...
Hold your tongue.
has been captive for than Sixty s. Stripped possessions. eaned, abused, urt.
.. know she must eel.
d you will free her ause "You the ideas?"
You disgust me, Richard Madoc.
You want ideas? You want dreams? You want stories?
Then ideas you will have. IDEAS IN ABUNDANCE.

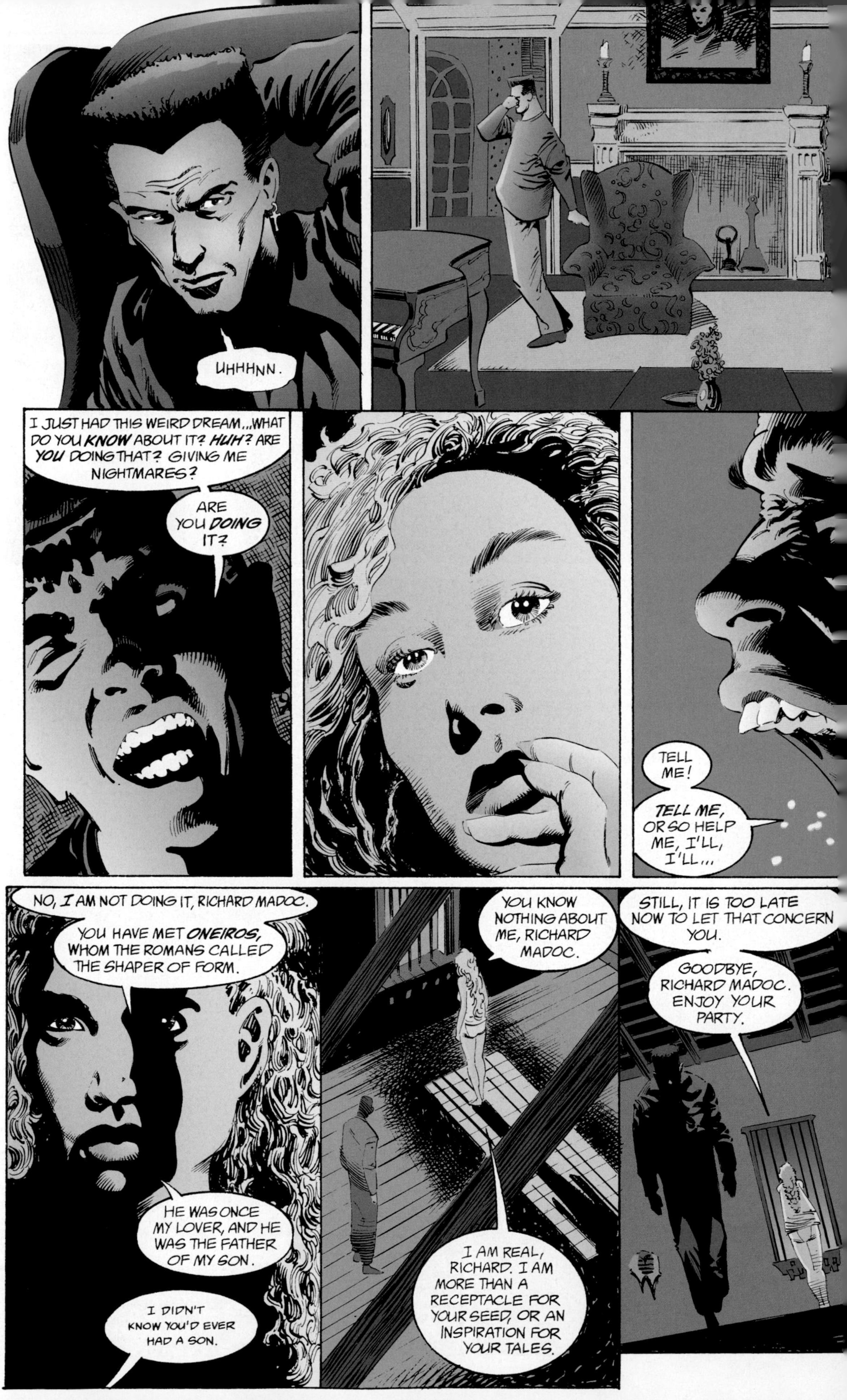
UHHHNN.
I JUST HAD THIS WEIRD DREAM... WHAT DO YOU **KNOW** ABOUT IT? **HUH**? ARE **YOU** DOING THAT? GIVING ME NIGHTMARES?
ARE YOU **DOING** IT?
TELL ME!
TELL ME, OR SO HELP ME, I'LL, I'LL...
NO, **I** AM NOT DOING IT, RICHARD MADOC.
YOU HAVE MET **ONEIROS**, WHOM THE ROMANS CALLED THE SHAPER OF FORM.
HE WAS ONCE MY LOVER, AND HE WAS THE FATHER OF MY SON.
I DIDN'T KNOW YOU'D EVER HAD A SON.
YOU KNOW NOTHING ABOUT ME, RICHARD MADOC.
I AM REAL, RICHARD. I AM MORE THAN A RECEPTACLE FOR YOUR SEED, OR AN INSPIRATION FOR YOUR TALES.
STILL, IT IS TOO LATE NOW TO LET THAT CONCERN YOU.
GOODBYE, RICHARD MADOC. ENJOY YOUR PARTY.

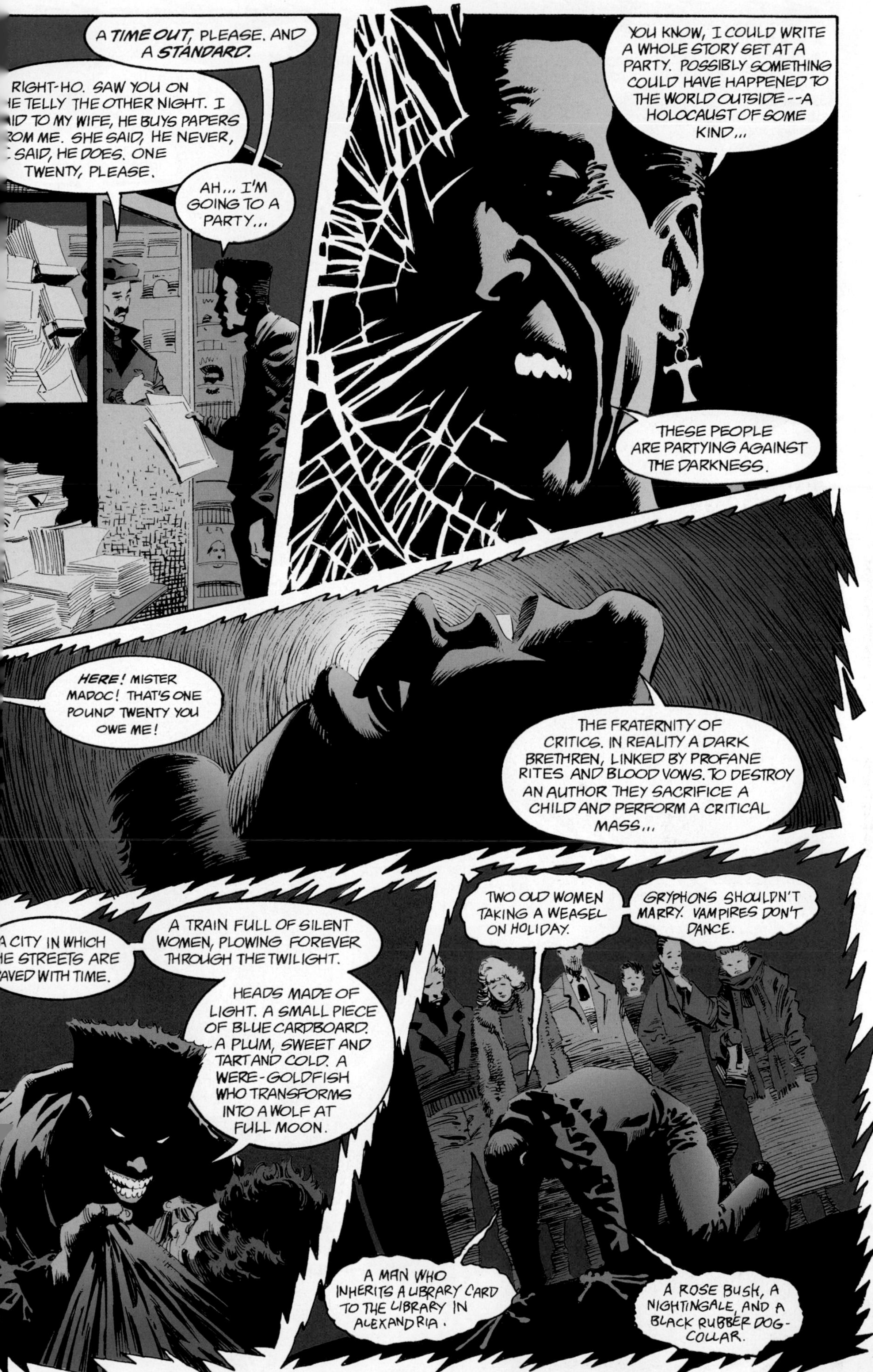
A TIME OUT, PLEASE. AND A STANDARD.
RIGHT-HO. SAW YOU ON HE TELLY THE OTHER NIGHT. I AID TO MY WIFE, HE BUYS PAPERS ROM ME. SHE SAID, HE NEVER, SAID, HE DOES. ONE TWENTY, PLEASE.
AH... I'M GOING TO A PARTY...
YOU KNOW, I COULD WRITE A WHOLE STORY SET AT A PARTY. POSSIBLY SOMETHING COULD HAVE HAPPENED TO THE WORLD OUTSIDE--A HOLOCAUST OF SOME KIND...
THESE PEOPLE ARE PARTYING AGAINST THE DARKNESS.
HERE! MISTER MADOC! THAT'S ONE POUND TWENTY YOU OWE ME!
THE FRATERNITY OF CRITICS. IN REALITY A DARK BRETHREN, LINKED BY PROFANE RITES AND BLOOD VOWS. TO DESTROY AN AUTHOR THEY SACRIFICE A CHILD AND PERFORM A CRITICAL MASS...
A CITY IN WHICH HE STREETS ARE AVED WITH TIME.
A TRAIN FULL OF SILENT WOMEN, PLOWING FOREVER THROUGH THE TWILIGHT.
HEADS MADE OF LIGHT. A SMALL PIECE OF BLUE CARDBOARD. A PLUM, SWEET AND TART AND COLD. A WERE-GOLDFISH WHO TRANSFORMS INTO A WOLF AT FULL MOON.
TWO OLD WOMEN TAKING A WEASEL ON HOLIDAY.
GRYPHONS SHOULDN'T MARRY. VAMPIRES DON'T DANCE.
A MAN WHO INHERITS A LIBRARY CARD TO THE LIBRARY IN ALEXANDRIA.
A ROSE BUSH, A NIGHTINGALE, AND A BLACK RUBBER DOG-COLLAR.

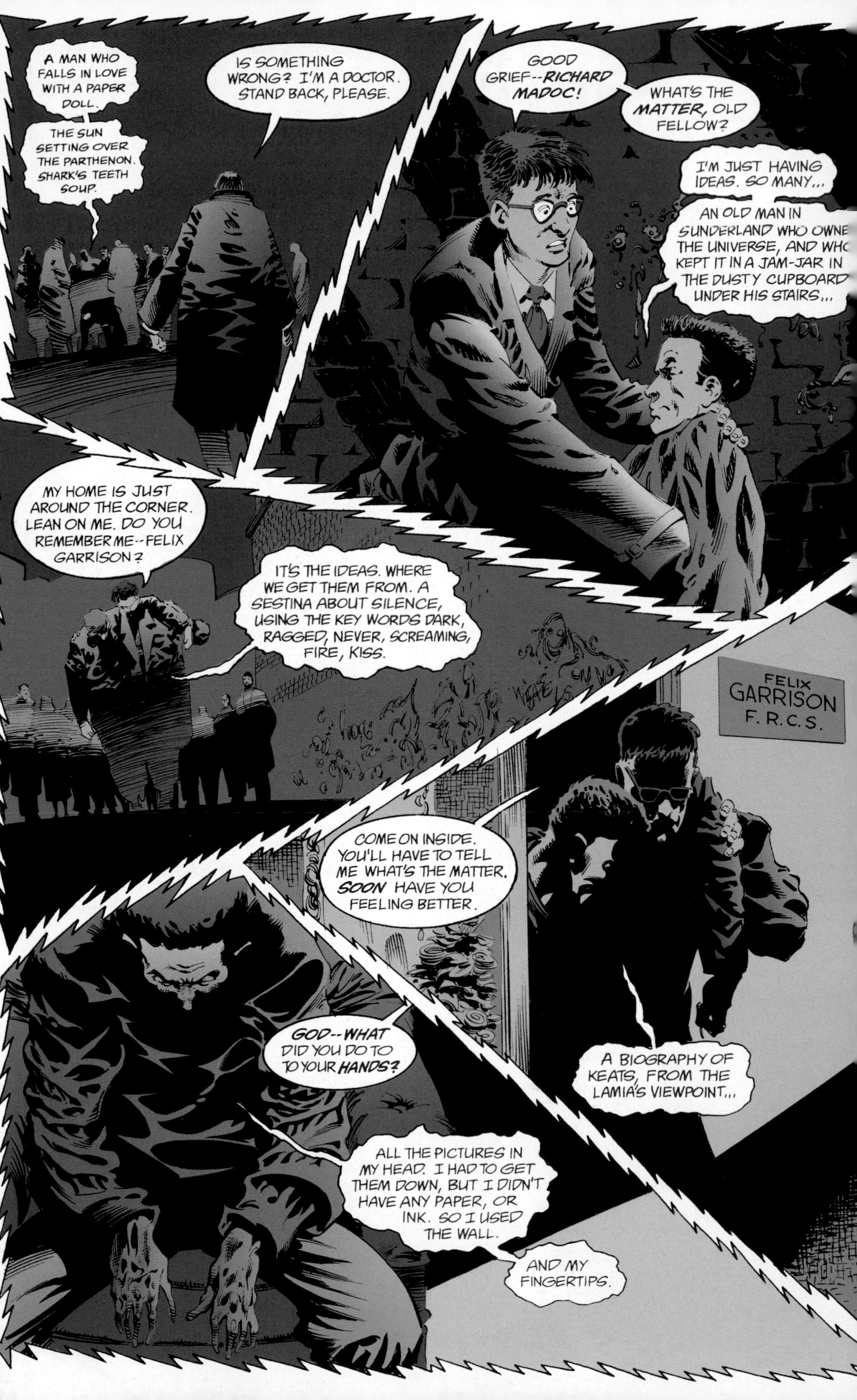

A MAN WHO FALLS IN LOVE WITH A PAPER DOLL.
THE SUN SETTING OVER THE PARTHENON. SHARK'S TEETH SOUP.
IS SOMETHING WRONG? I'M A DOCTOR. STAND BACK, PLEASE.
GOOD GRIEF--**RICHARD MADOC!**
WHAT'S THE **MATTER,** OLD FELLOW?
I'M JUST HAVING IDEAS. SO MANY...
AN OLD MAN IN SUNDERLAND WHO OWNE THE UNIVERSE, AND WHO KEPT IT IN A JAM-JAR IN THE DUSTY CUPBOARD UNDER HIS STAIRS...
MY HOME IS JUST AROUND THE CORNER. LEAN ON ME. DO YOU REMEMBER ME--FELIX GARRISON?
IT'S THE IDEAS. WHERE WE GET THEM FROM. A SESTINA ABOUT SILENCE, USING THE KEY WORDS DARK, RAGGED, NEVER, SCREAMING, FIRE, KISS.
FELIX GARRISON F. R. C. S.
COME ON INSIDE. YOU'LL HAVE TO TELL ME WHAT'S THE MATTER. **SOON** HAVE YOU FEELING BETTER.
A BIOGRAPHY OF KEATS, FROM THE LAMIA'S VIEWPOINT...
GOD--WHAT DID YOU DO TO YOUR **HANDS?**
ALL THE PICTURES IN MY HEAD. I HAD TO GET THEM DOWN, BUT I DIDN'T HAVE ANY PAPER, OR INK. SO I USED THE WALL.
AND MY FINGERTIPS.

THE IDEAS, INSIDE. ALL THE [PICT]URES AND POEMS AND TALES [AND] SONGS AND PLAYS AND [S]PEECHES AND FRAGMENTS... THEY'RE ALL COMING OUT. YOU MUST HELP ME.

I'LL GIVE YOU A SEDATIVE, AND BANDAGE THOSE FINGERS.

NO! NO... I'M SORRY. NOTHING LIKE THAT.

IT'S HER REVENGE, YOU SEE. OR HIS REVENGE. I SAID I NEEDED THE IDEAS--BUT THEY'RE COMING SO FAST, SWAMPING ME, OVER-WHELMING ME...

YOU HAVE TO MAKE THEM STOP.

HERE-- THIS WILL CALM YOUR NERVES.

NO! I TOLD YOU.

LOOK-- GO TO MY HOUSE. THE KEYS ARE IN MY POCKET IF-- IF YOU CAN TAKE THEM OUT FOR ME. I DON'T THINK I CAN USE MY HANDS ANYMORE.

GO UPSTAIRS. [A]T THE TOP OF THE [HO]USE THERE'S A ROOM. [TH]ERE'S A WOMAN IN THERE.

LET HER OUT. [S]HE'S LOCKED UP [I]N THERE, YOU SEE.

TELL HER--TELL [H]ER SHE CAN GO. THAT [I] FREE HER. MAKE [H]ER LEAVE. MAKE HER GO AWAY.

I SIGNED A BOOK FOR YOU ONCE, DIDN'T I?

OH GOD. PLEASE.

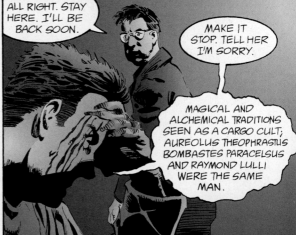

ALL RIGHT. STAY HERE. I'LL BE BACK SOON.

MAKE IT STOP. TELL HER I'M SORRY.

MAGICAL AND ALCHEMICAL TRADITIONS SEEN AS A CARGO CULT; AUREOLUS THEOPHRASTUS BOMBASTUS PARACELSUS AND RAYMOND LULLI WERE THE SAME MAN.

UM. **HELLO?**

IS THERE, UM, ANYONE HERE? HE SAYS -- RIC, UH, SAYS YOU'RE FREE TO GO. **HELLO?**

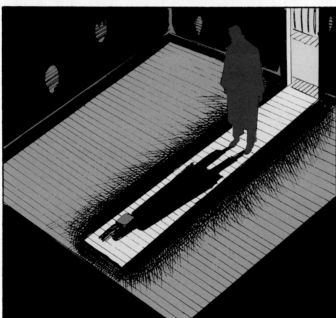

HERE COMES A CANDLE
BY ERASMUS FRY

'SHE WAS HIS MUSE -- AND THE SLAVE OF HIS LUST!'

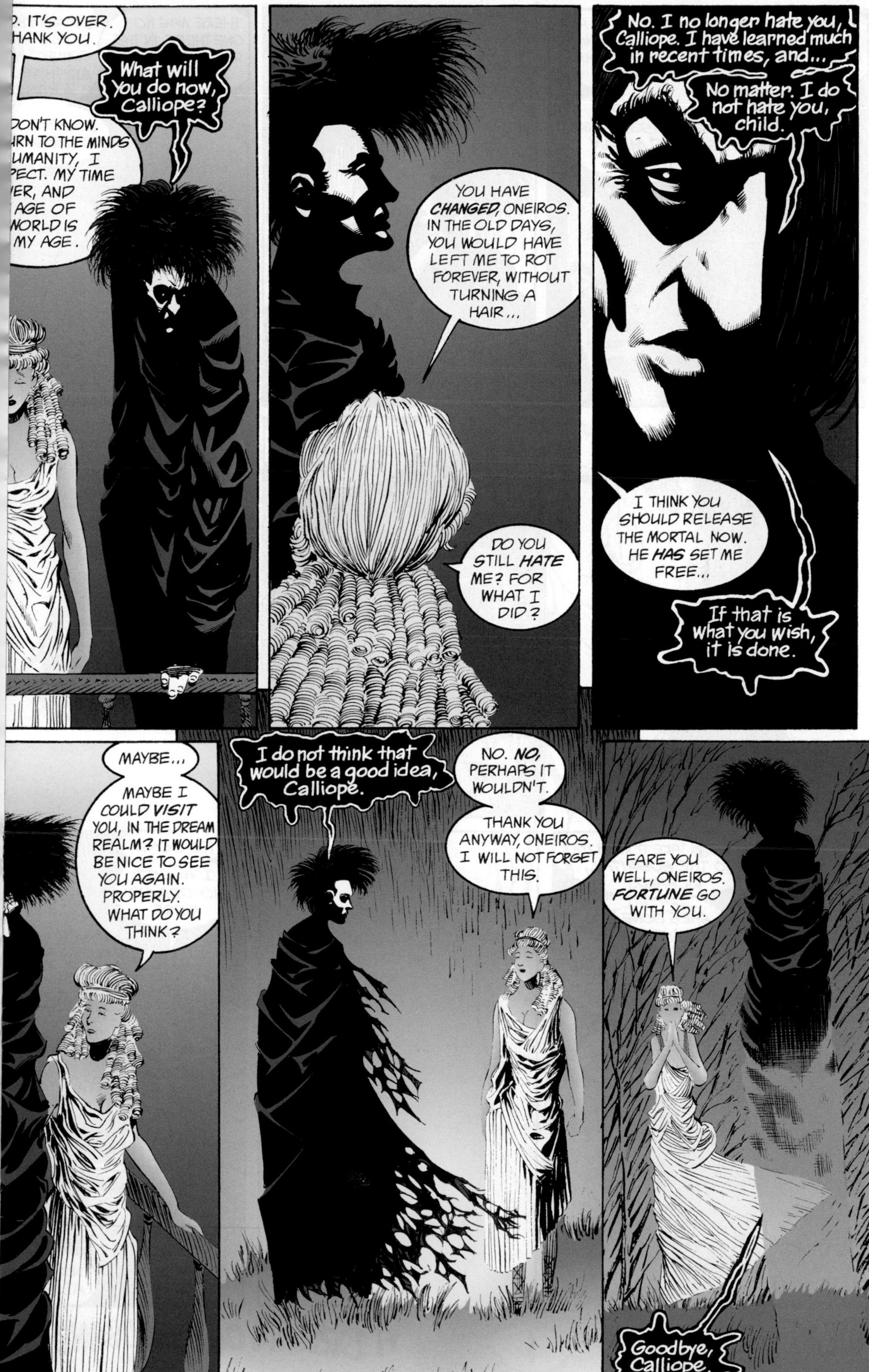

O. IT'S OVER. HANK YOU.
What will You do now, Calliope?
DON'T KNOW. URN TO THE MINDS UMANITY, I PECT. MY TIME VER, AND AGE OF WORLD IS MY AGE.
YOU HAVE CHANGED, ONEIROS. IN THE OLD DAYS, YOU WOULD HAVE LEFT ME TO ROT FOREVER, WITHOUT TURNING A HAIR...
DO YOU STILL HATE ME? FOR WHAT I DID?
No. I no longer hate you, Calliope. I have learned much in recent times, and...
No matter. I do not hate you, child.
I THINK YOU SHOULD RELEASE THE MORTAL NOW. HE HAS SET ME FREE...
If that is what you wish, it is done.
MAYBE...
MAYBE I COULD VISIT YOU, IN THE DREAM REALM? IT WOULD BE NICE TO SEE YOU AGAIN. PROPERLY. WHAT DO YOU THINK?
I do not think that would be a good idea, Calliope.
NO. NO, PERHAPS IT WOULDN'T.
THANK YOU ANYWAY, ONEIROS. I WILL NOT FORGET THIS.
FARE YOU WELL, ONEIROS. FORTUNE GO WITH YOU.
Goodbye, Calliope.

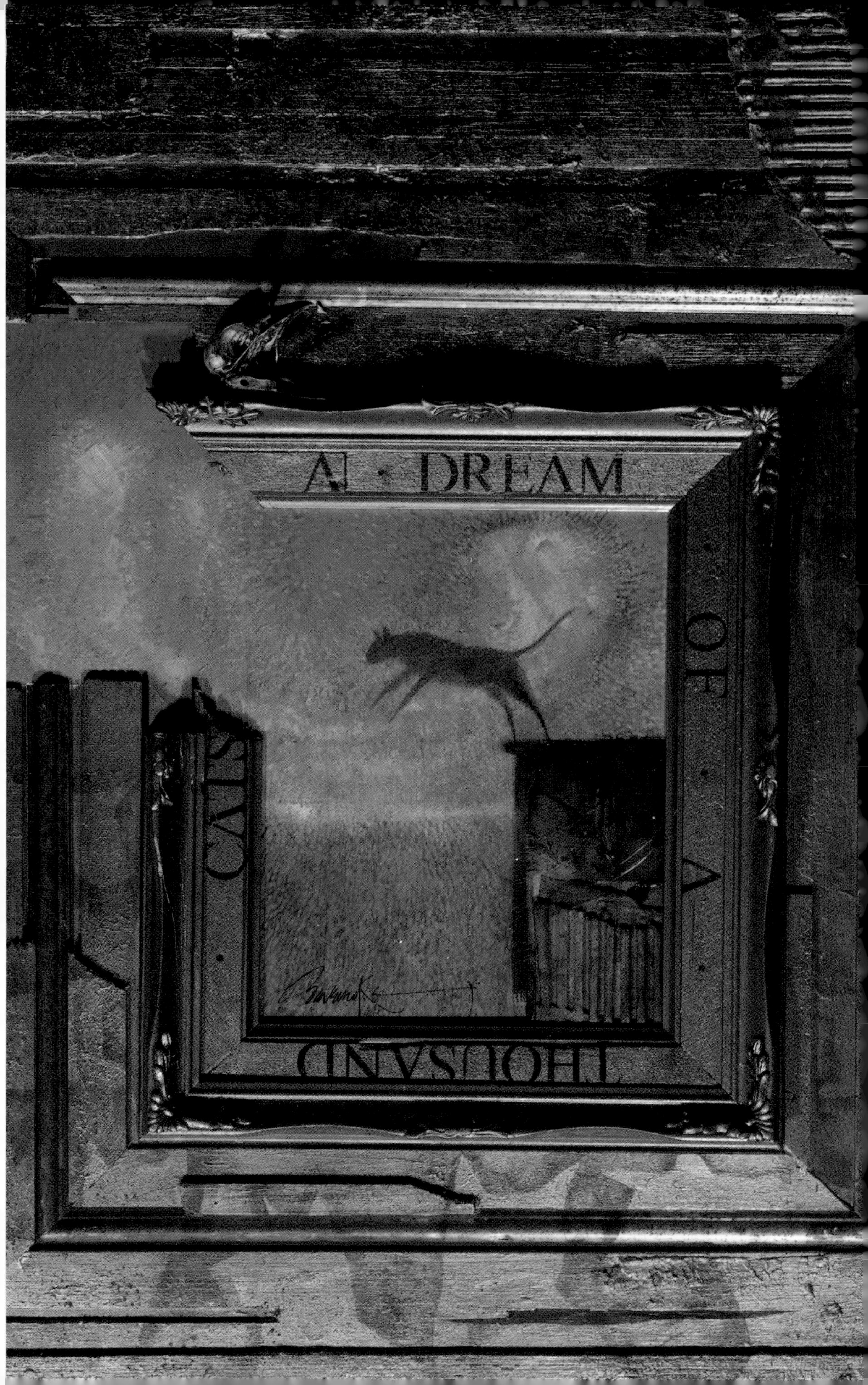
A · DREAM
OF · A
THOUSAND
CATS

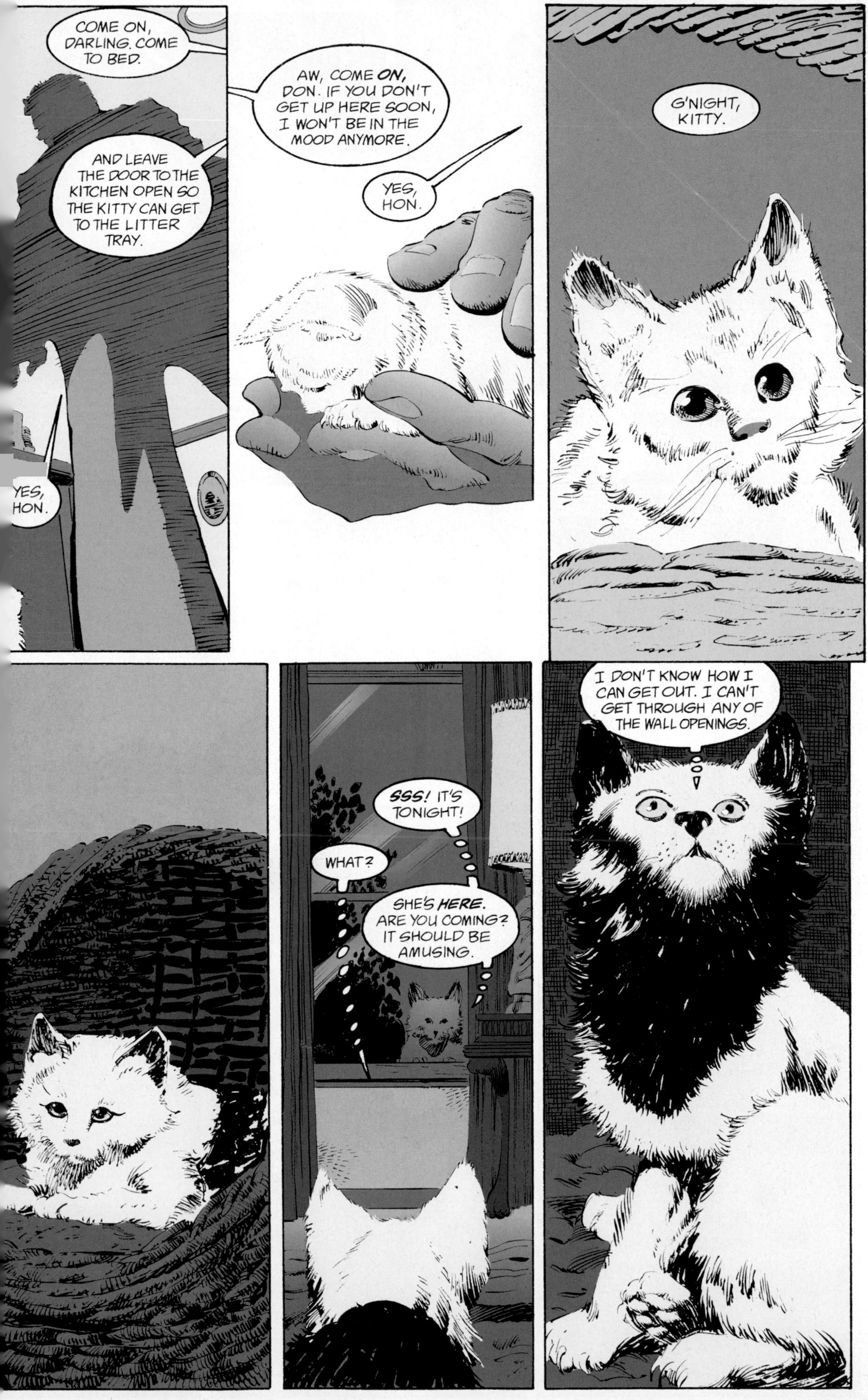
COME ON, DARLING. COME TO BED.
AND LEAVE THE DOOR TO THE KITCHEN OPEN SO THE KITTY CAN GET TO THE LITTER TRAY.
YES, HON.
AW, COME **ON,** DON. IF YOU DON'T GET UP HERE SOON, I WON'T BE IN THE MOOD ANYMORE.
YES, HON.
G'NIGHT, KITTY.
SSS! IT'S TONIGHT!
WHAT?
SHE'S **HERE.** ARE YOU COMING? IT SHOULD BE AMUSING.
I DON'T KNOW HOW I CAN GET OUT. I CAN'T GET THROUGH ANY OF THE WALL OPENINGS.

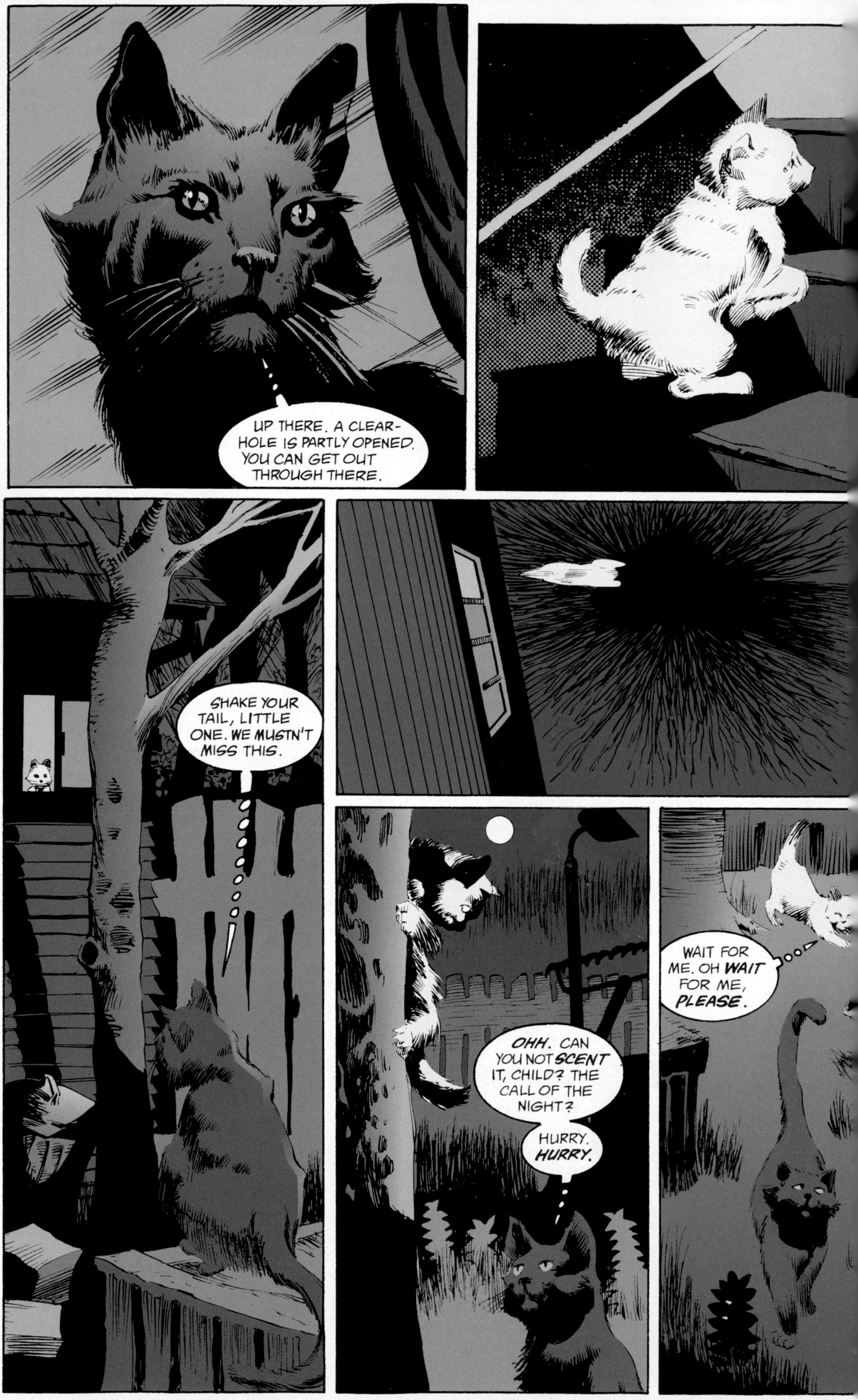
UP THERE. A CLEAR-HOLE IS PARTLY OPENED. YOU CAN GET OUT THROUGH THERE.
SHAKE YOUR TAIL, LITTLE ONE. WE MUSTN'T MISS THIS.
OHH. CAN YOU NOT SCENT IT, CHILD? THE CALL OF THE NIGHT?
HURRY. HURRY.
WAIT FOR ME. OH WAIT FOR ME, PLEASE.

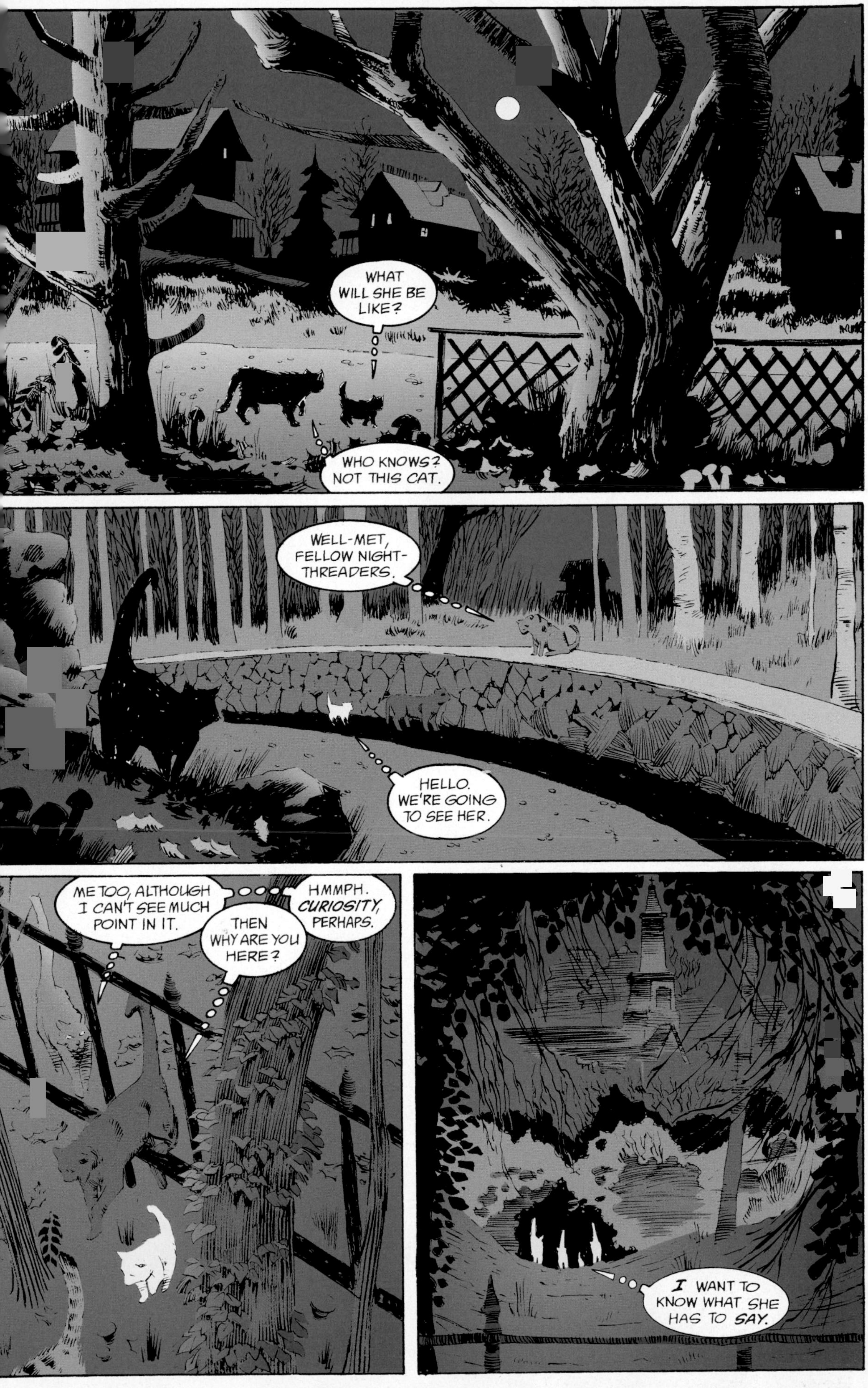
WHAT WILL SHE BE LIKE?
WHO KNOWS? NOT THIS CAT.
WELL-MET, FELLOW NIGHT-THREADERS.
HELLO. WE'RE GOING TO SEE HER.
ME TOO, ALTHOUGH I CAN'T SEE MUCH POINT IN IT.
HMMPH. *CURIOSITY,* PERHAPS.
THEN WHY ARE YOU HERE?
I WANT TO KNOW WHAT SHE HAS TO *SAY.*

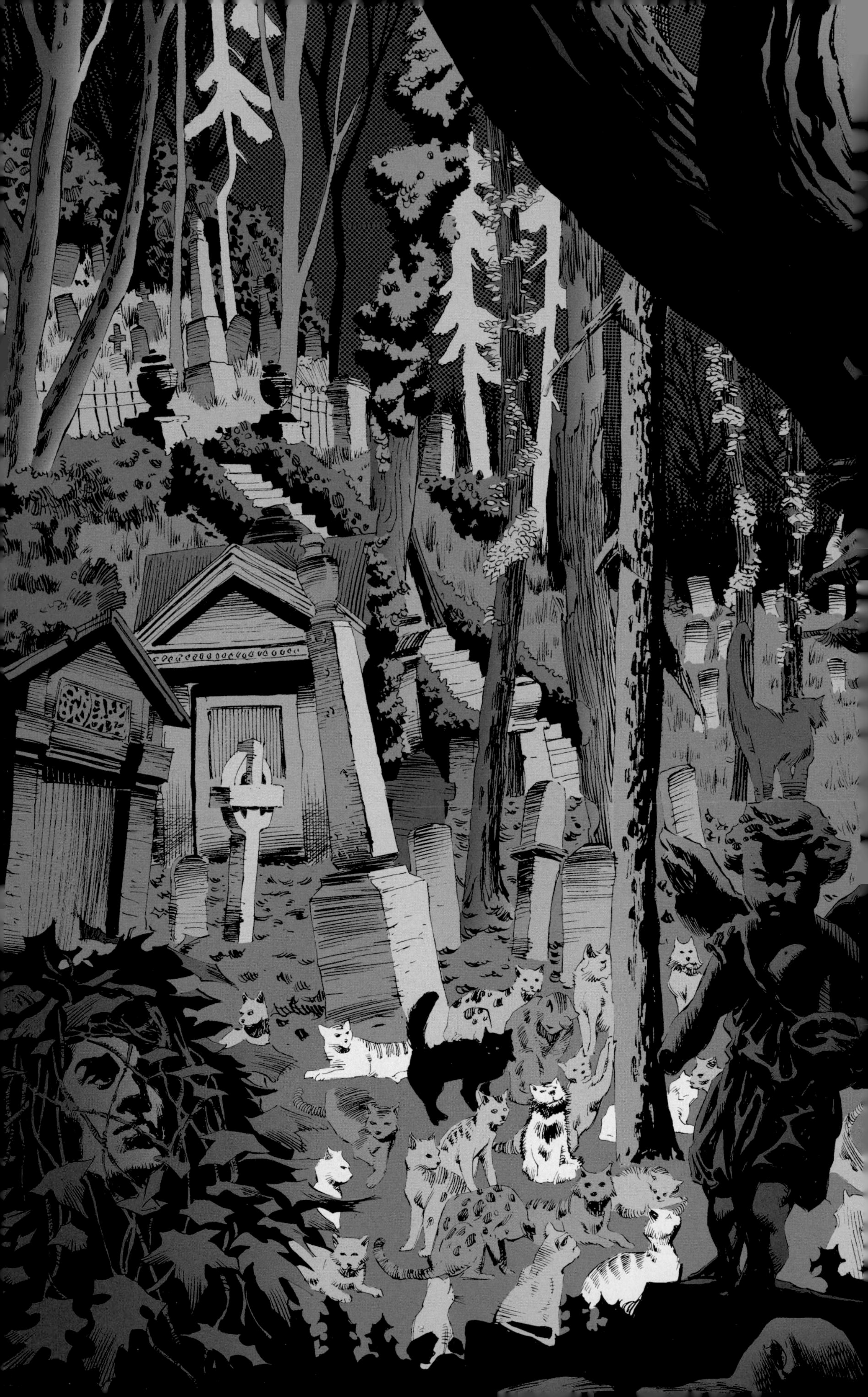

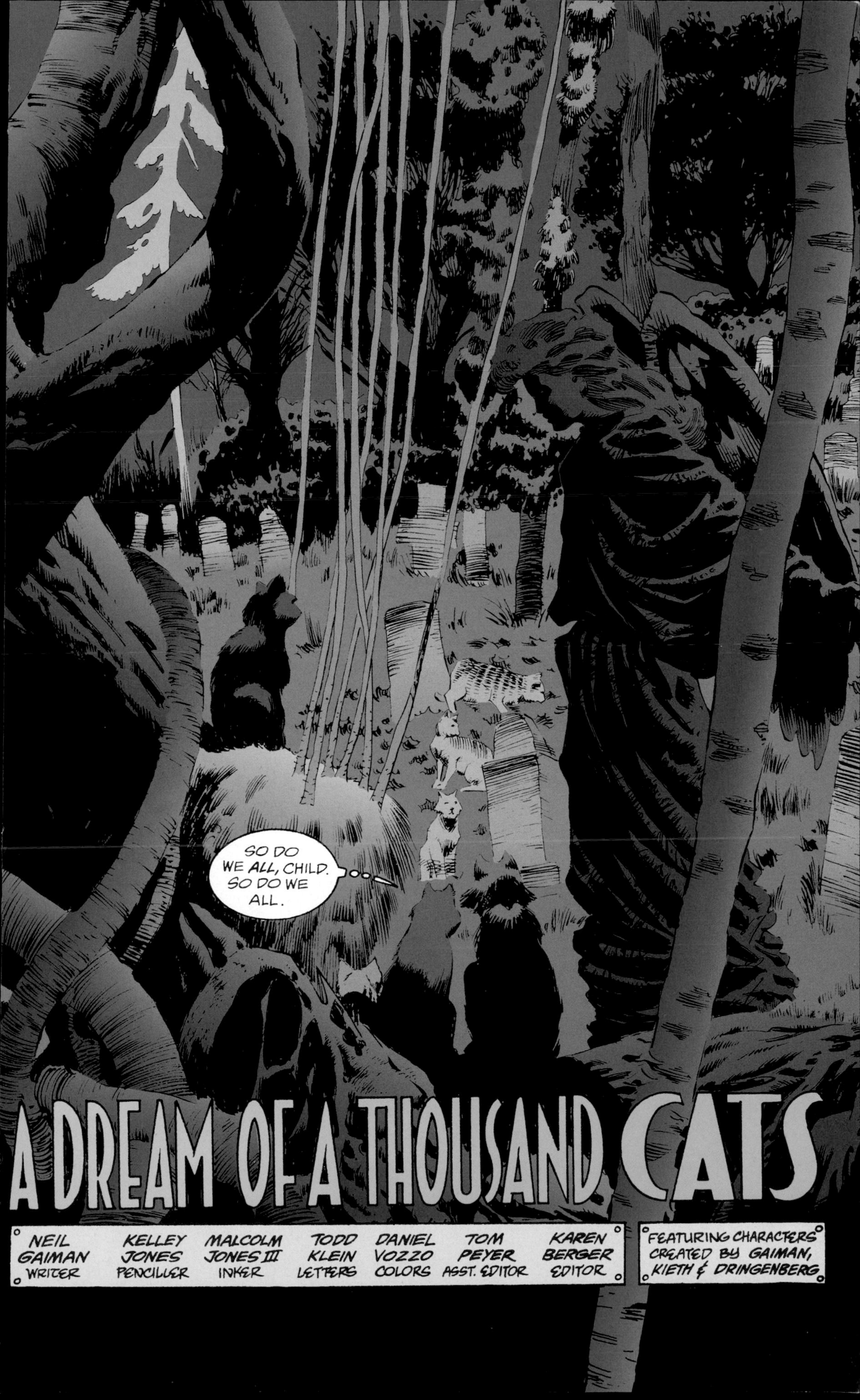
SO DO WE ALL, CHILD. SO DO WE ALL.
A DREAM OF A THOUSAND CATS
NEIL GAIMAN WRITER
KELLEY JONES PENCILLER
MALCOLM JONES III INKER
TODD KLEIN LETTERS
DANIEL VOZZO COLORS
TOM PEYER ASST. EDITOR
KAREN BERGER EDITOR
FEATURING CHARACTERS CREATED BY GAIMAN, KIETH & DRINGENBERG

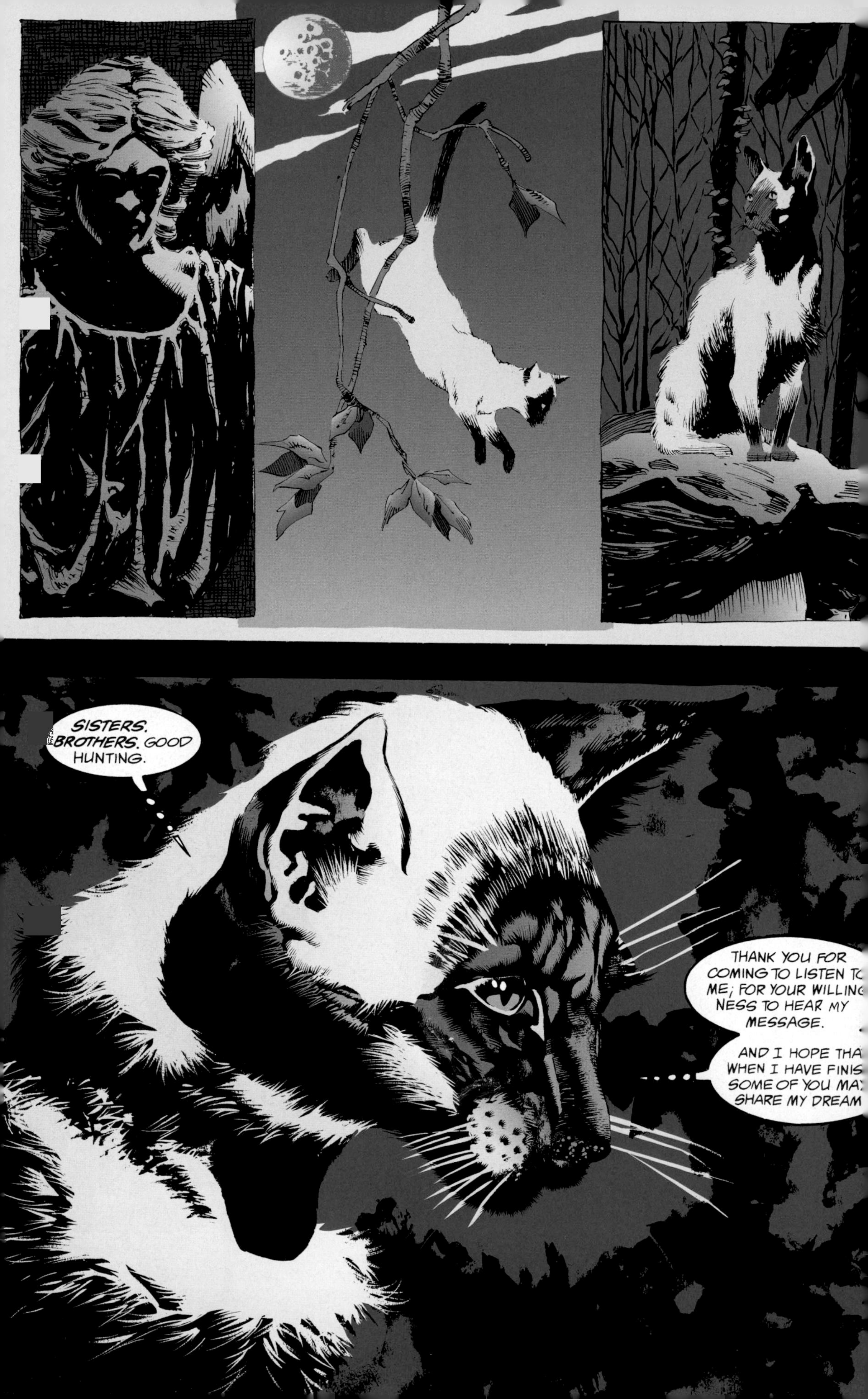
SISTERS. BROTHERS. GOOD HUNTING.
THANK YOU FOR COMING TO LISTEN T ME; FOR YOUR WILLIN NESS TO HEAR MY MESSAGE.
AND I HOPE THA WHEN I HAVE FINIS SOME OF YOU MA SHARE MY DREAM

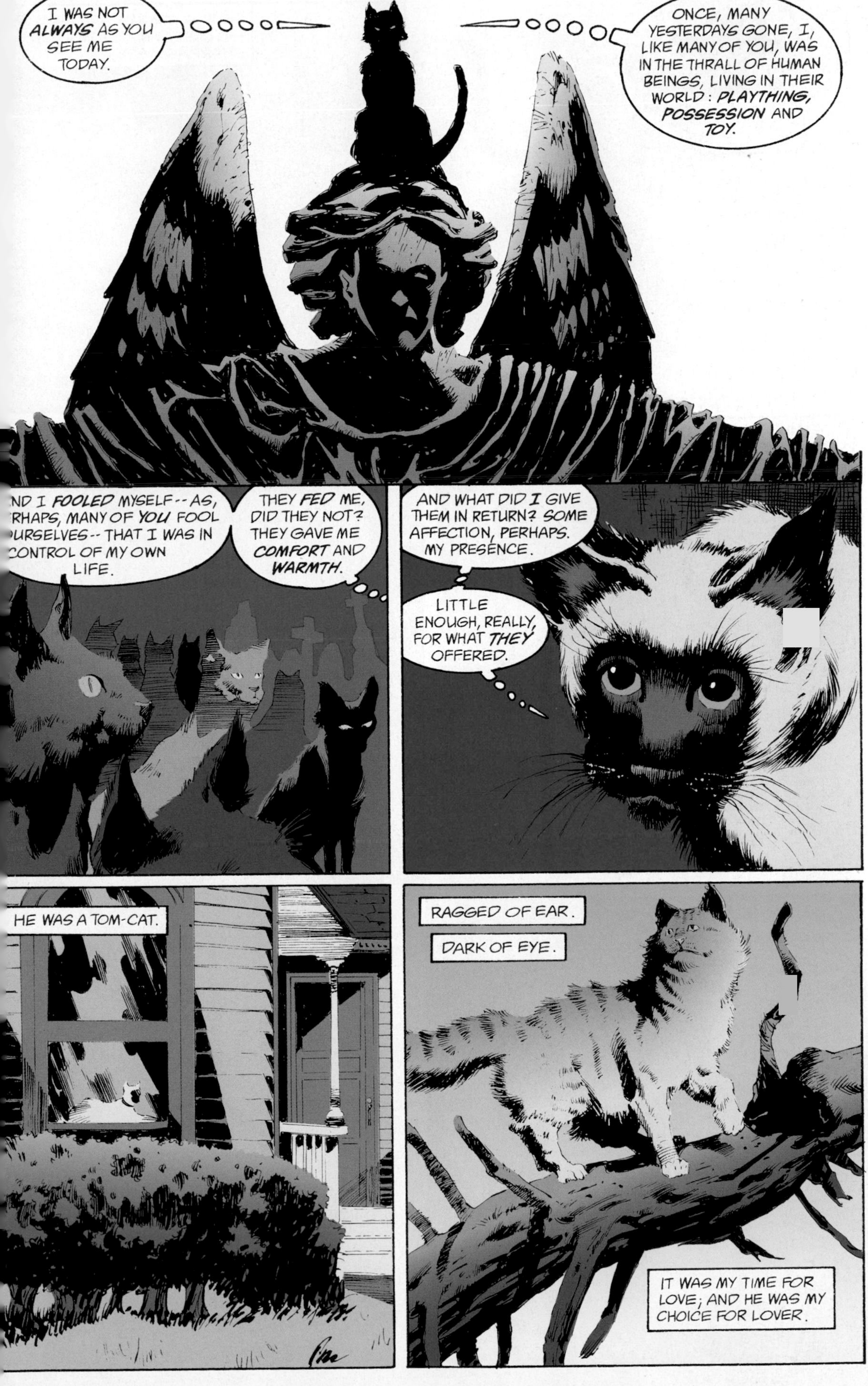

I WAS NOT ALWAYS AS YOU SEE ME TODAY.
ONCE, MANY YESTERDAYS GONE, I, LIKE MANY OF YOU, WAS IN THE THRALL OF HUMAN BEINGS, LIVING IN THEIR WORLD: PLAYTHING, POSSESSION AND TOY.
ND I FOOLED MYSELF-- AS, RHAPS, MANY OF YOU FOOL URSELVES-- THAT I WAS IN CONTROL OF MY OWN LIFE.
THEY FED ME, DID THEY NOT? THEY GAVE ME COMFORT AND WARMTH.
AND WHAT DID I GIVE THEM IN RETURN? SOME AFFECTION, PERHAPS. MY PRESENCE.
LITTLE ENOUGH, REALLY, FOR WHAT THEY OFFERED.
HE WAS A TOM-CAT.
RAGGED OF EAR.
DARK OF EYE.
IT WAS MY TIME FOR LOVE; AND HE WAS MY CHOICE FOR LOVER.

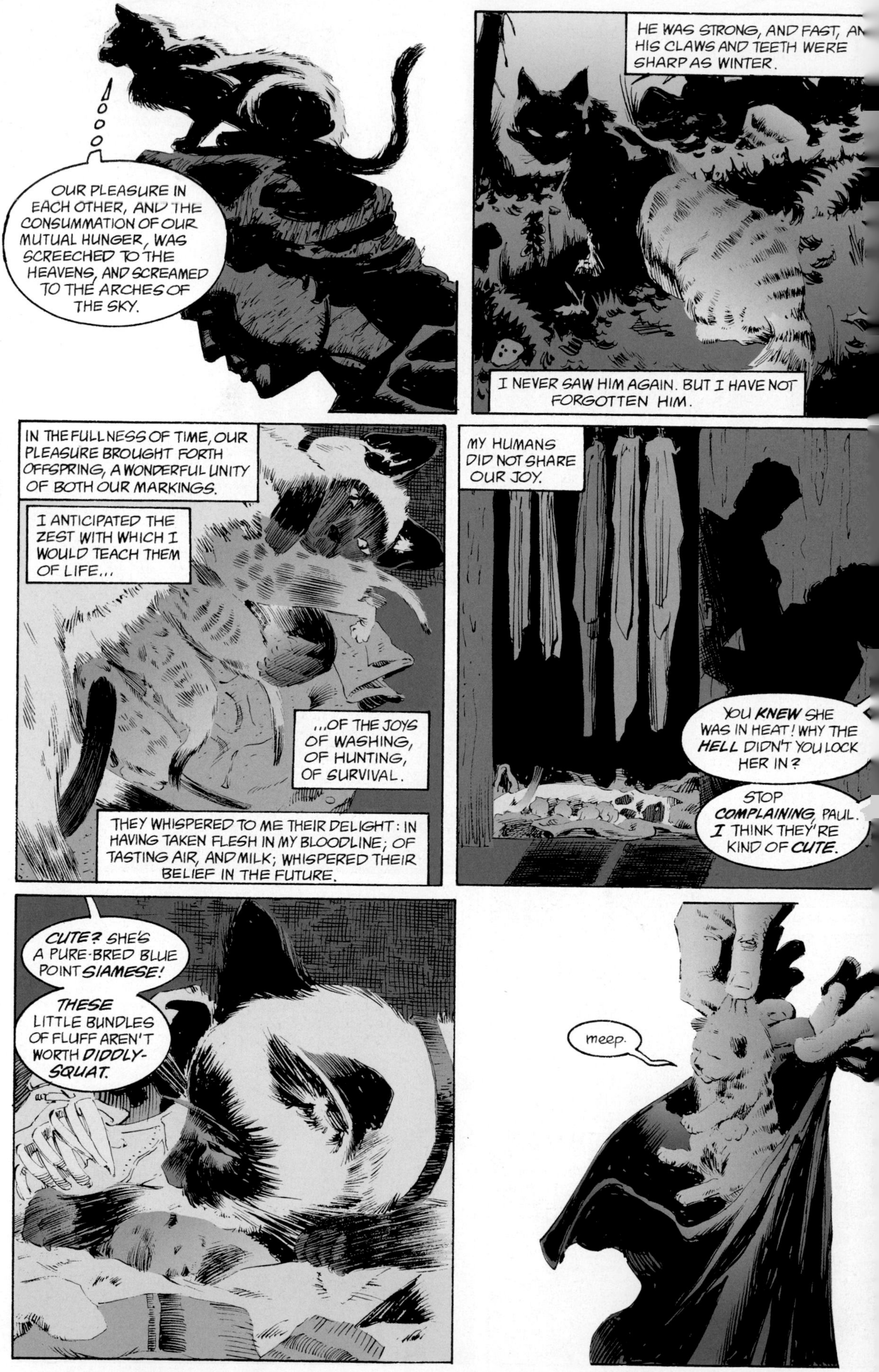
OUR PLEASURE IN EACH OTHER, AND THE CONSUMMATION OF OUR MUTUAL HUNGER, WAS SCREECHED TO THE HEAVENS, AND SCREAMED TO THE ARCHES OF THE SKY.
HE WAS STRONG, AND FAST, AN HIS CLAWS AND TEETH WERE SHARP AS WINTER.
I NEVER SAW HIM AGAIN. BUT I HAVE NOT FORGOTTEN HIM.
IN THE FULLNESS OF TIME, OUR PLEASURE BROUGHT FORTH OFFSPRING, A WONDERFUL UNITY OF BOTH OUR MARKINGS.
I ANTICIPATED THE ZEST WITH WHICH I WOULD TEACH THEM OF LIFE...
...OF THE JOYS OF WASHING, OF HUNTING, OF SURVIVAL.
THEY WHISPERED TO ME THEIR DELIGHT: IN HAVING TAKEN FLESH IN MY BLOODLINE; OF TASTING AIR, AND MILK; WHISPERED THEIR BELIEF IN THE FUTURE.
MY HUMANS DID NOT SHARE OUR JOY.
YOU KNEW SHE WAS IN HEAT! WHY THE HELL DIDN'T YOU LOCK HER IN?
STOP COMPLAINING, PAUL. I THINK THEY'RE KIND OF CUTE.
CUTE? SHE'S A PURE-BRED BLUE POINT SIAMESE!
THESE LITTLE BUNDLES OF FLUFF AREN'T WORTH DIDDLY-SQUAT.
meep.

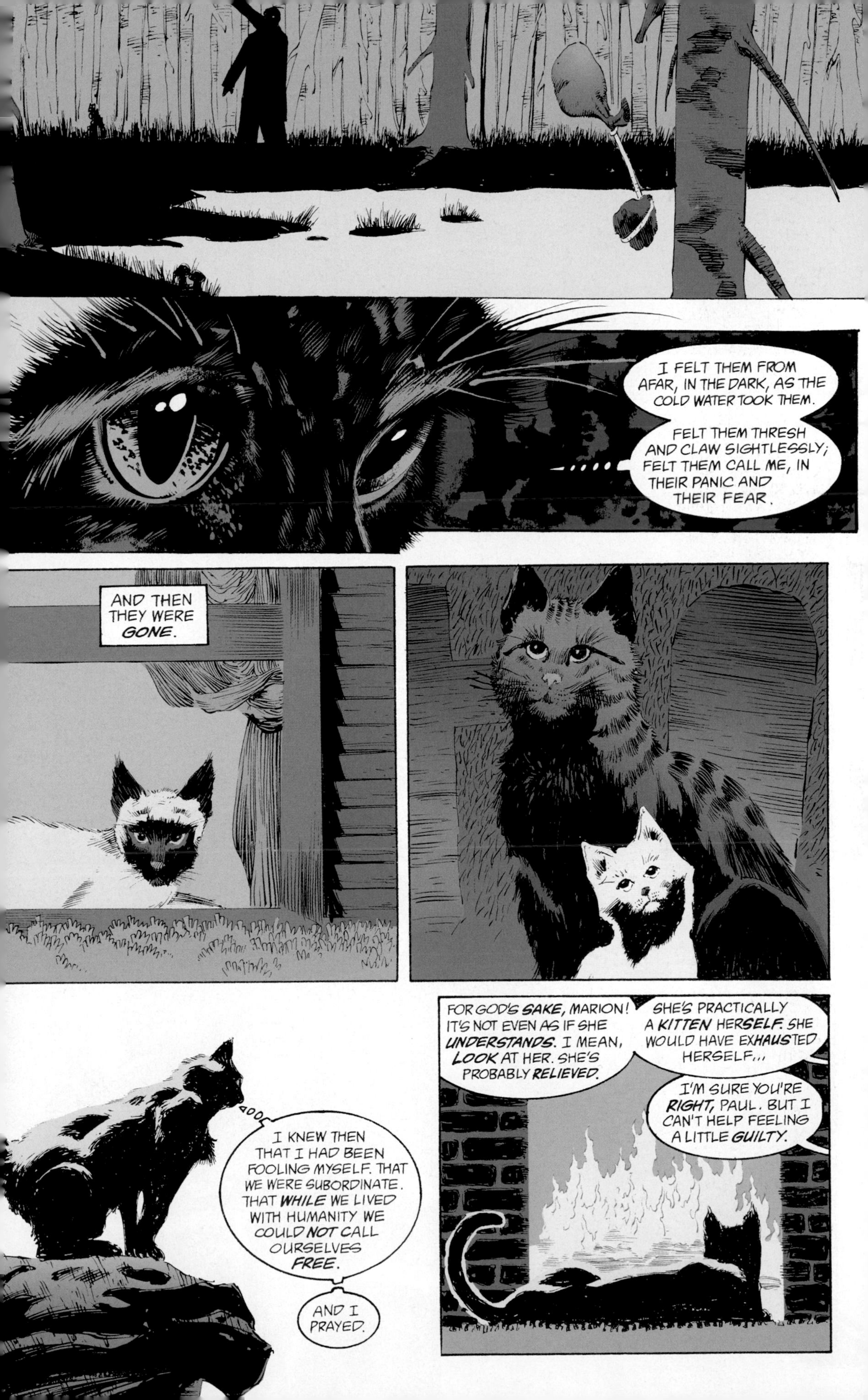
I FELT THEM FROM AFAR, IN THE DARK, AS THE COLD WATER TOOK THEM.
FELT THEM THRESH AND CLAW SIGHTLESSLY; FELT THEM CALL ME, IN THEIR PANIC AND THEIR FEAR.
AND THEN THEY WERE GONE.
I KNEW THEN THAT I HAD BEEN FOOLING MYSELF. THAT WE WERE SUBORDINATE. THAT WHILE WE LIVED WITH HUMANITY WE COULD NOT CALL OURSELVES FREE.
AND I PRAYED.
FOR GOD'S SAKE, MARION! IT'S NOT EVEN AS IF SHE UNDERSTANDS. I MEAN, LOOK AT HER. SHE'S PROBABLY RELIEVED.
SHE'S PRACTICALLY A KITTEN HERSELF. SHE WOULD HAVE EXHAUSTED HERSELF...
I'M SURE YOU'RE RIGHT, PAUL. BUT I CAN'T HELP FEELING A LITTLE GUILTY.

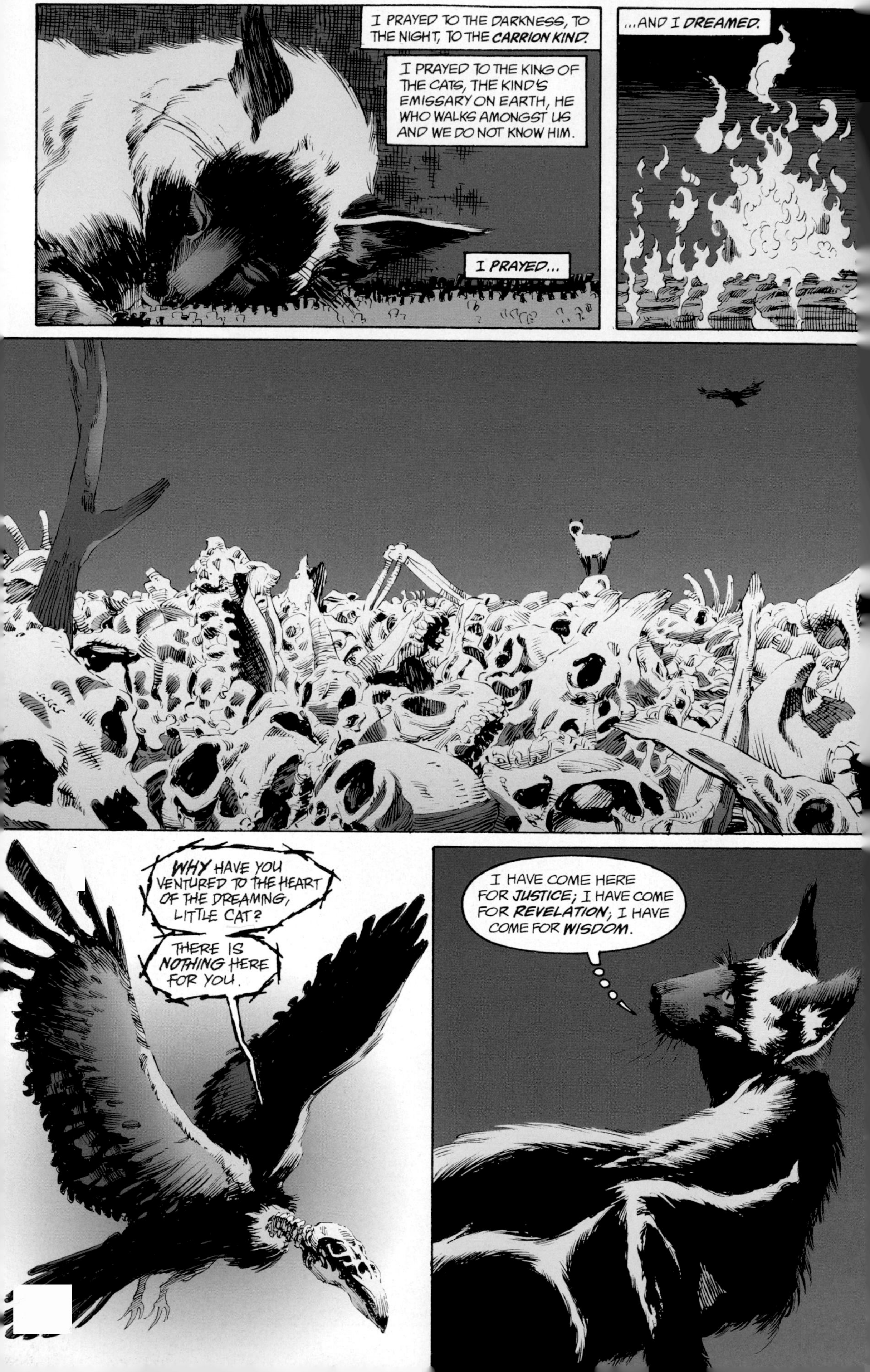
I PRAYED TO THE DARKNESS, TO THE NIGHT, TO THE CARRION KIND.
I PRAYED TO THE KING OF THE CATS, THE KIND'S EMISSARY ON EARTH, HE WHO WALKS AMONGST US AND WE DO NOT KNOW HIM.
I PRAYED...
...AND I DREAMED.
WHY HAVE YOU VENTURED TO THE HEART OF THE DREAMING, LITTLE CAT?
THERE IS NOTHING HERE FOR YOU.
I HAVE COME HERE FOR JUSTICE; I HAVE COME FOR REVELATION; I HAVE COME FOR WISDOM.

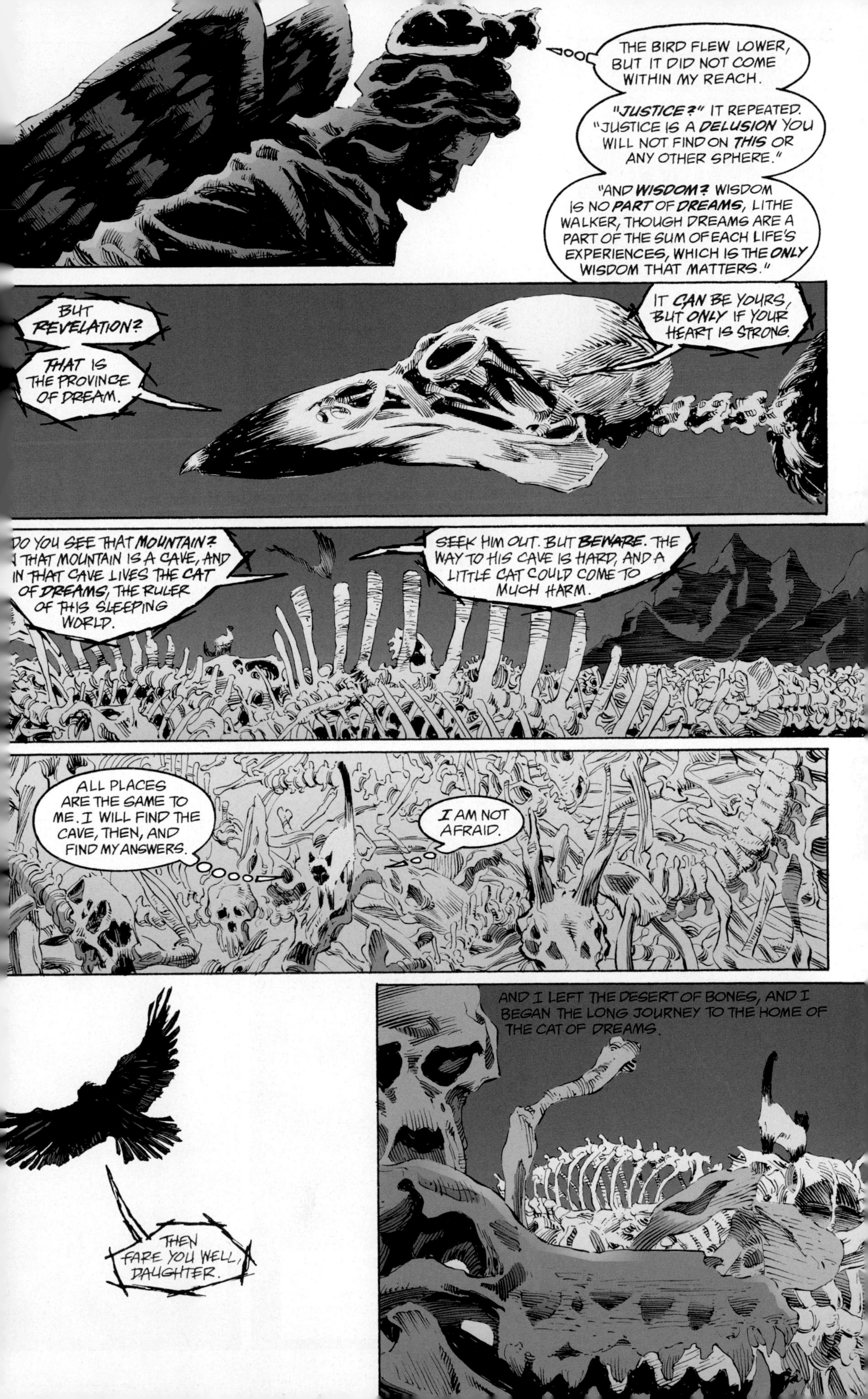
THE BIRD FLEW LOWER, BUT IT DID NOT COME WITHIN MY REACH.
"JUSTICE?" IT REPEATED. "JUSTICE IS A DELUSION YOU WILL NOT FIND ON THIS OR ANY OTHER SPHERE."
"AND WISDOM? WISDOM IS NO PART OF DREAMS, LITHE WALKER, THOUGH DREAMS ARE A PART OF THE SUM OF EACH LIFE'S EXPERIENCES, WHICH IS THE ONLY WISDOM THAT MATTERS."
BUT REVELATION?
THAT IS THE PROVINCE OF DREAM.
IT CAN BE YOURS, BUT ONLY IF YOUR HEART IS STRONG.
DO YOU SEE THAT MOUNTAIN? IN THAT MOUNTAIN IS A CAVE, AND IN THAT CAVE LIVES THE CAT OF DREAMS, THE RULER OF THIS SLEEPING WORLD.
SEEK HIM OUT. BUT BEWARE. THE WAY TO HIS CAVE IS HARD, AND A LITTLE CAT COULD COME TO MUCH HARM.
ALL PLACES ARE THE SAME TO ME. I WILL FIND THE CAVE, THEN, AND FIND MY ANSWERS.
I AM NOT AFRAID.
THEN FARE YOU WELL, DAUGHTER.
AND I LEFT THE DESERT OF BONES, AND I BEGAN THE LONG JOURNEY TO THE HOME OF THE CAT OF DREAMS.

I WALKED THROUGH THE WOOD OF GHOSTS, WHERE THE DEAD AND THE LOST WHISPERED CONTINUALLY, PROMISED ME WORLDS IF I WOULD ONLY STOP AND PLAY WITH THEM.

I CLOSED MY EARS TO THEIR ENTREATIES.

AT ONE POINT I THOUGHT I HEARD MY CHILDREN CALLING ME. BUT I STRAIGHTENED MY TAIL, AND I WALKED FORWARD.

I WALKED THROUGH THE COLD PLACES, HARD AND FROZEN, WHERE EVERY STEP WAS PAIN, EVERY MOVEMENT WAS TORMENT.

I WALKED ON.

I WALKED THROUGH THE WETNESS THAT NUMBED MY PAWS, DRENCHED MY FUR, TRIED TO WASH AWAY MY MEMORIES.

I WALKED THROUGH THE DARKNESS, THROUGH THE VOID, WHERE EVERYTHING WAS SUCKED FROM ME--EVERYTHING THAT MAKES ME WHAT I AM.

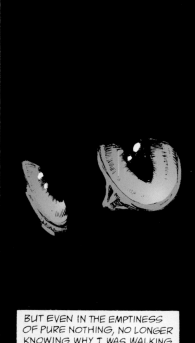

BUT EVEN IN THE EMPTINESS OF PURE NOTHING, NO LONGER KNOWING WHY I WAS WALKING OR WHAT I WAS SEEKING, I WALKED ONWARD.

AND, AFTER A TIME, MY SELF RETURNED TO ME, AND I LEFT THAT PLACE, AND I FOUND MYSELF AT THE MOUNTAIN OF THE CAT OF DREAMS.

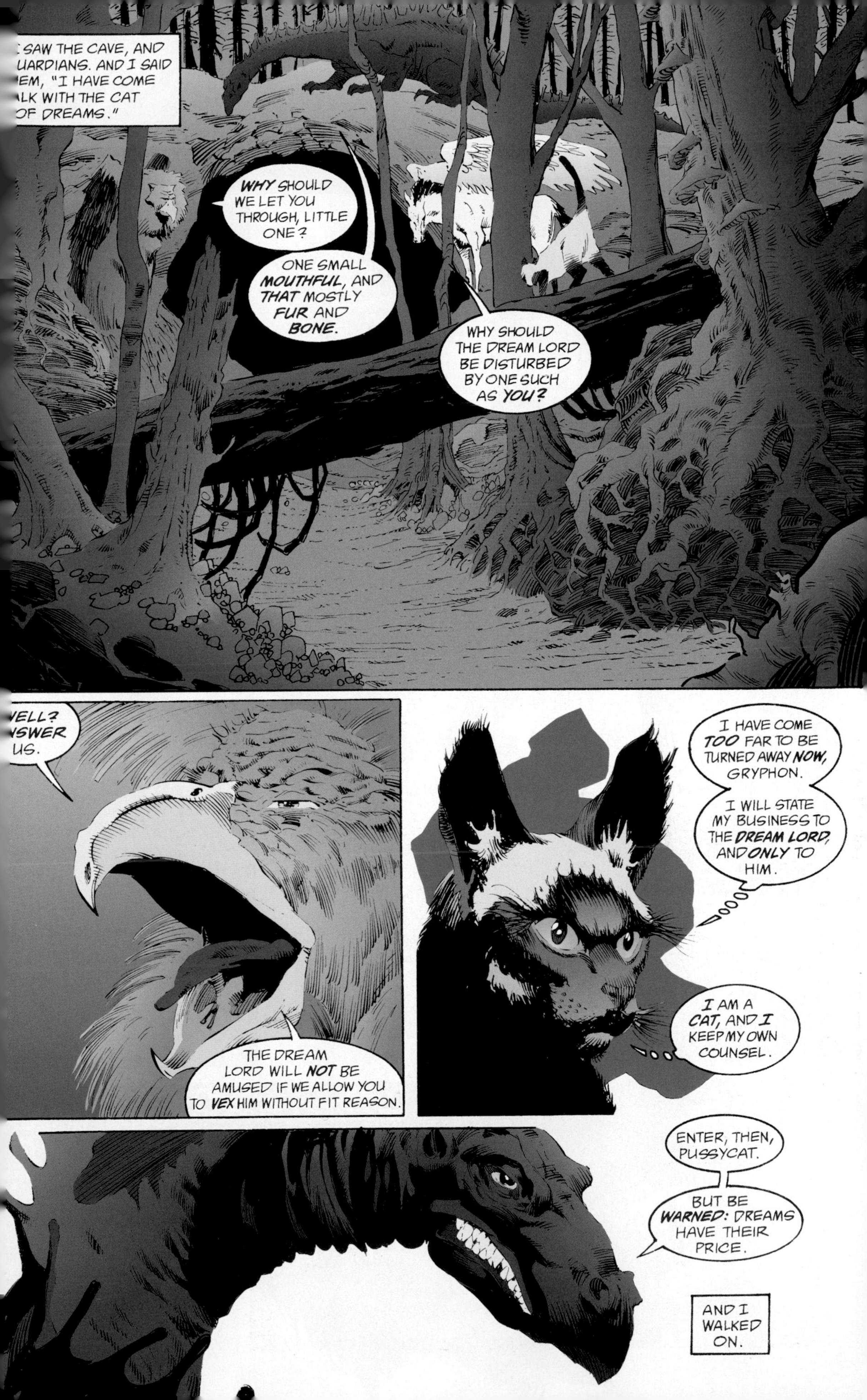

SAW THE CAVE, AND UARDIANS. AND I SAID EM, "I HAVE COME LK WITH THE CAT OF DREAMS."
WHY SHOULD WE LET YOU THROUGH, LITTLE ONE?
ONE SMALL MOUTHFUL, AND THAT MOSTLY FUR AND BONE.
WHY SHOULD THE DREAM LORD BE DISTURBED BY ONE SUCH AS YOU?
ELL? NSWER US.
THE DREAM LORD WILL NOT BE AMUSED IF WE ALLOW YOU TO VEX HIM WITHOUT FIT REASON.
I HAVE COME TOO FAR TO BE TURNED AWAY NOW, GRYPHON.
I WILL STATE MY BUSINESS TO THE DREAM LORD, AND ONLY TO HIM.
I AM A CAT, AND I KEEP MY OWN COUNSEL.
ENTER, THEN, PUSSYCAT.
BUT BE WARNED: DREAMS HAVE THEIR PRICE.
AND I WALKED ON.

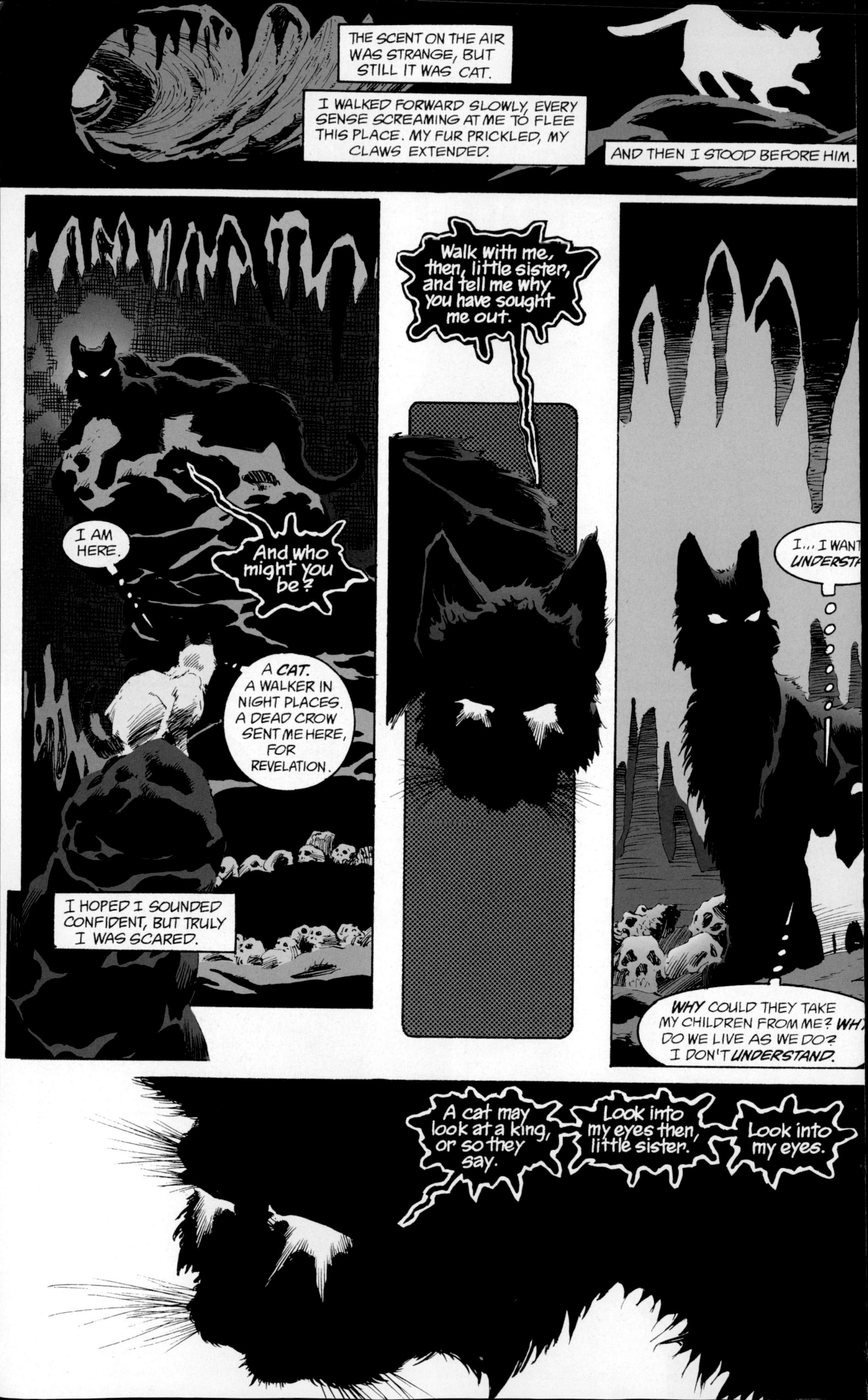
THE SCENT ON THE AIR WAS STRANGE, BUT STILL IT WAS CAT.
I WALKED FORWARD SLOWLY, EVERY SENSE SCREAMING AT ME TO FLEE THIS PLACE. MY FUR PRICKLED, MY CLAWS EXTENDED.
AND THEN I STOOD BEFORE HIM.
I AM HERE.
And who might you be?
A CAT. A WALKER IN NIGHT PLACES. A DEAD CROW SENT ME HERE, FOR REVELATION.
I HOPED I SOUNDED CONFIDENT, BUT TRULY I WAS SCARED.
Walk with me, then, little sister, and tell me why you have sought me out.
I... I WANT
WHY COULD THEY TAKE MY CHILDREN FROM ME? WHY DO WE LIVE AS WE DO? I DON'T UNDERSTAND.
A cat may look at a king, or so they say.
Look into my eyes then, little sister.
Look into my eyes.

AND IT SHOWED ME. IT TOLD ME THE TRUTH, EVEN AS I AM TELLING IT TO YOU NOW.

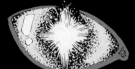

R IN ITS EYES SAW PICTURES. D IN THE CTURES I SAW E *TRUTH*.

ALL CATS CAN SEE FUTURES, AND SEE ECHOES OF THE PAST. WE CAN WATCH THE PASSAGE OF CREATURES FROM THE INFINITY OF NOW, FROM ALL THE WORLDS LIKE OURS, ONLY FRACTIONALLY DIFFERENT.

AND WE FOLLOW THEM WITH OUR EYES, GHOST THINGS, AND THE HUMANS SEE NOTHING.

BUT THE REALITY THE CAT OF DREAMS SHOWED ME TRANSCENDED ANYTHING I HAD IMAGINED.

MANY, MANY SEASONS AGO, CATS TRULY RULED THIS WORLD.

WE WERE LARGER THEN, AND THIS WHOLE WORLD WAS CREATED FOR OUR PLEASURE. WE ROAMED IT AS WE WOULD, TAKING WHAT WE WANTED.

IN THOSE TIMES HUMANS WERE TINY CREATURES, NO LARGER THAN WE ARE NOW.

AND THE HUMANS WOULD GROOM US, AND FEED US, AND PET US.

AND WHEN THE MOON SHONE FULL, WE WOULD *HUNT* THEM, AND WE WOULD EAT *PART* OF THEM, BUT CHIEFLY WE WOULD HUNT THEM...

...FOR THEY WERE MORE DELIGHTFUL TO HUNT EVEN THAN BIRDS, AND BACK THEN, MICE WERE TOO SMALL AND INSIGNIFICANT FOR US TO DEIGN TO TOUCH.

OH, THE *JOY* OF THOSE HUNTING DAYS, BENEATH THE CAT'S MOON. THE *GAME* OF *CAT* AND *MAN*...

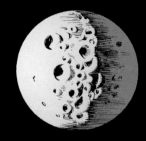

PRRRRRR.

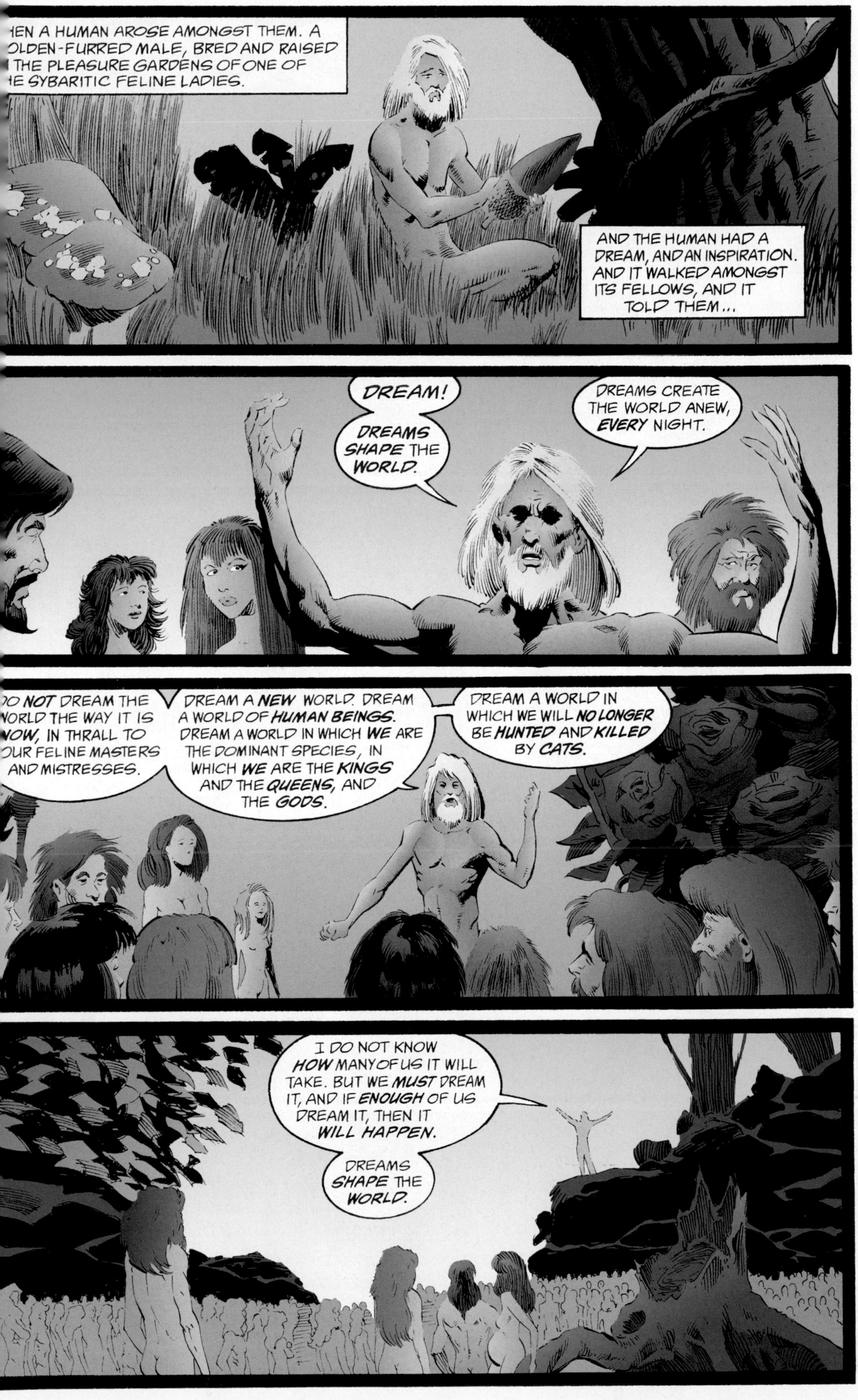
HEN A HUMAN AROSE AMONGST THEM. A OLDEN-FURRED MALE, BRED AND RAISED THE PLEASURE GARDENS OF ONE OF HE SYBARITIC FELINE LADIES.
AND THE HUMAN HAD A DREAM, AND AN INSPIRATION. AND IT WALKED AMONGST ITS FELLOWS, AND IT TOLD THEM...
DREAM! DREAMS SHAPE THE WORLD.
DREAMS CREATE THE WORLD ANEW, EVERY NIGHT.
O NOT DREAM THE ORLD THE WAY IT IS NOW, IN THRALL TO OUR FELINE MASTERS AND MISTRESSES.
DREAM A NEW WORLD. DREAM A WORLD OF HUMAN BEINGS. DREAM A WORLD IN WHICH WE ARE THE DOMINANT SPECIES, IN WHICH WE ARE THE KINGS AND THE QUEENS, AND THE GODS.
DREAM A WORLD IN WHICH WE WILL NO LONGER BE HUNTED AND KILLED BY CATS.
I DO NOT KNOW HOW MANY OF US IT WILL TAKE. BUT WE MUST DREAM IT, AND IF ENOUGH OF US DREAM IT, THEN IT WILL HAPPEN.
DREAMS SHAPE THE WORLD.

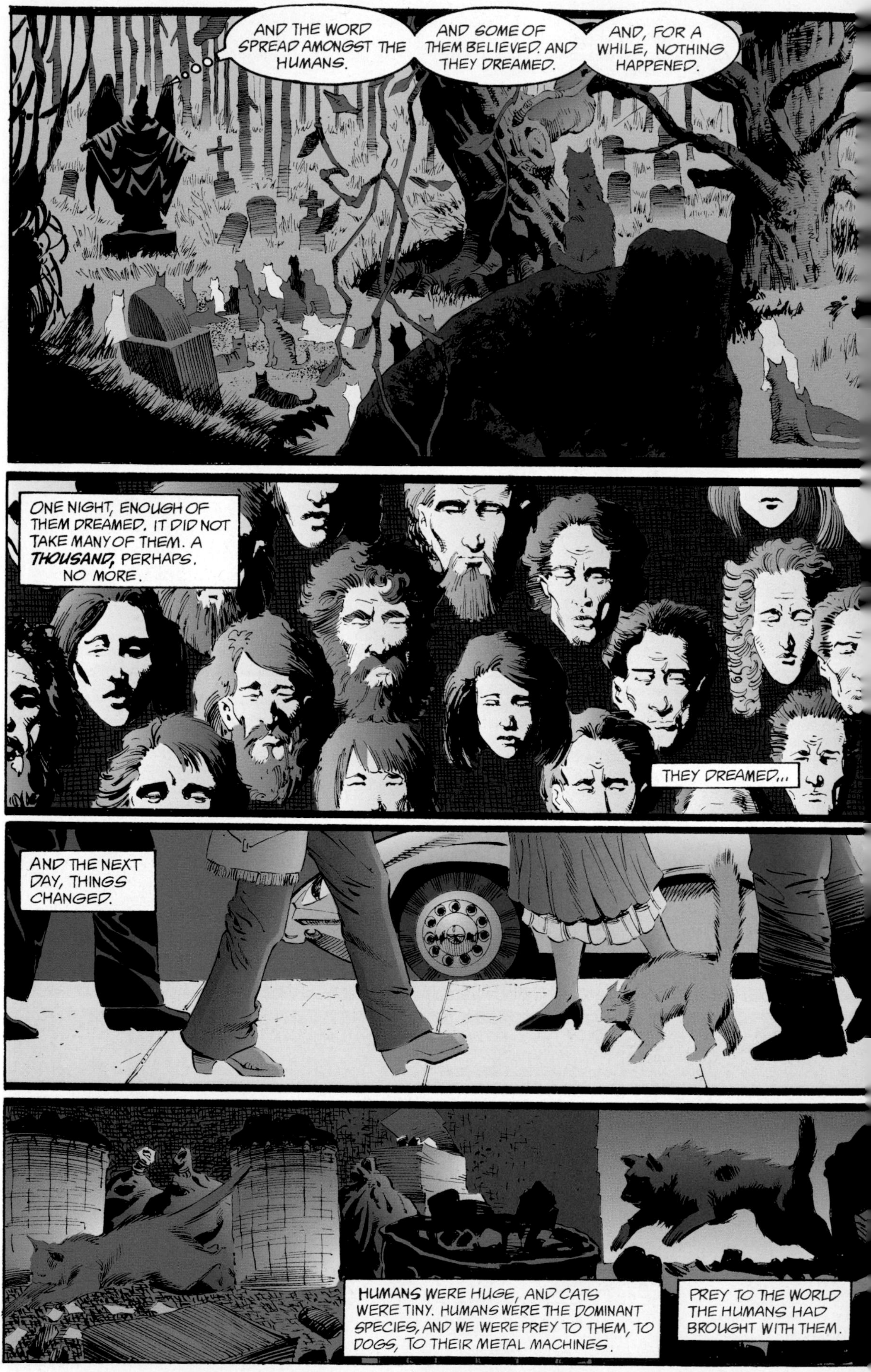
AND THE WORD SPREAD AMONGST THE HUMANS.
AND SOME OF THEM BELIEVED. AND THEY DREAMED.
AND, FOR A WHILE, NOTHING HAPPENED.
ONE NIGHT, ENOUGH OF THEM DREAMED. IT DID NOT TAKE MANY OF THEM. A THOUSAND, PERHAPS. NO MORE.
THEY DREAMED...
AND THE NEXT DAY, THINGS CHANGED.
HUMANS WERE HUGE, AND CATS WERE TINY. HUMANS WERE THE DOMINANT SPECIES, AND WE WERE PREY TO THEM, TO DOGS, TO THEIR METAL MACHINES.
PREY TO THE WORLD THE HUMANS HAD BROUGHT WITH THEM.

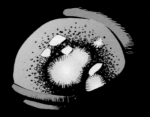

ALL THIS I SAW, WHEN I LOOKED INTO THE DREAM CAT'S EYES.

...O THEY DREAMED ...E WORLD INTO ...E FORM IT IS NOW?

Not exactly.

They dreamed the world so it ALWAYS WAS the way it is now, little one. There never WAS a world of high cat-ladies and cat-lords.

They changed the universe from the beginning of all things, until the end of time.

Do you understand now?

YES.

YES, I DO.

Then you know what your task must be. You know the burden you must bear.

Are you strong enough?

YES. I HOPE SO.

Then wake, child. With my blessing."

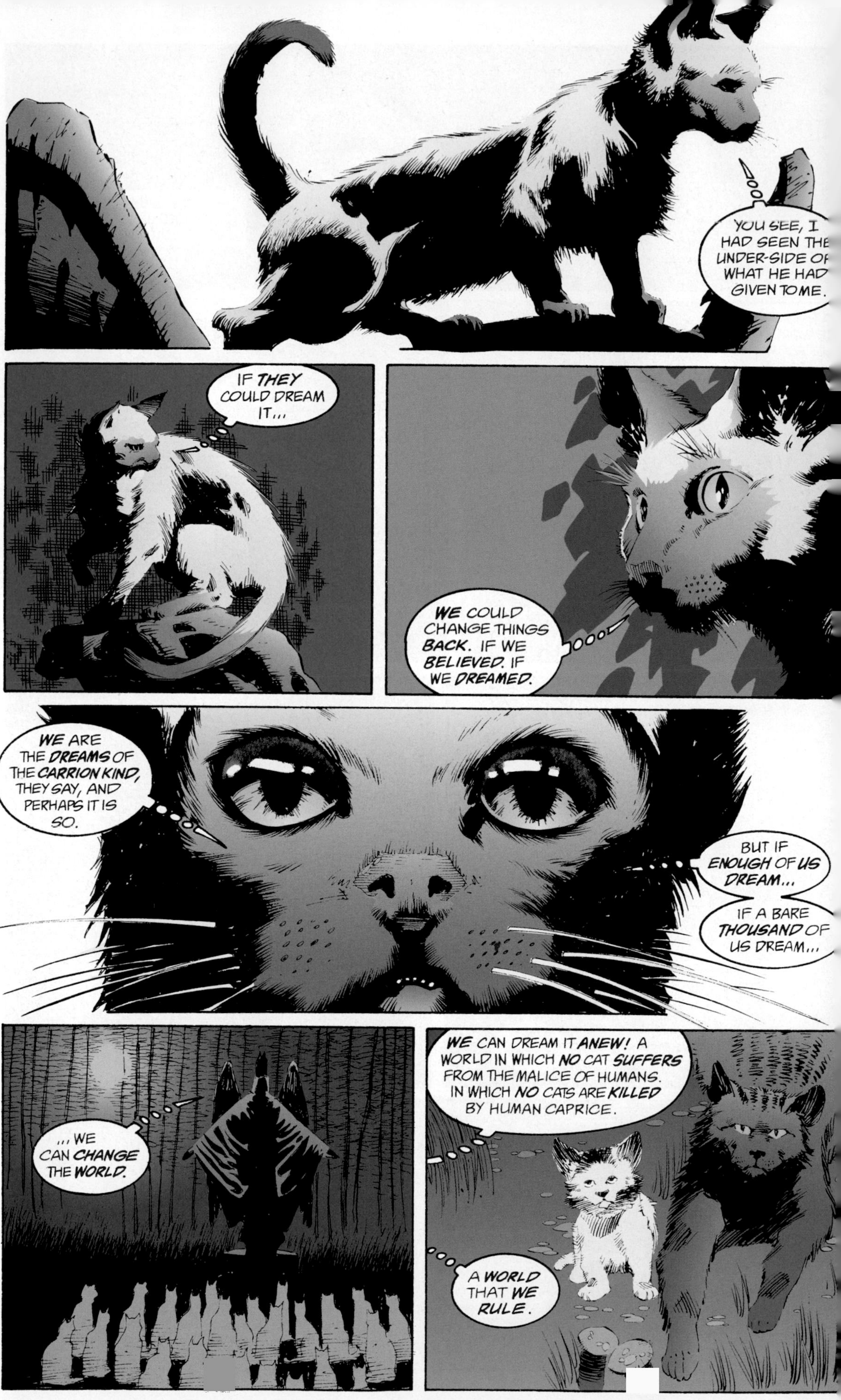

YOU SEE, I HAD SEEN THE UNDER-SIDE OF WHAT HE HAD GIVEN TO ME.
IF THEY COULD DREAM IT...
WE COULD CHANGE THINGS BACK. IF WE BELIEVED. IF WE DREAMED.
WE ARE THE DREAMS OF THE CARRION KIND, THEY SAY, AND PERHAPS IT IS SO.
BUT IF ENOUGH OF US DREAM...
IF A BARE THOUSAND OF US DREAM...
...WE CAN CHANGE THE WORLD.
WE CAN DREAM IT ANEW! A WORLD IN WHICH NO CAT SUFFERS FROM THE MALICE OF HUMANS. IN WHICH NO CATS ARE KILLED BY HUMAN CAPRICE.
A WORLD THAT WE RULE.

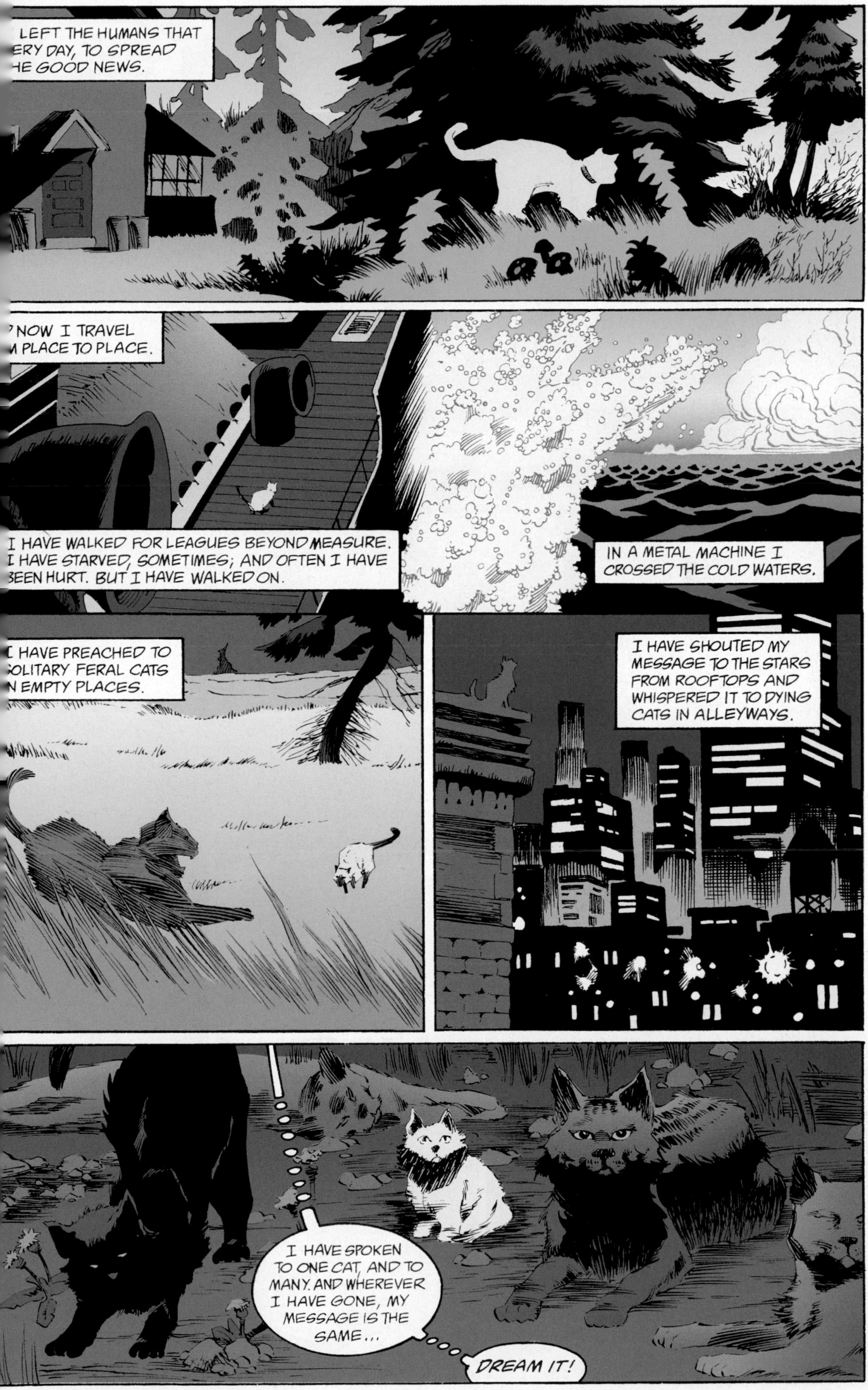
LEFT THE HUMANS THAT
ERY DAY, TO SPREAD
HE GOOD NEWS.
NOW I TRAVEL
M PLACE TO PLACE.
I HAVE WALKED FOR LEAGUES BEYOND MEASURE. I HAVE STARVED, SOMETIMES; AND OFTEN I HAVE BEEN HURT. BUT I HAVE WALKED ON.
IN A METAL MACHINE I CROSSED THE COLD WATERS.
I HAVE PREACHED TO SOLITARY FERAL CATS N EMPTY PLACES.
I HAVE SHOUTED MY MESSAGE TO THE STARS FROM ROOFTOPS AND WHISPERED IT TO DYING CATS IN ALLEYWAYS.
I HAVE SPOKEN TO ONE CAT, AND TO MANY. AND WHEREVER I HAVE GONE, MY MESSAGE IS THE SAME...
DREAM IT!

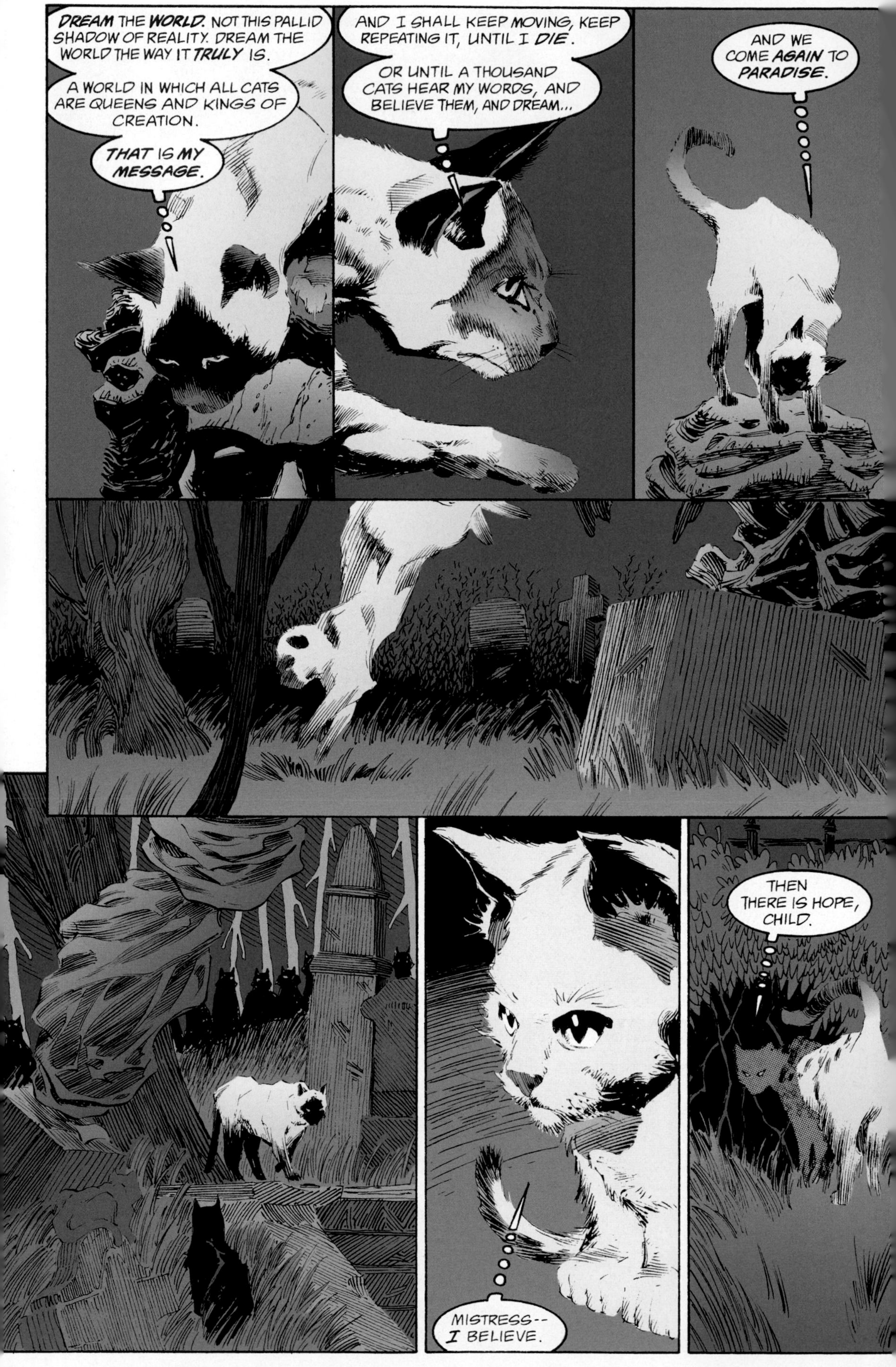
DREAM THE WORLD. NOT THIS PALLID SHADOW OF REALITY. DREAM THE WORLD THE WAY IT TRULY IS.
A WORLD IN WHICH ALL CATS ARE QUEENS AND KINGS OF CREATION.
THAT IS MY MESSAGE.
AND I SHALL KEEP MOVING, KEEP REPEATING IT, UNTIL I DIE.
OR UNTIL A THOUSAND CATS HEAR MY WORDS, AND BELIEVE THEM, AND DREAM...
AND WE COME AGAIN TO PARADISE.
MISTRESS-- I BELIEVE.
THEN THERE IS HOPE, CHILD.

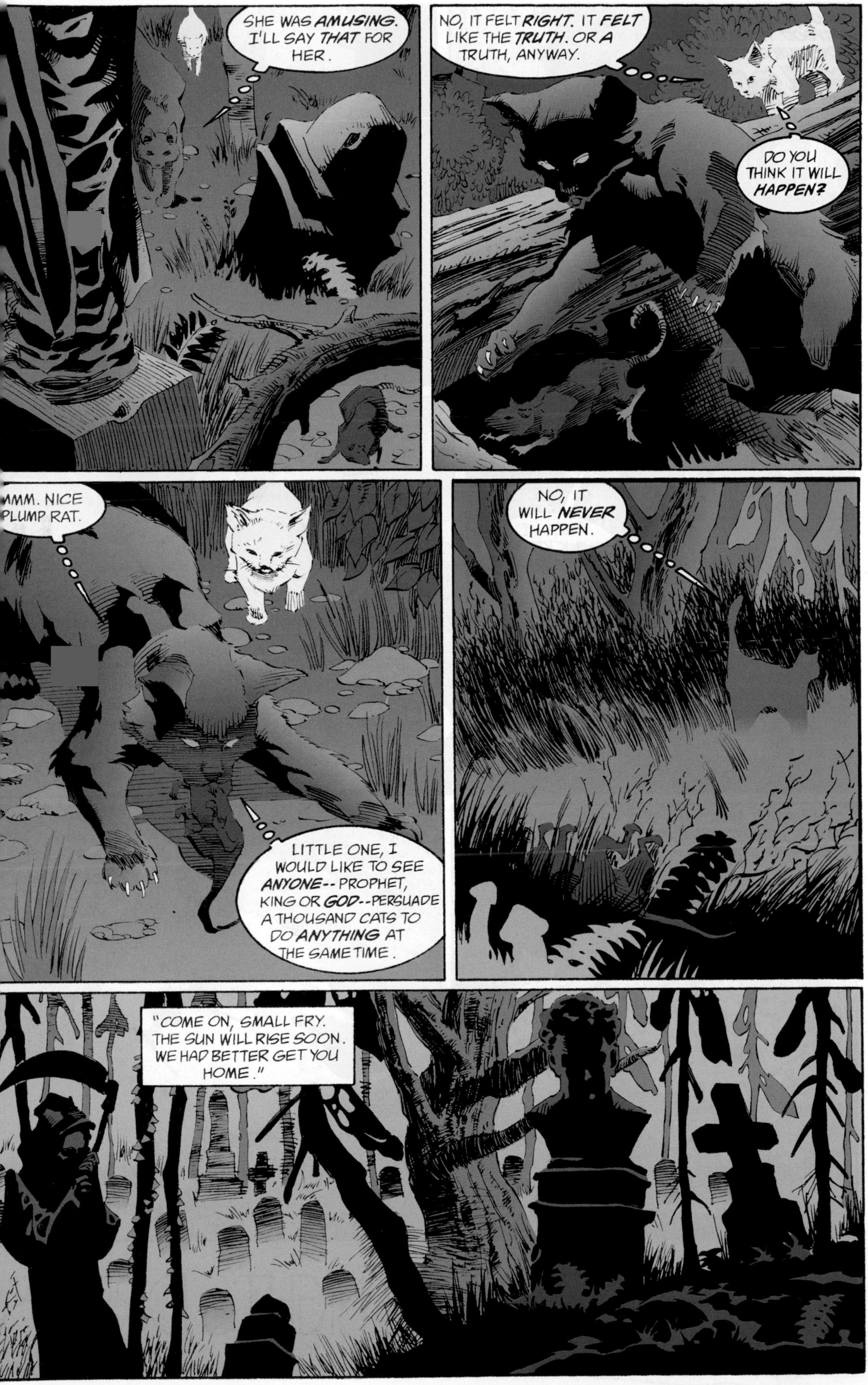
SHE WAS AMUSING. I'LL SAY THAT FOR HER.
NO, IT FELT RIGHT. IT FELT LIKE THE TRUTH. OR A TRUTH, ANYWAY.
DO YOU THINK IT WILL HAPPEN?
MMM. NICE PLUMP RAT.
LITTLE ONE, I WOULD LIKE TO SEE ANYONE--PROPHET, KING OR GOD--PERSUADE A THOUSAND CATS TO DO ANYTHING AT THE SAME TIME.
NO, IT WILL NEVER HAPPEN.
"COME ON, SMALL FRY. THE SUN WILL RISE SOON. WE HAD BETTER GET YOU HOME."

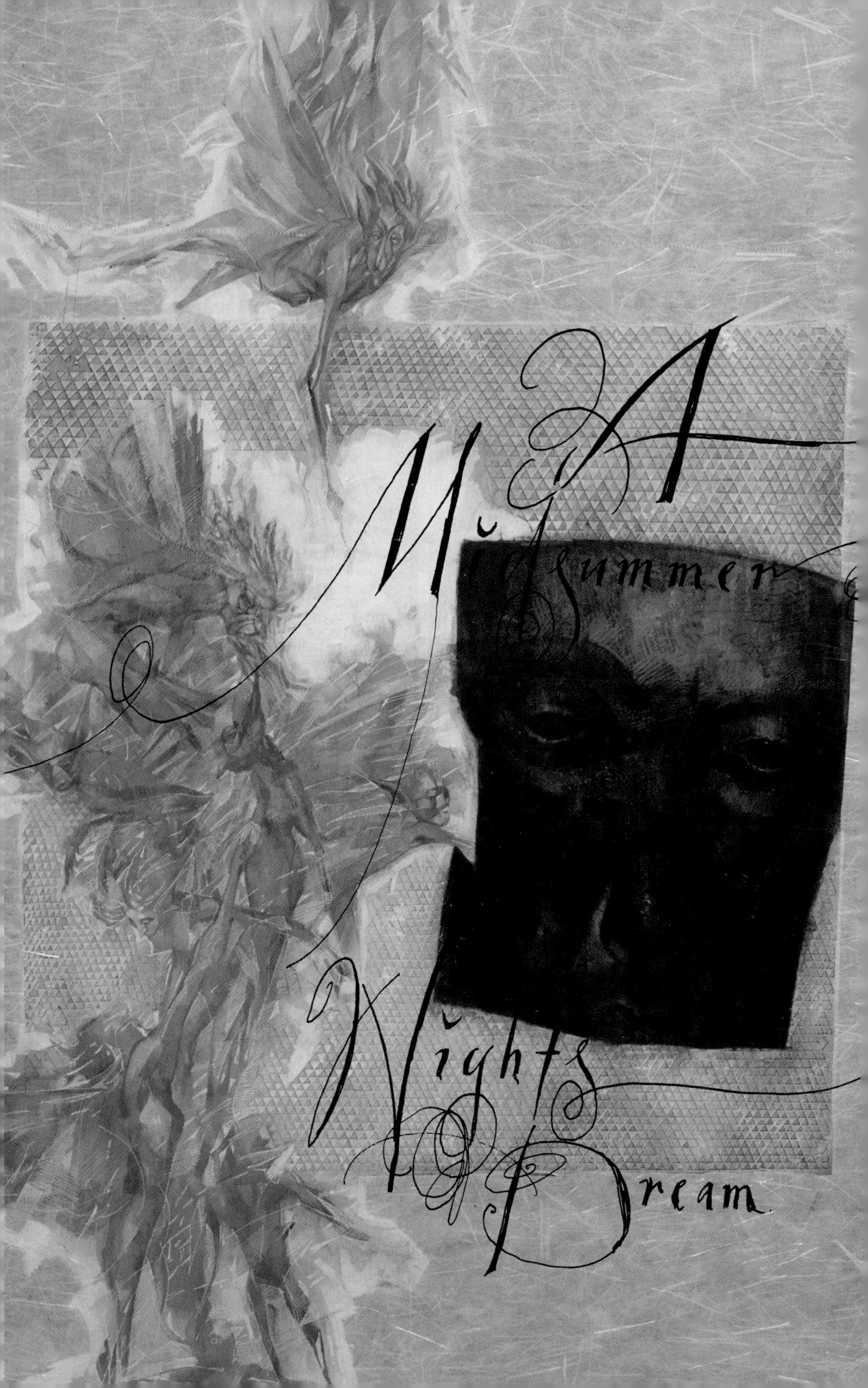
A
Midsummer
Nights
Dream

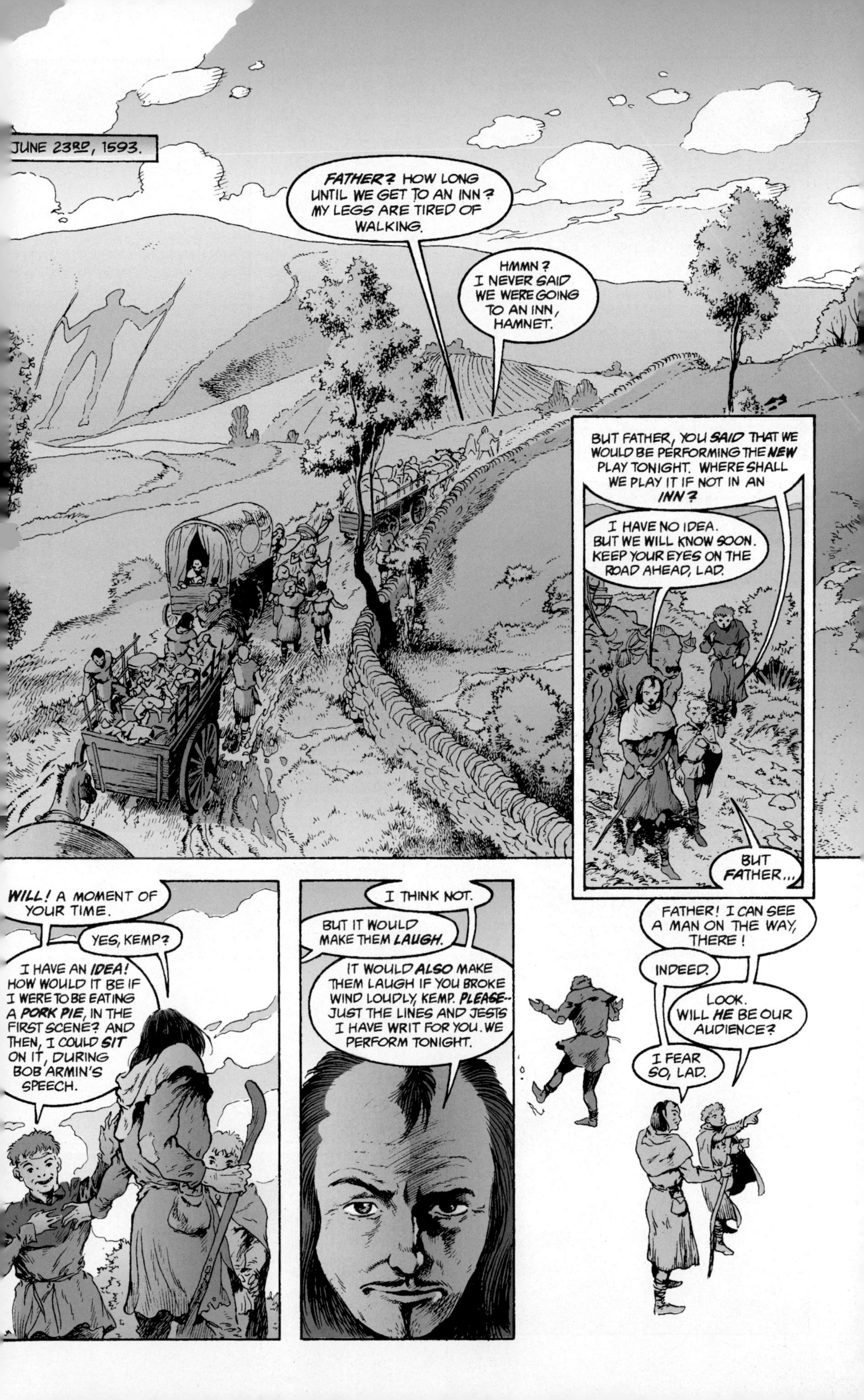
JUNE 23RD, 1593.
FATHER? HOW LONG UNTIL WE GET TO AN INN? MY LEGS ARE TIRED OF WALKING.
HMMN? I NEVER SAID WE WERE GOING TO AN INN, HAMNET.
BUT FATHER, YOU SAID THAT WE WOULD BE PERFORMING THE NEW PLAY TONIGHT. WHERE SHALL WE PLAY IT IF NOT IN AN INN?
I HAVE NO IDEA. BUT WE WILL KNOW SOON. KEEP YOUR EYES ON THE ROAD AHEAD, LAD.
BUT FATHER...
WILL! A MOMENT OF YOUR TIME.
YES, KEMP?
I HAVE AN IDEA! HOW WOULD IT BE IF I WERE TO BE EATING A PORK PIE, IN THE FIRST SCENE? AND THEN, I COULD SIT ON IT, DURING BOB ARMIN'S SPEECH.
I THINK NOT.
BUT IT WOULD MAKE THEM LAUGH.
IT WOULD ALSO MAKE THEM LAUGH IF YOU BROKE WIND LOUDLY, KEMP. PLEASE-- JUST THE LINES AND JESTS I HAVE WRIT FOR YOU. WE PERFORM TONIGHT.
FATHER! I CAN SEE A MAN ON THE WAY, THERE!
INDEED.
LOOK. WILL HE BE OUR AUDIENCE?
I FEAR SO, LAD.

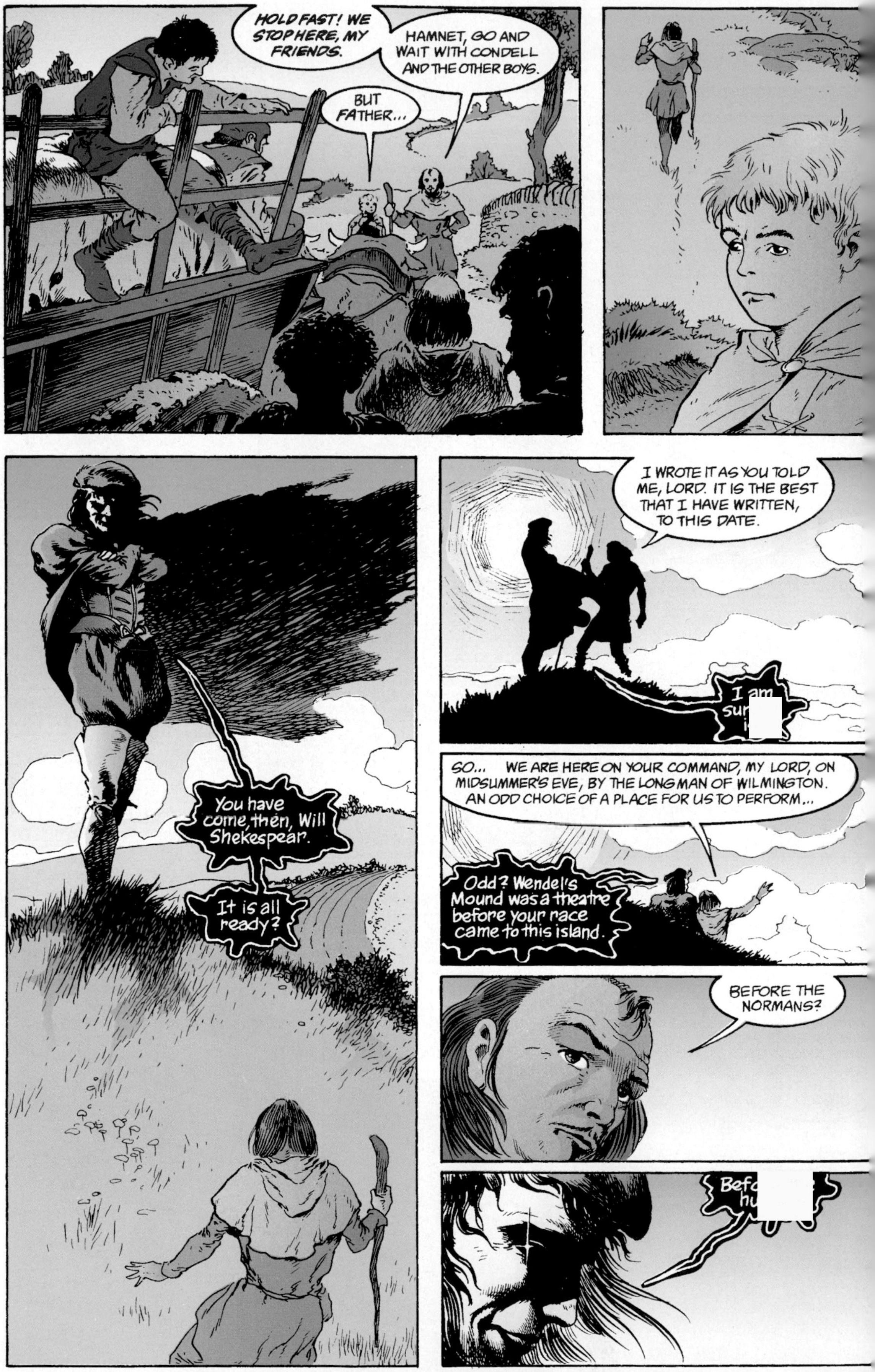
HOLD FAST! WE STOP HERE, MY FRIENDS.
HAMNET, GO AND WAIT WITH CONDELL AND THE OTHER BOYS.
BUT FATHER...
You have come, then, Will Shekespear.
It is all ready?
I WROTE IT AS YOU TOLD ME, LORD. IT IS THE BEST THAT I HAVE WRITTEN, TO THIS DATE.
I am
SO... WE ARE HERE ON YOUR COMMAND, MY LORD, ON MIDSUMMER'S EVE, BY THE LONG MAN OF WILMINGTON. AN ODD CHOICE OF A PLACE FOR US TO PERFORM...
Odd? Wendel's Mound was a theatre before your race came to this island.
BEFORE THE NORMANS?

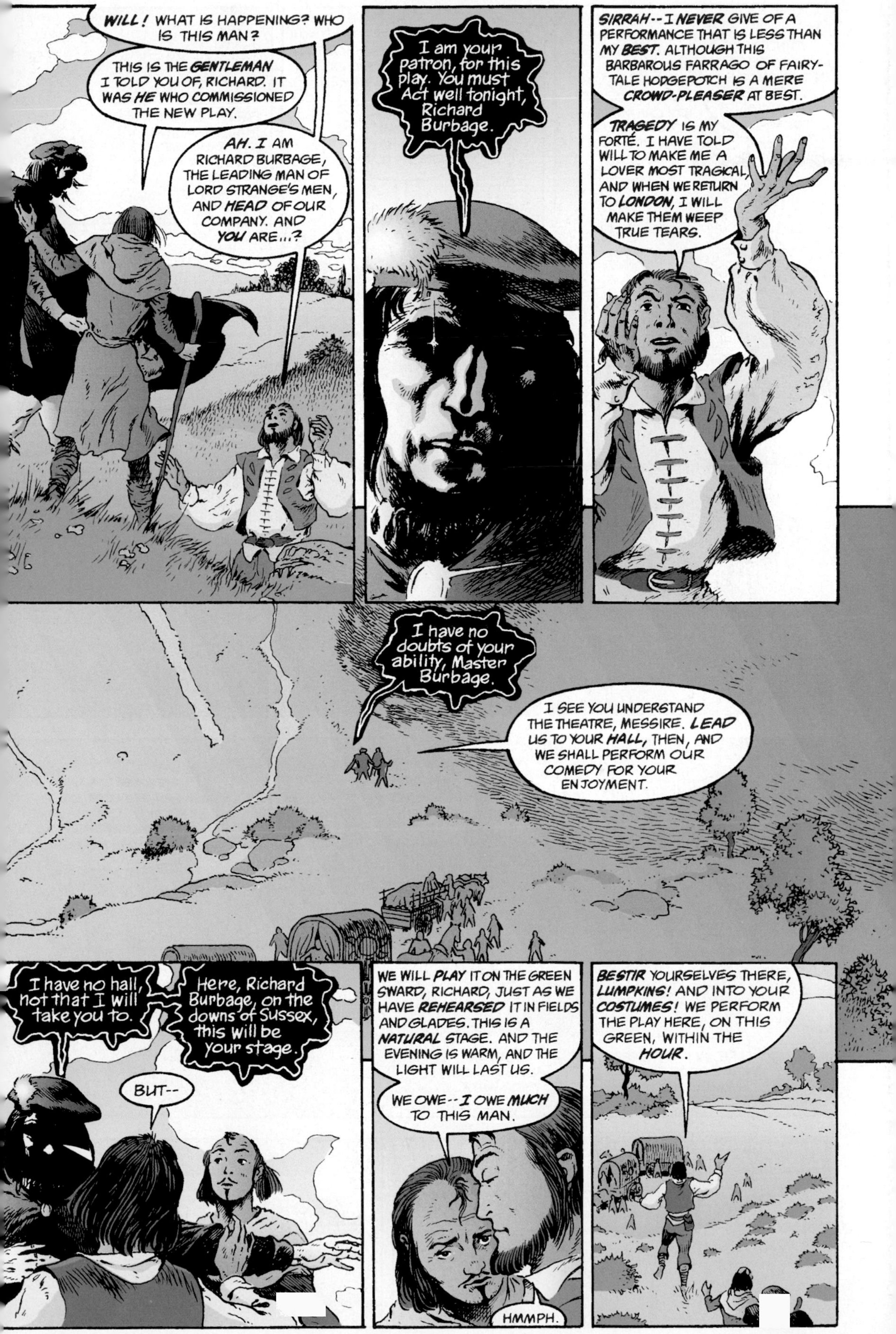
WILL! WHAT IS HAPPENING? WHO IS THIS MAN?
THIS IS THE GENTLEMAN I TOLD YOU OF, RICHARD. IT WAS HE WHO COMMISSIONED THE NEW PLAY.
AH. I AM RICHARD BURBAGE, THE LEADING MAN OF LORD STRANGE'S MEN, AND HEAD OF OUR COMPANY. AND YOU ARE...?
I am your patron, for this play. You must Act well tonight, Richard Burbage.
SIRRAH--I NEVER GIVE OF A PERFORMANCE THAT IS LESS THAN MY BEST. ALTHOUGH THIS BARBAROUS FARRAGO OF FAIRY-TALE HODGEPOTCH IS A MERE CROWD-PLEASER AT BEST.
TRAGEDY IS MY FORTÉ. I HAVE TOLD WILL TO MAKE ME A LOVER MOST TRAGICAL, AND WHEN WE RETURN TO LONDON, I WILL MAKE THEM WEEP TRUE TEARS.
I have no doubts of your ability, Master Burbage.
I SEE YOU UNDERSTAND THE THEATRE, MESSIRE. LEAD US TO YOUR HALL, THEN, AND WE SHALL PERFORM OUR COMEDY FOR YOUR ENJOYMENT.
I have no hall, not that I will take you to.
Here, Richard Burbage, on the downs of Sussex, this will be your stage.
BUT--
WE WILL PLAY IT ON THE GREEN SWARD, RICHARD, JUST AS WE HAVE REHEARSED IT IN FIELDS AND GLADES. THIS IS A NATURAL STAGE. AND THE EVENING IS WARM, AND THE LIGHT WILL LAST US.
WE OWE--I OWE MUCH TO THIS MAN.
HMMPH.
BESTIR YOURSELVES THERE, LUMPKINS! AND INTO YOUR COSTUMES! WE PERFORM THE PLAY HERE, ON THIS GREEN, WITHIN THE HOUR.

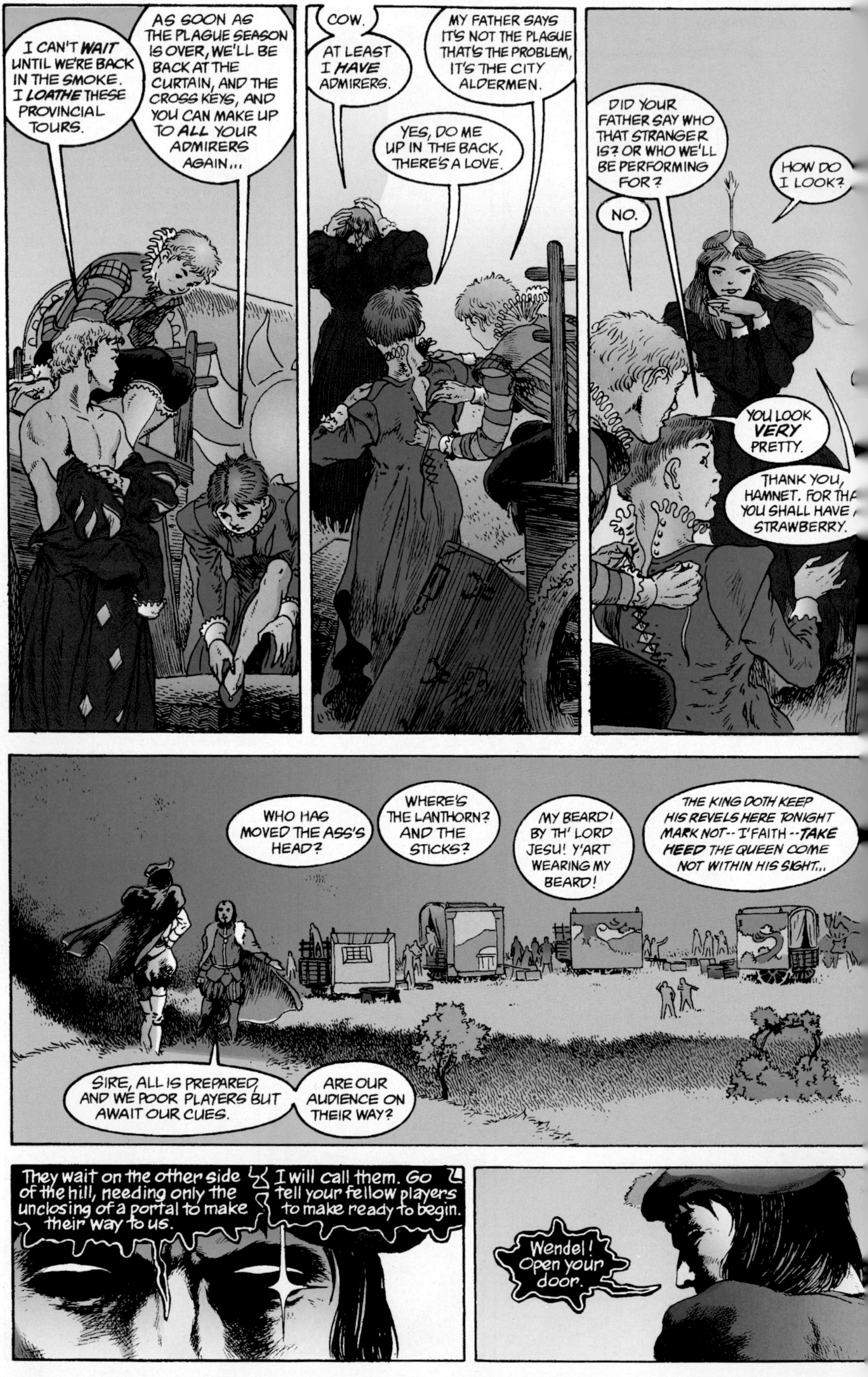
I CAN'T WAIT UNTIL WE'RE BACK IN THE SMOKE. I LOATHE THESE PROVINCIAL TOURS.
AS SOON AS THE PLAGUE SEASON IS OVER, WE'LL BE BACK AT THE CURTAIN, AND THE CROSS KEYS, AND YOU CAN MAKE UP TO ALL YOUR ADMIRERS AGAIN...
COW.
AT LEAST I HAVE ADMIRERS.
MY FATHER SAYS IT'S NOT THE PLAGUE THAT'S THE PROBLEM, IT'S THE CITY ALDERMEN.
YES, DO ME UP IN THE BACK, THERE'S A LOVE.
DID YOUR FATHER SAY WHO THAT STRANGER IS? OR WHO WE'LL BE PERFORMING FOR?
NO.
HOW DO I LOOK?
YOU LOOK VERY PRETTY.
THANK YOU, HAMNET. FOR THA YOU SHALL HAVE STRAWBERRY.
WHO HAS MOVED THE ASS'S HEAD?
WHERE'S THE LANTHORN? AND THE STICKS?
MY BEARD! BY TH' LORD JESU! Y'ART WEARING MY BEARD!
THE KING DOTH KEEP HIS REVELS HERE TONIGHT MARK NOT-- I'FAITH --TAKE HEED THE QUEEN COME NOT WITHIN HIS SIGHT...
SIRE, ALL IS PREPARED, AND WE POOR PLAYERS BUT AWAIT OUR CUES.
ARE OUR AUDIENCE ON THEIR WAY?
They wait on the other side of the hill, needing only the unclosing of a portal to make their way to us.
I will call them. Go tell your fellow players to make ready to begin.
Wendel! Open your door.

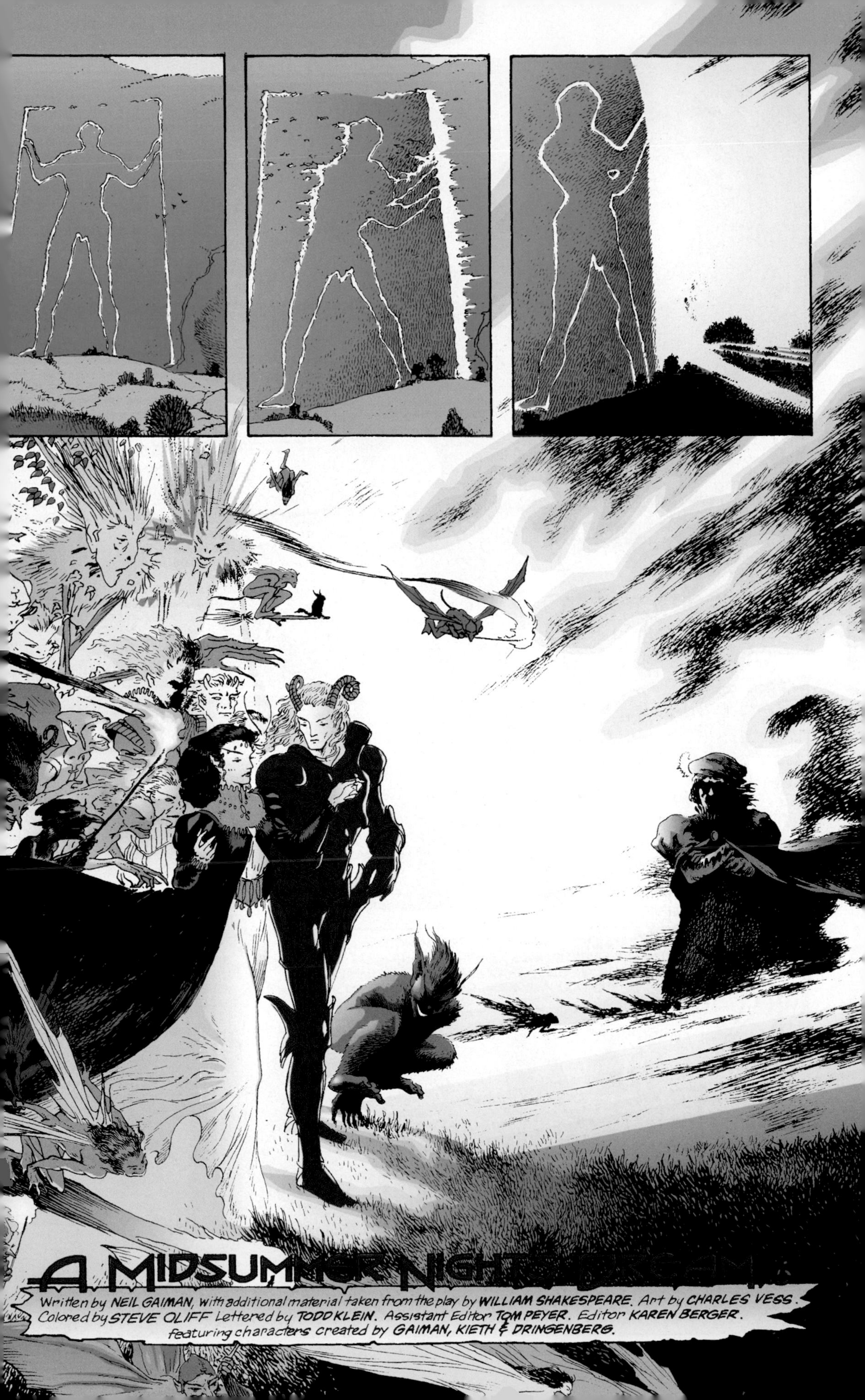
A MIDSUMMER NIGHT'S DREAM
Written by NEIL GAIMAN, with additional material taken from the play by WILLIAM SHAKESPEARE. Art by CHARLES VESS.
Colored by STEVE OLIFF Lettered by TODD KLEIN. Assistant Editor TOM PEYER. Editor KAREN BERGER.
featuring characters created by GAIMAN, KIETH & DRINGENBERG.

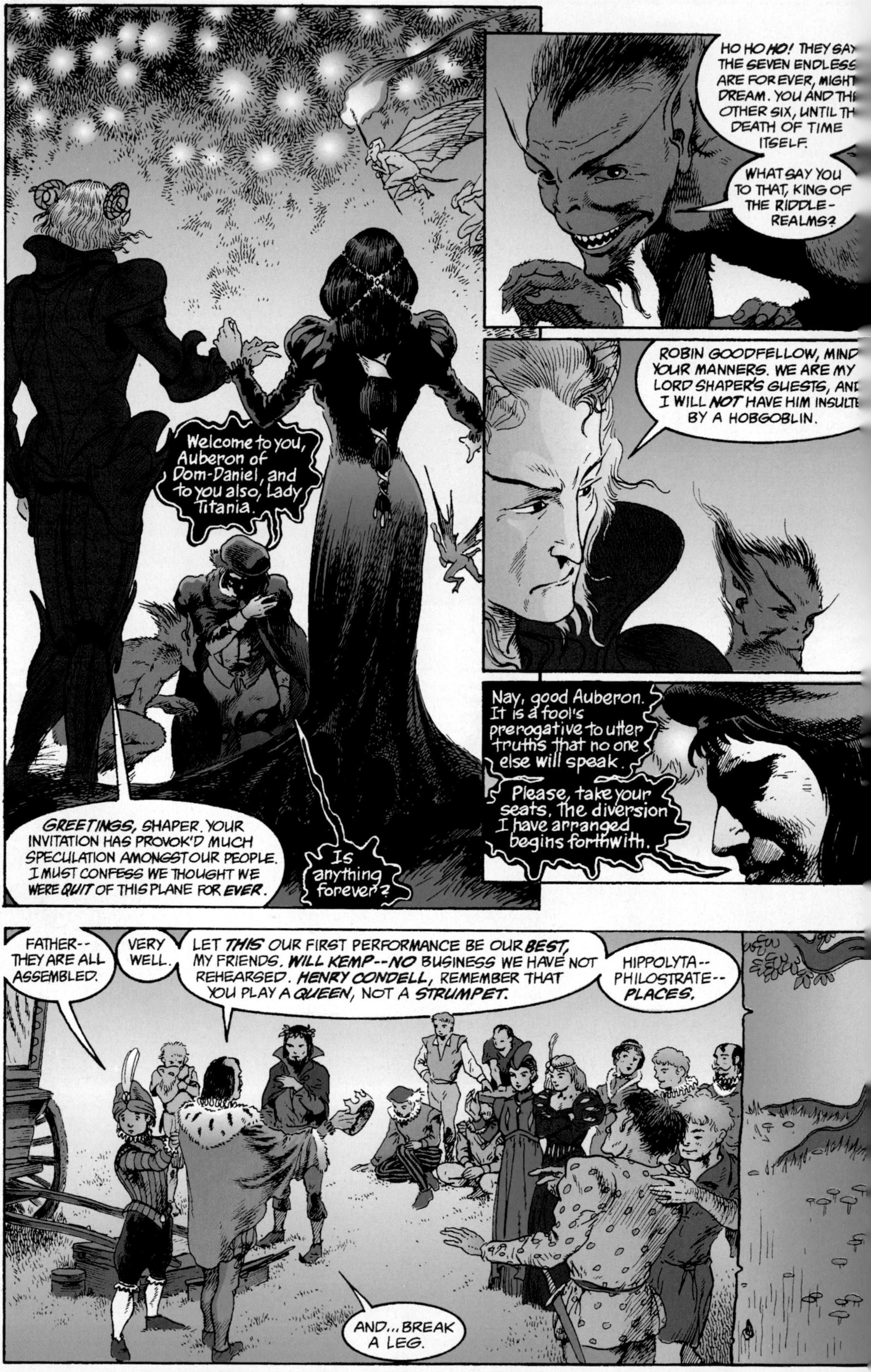

Welcome to you, Auberon of Dom-Daniel, and to you also, Lady Titania.
GREETINGS, SHAPER. YOUR INVITATION HAS PROVOK'D MUCH SPECULATION AMONGST OUR PEOPLE. I MUST CONFESS WE THOUGHT WE WERE QUIT OF THIS PLANE FOR EVER.
Is anything forever?
HO HO HO! THEY SAY THE SEVEN ENDLESS ARE FOREVER, MIGHT DREAM. YOU AND TH OTHER SIX, UNTIL TH DEATH OF TIME ITSELF.
WHAT SAY YOU TO THAT, KING OF THE RIDDLE-REALMS?
ROBIN GOODFELLOW, MIND YOUR MANNERS. WE ARE MY LORD SHAPER'S GUESTS, AND I WILL NOT HAVE HIM INSULTE BY A HOBGOBLIN.
Nay, good Auberon. It is a fool's prerogative to utter truths that no one else will speak.
Please, take your seats. The diversion I have arranged begins forthwith.
FATHER-- THEY ARE ALL ASSEMBLED.
VERY WELL.
LET THIS OUR FIRST PERFORMANCE BE OUR BEST, MY FRIENDS. WILL KEMP--NO BUSINESS WE HAVE NOT REHEARSED. HENRY CONDELL, REMEMBER THAT YOU PLAY A QUEEN, NOT A STRUMPET.
HIPPOLYTA-- PHILOSTRATE-- PLACES.
AND... BREAK A LEG.

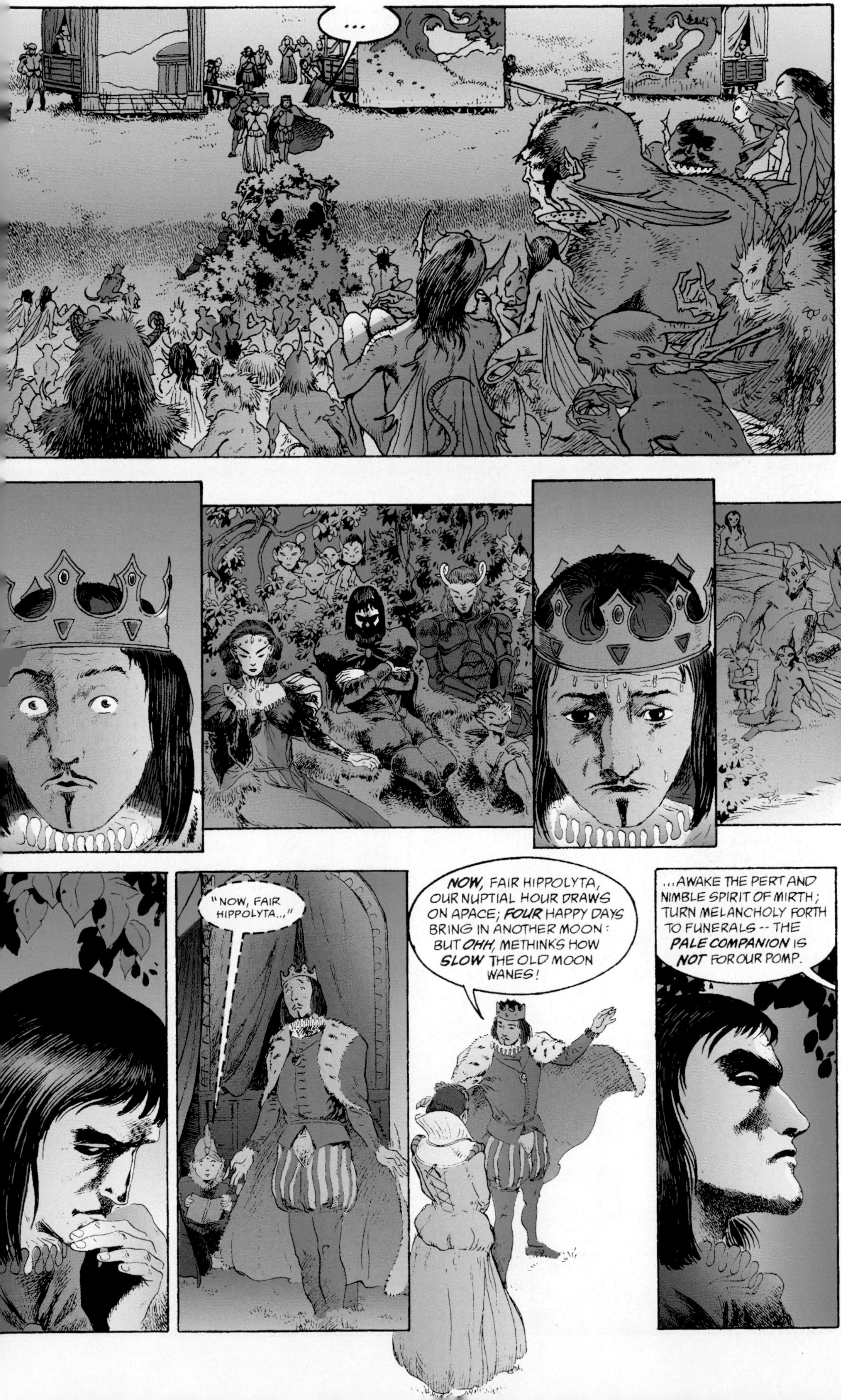
...
"NOW, FAIR HIPPOLYTA..."
NOW, FAIR HIPPOLYTA, OUR NUPTIAL HOUR DRAWS ON APACE; FOUR HAPPY DAYS BRING IN ANOTHER MOON: BUT OHH, METHINKS HOW SLOW THE OLD MOON WANES!
...AWAKE THE PERT AND NIMBLE SPIRIT OF MIRTH; TURN MELANCHOLY FORTH TO FUNERALS -- THE PALE COMPANION IS NOT FOR OUR POMP.

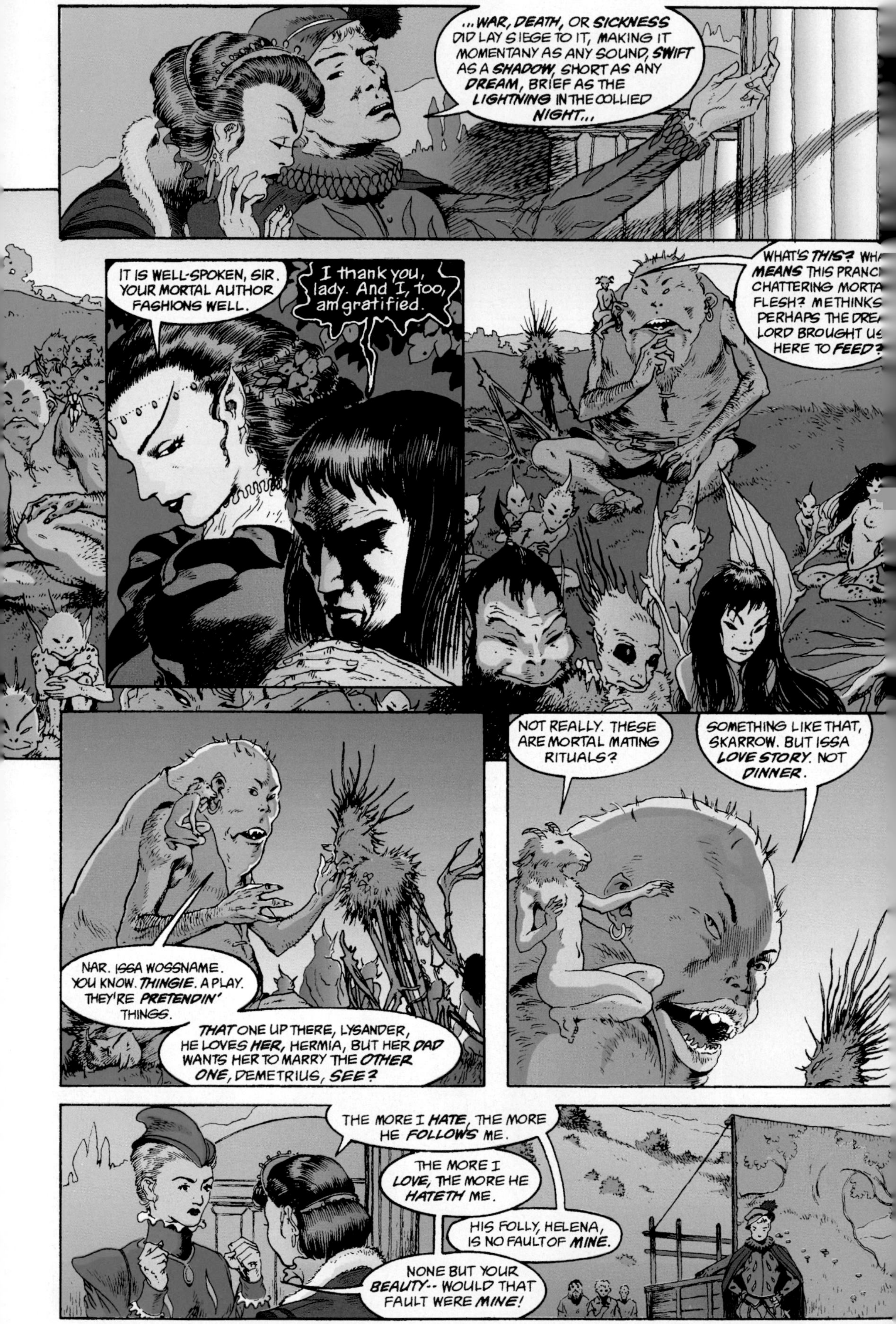
...WAR, DEATH, OR SICKNESS DID LAY SIEGE TO IT, MAKING IT MOMENTANY AS ANY SOUND, SWIFT AS A SHADOW, SHORT AS ANY DREAM, BRIEF AS THE LIGHTNING IN THE COLLIED NIGHT...
IT IS WELL-SPOKEN, SIR. YOUR MORTAL AUTHOR FASHIONS WELL.
I thank you, lady. And I, too, am gratified.
WHAT'S THIS? WHA MEANS THIS PRANC CHATTERING MORTA FLESH? METHINKS PERHAPS THE DRE LORD BROUGHT US HERE TO FEED?
NAR. ISSA WOSSNAME. YOU KNOW. THINGIE. A PLAY. THEY'RE PRETENDIN' THINGS.
THAT ONE UP THERE, LYSANDER, HE LOVES HER, HERMIA, BUT HER DAD WANTS HER TO MARRY THE OTHER ONE, DEMETRIUS, SEE?
NOT REALLY. THESE ARE MORTAL MATING RITUALS?
SOMETHING LIKE THAT, SKARROW. BUT ISSA LOVE STORY. NOT DINNER.
THE MORE I HATE, THE MORE HE FOLLOWS ME.
THE MORE I LOVE, THE MORE HE HATETH ME.
HIS FOLLY, HELENA, IS NO FAULT OF MINE.
NONE BUT YOUR BEAUTY-- WOULD THAT FAULT WERE MINE!

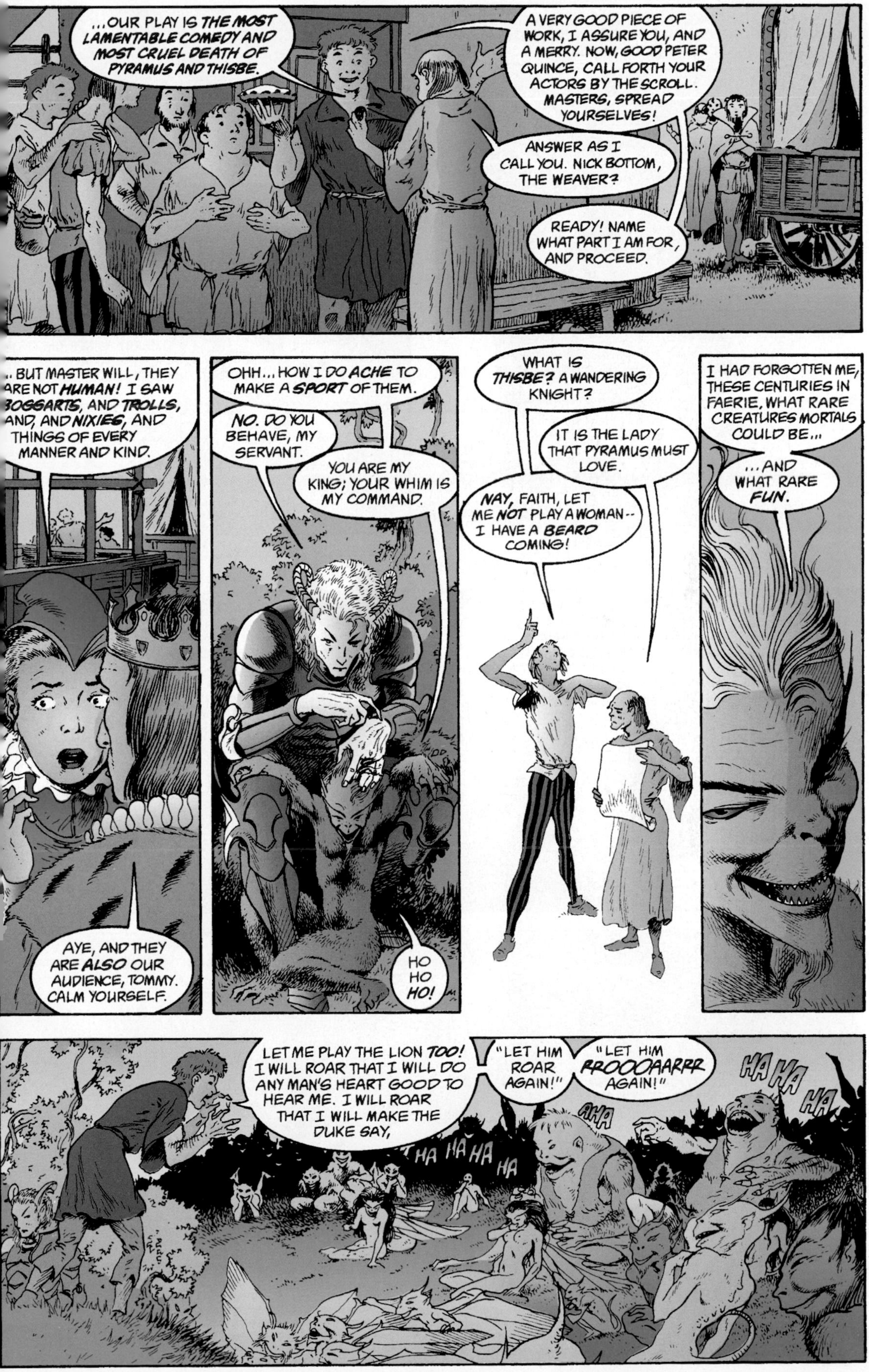
...OUR PLAY IS THE MOST LAMENTABLE COMEDY AND MOST CRUEL DEATH OF PYRAMUS AND THISBE.
A VERY GOOD PIECE OF WORK, I ASSURE YOU, AND A MERRY. NOW, GOOD PETER QUINCE, CALL FORTH YOUR ACTORS BY THE SCROLL. MASTERS, SPREAD YOURSELVES!
ANSWER AS I CALL YOU. NICK BOTTOM, THE WEAVER?
READY! NAME WHAT PART I AM FOR, AND PROCEED.
...BUT MASTER WILL, THEY ARE NOT HUMAN! I SAW BOGGARTS, AND TROLLS, AND, AND NIXIES, AND THINGS OF EVERY MANNER AND KIND.
AYE, AND THEY ARE ALSO OUR AUDIENCE, TOMMY. CALM YOURSELF.
OHH... HOW I DO ACHE TO MAKE A SPORT OF THEM.
NO. DO YOU BEHAVE, MY SERVANT.
YOU ARE MY KING; YOUR WHIM IS MY COMMAND.
HO HO HO!
WHAT IS THISBE? A WANDERING KNIGHT?
IT IS THE LADY THAT PYRAMUS MUST LOVE.
NAY, FAITH, LET ME NOT PLAY A WOMAN-- I HAVE A BEARD COMING!
I HAD FORGOTTEN ME, THESE CENTURIES IN FAERIE, WHAT RARE CREATURES MORTALS COULD BE...
...AND WHAT RARE FUN.
LET ME PLAY THE LION TOO! I WILL ROAR THAT I WILL DO ANY MAN'S HEART GOOD TO HEAR ME. I WILL ROAR THAT I WILL MAKE THE DUKE SAY,
"LET HIM ROAR AGAIN!"
"LET HIM RROOOAARRR AGAIN!"
HA HA HA
AHA
HA HA HA HA

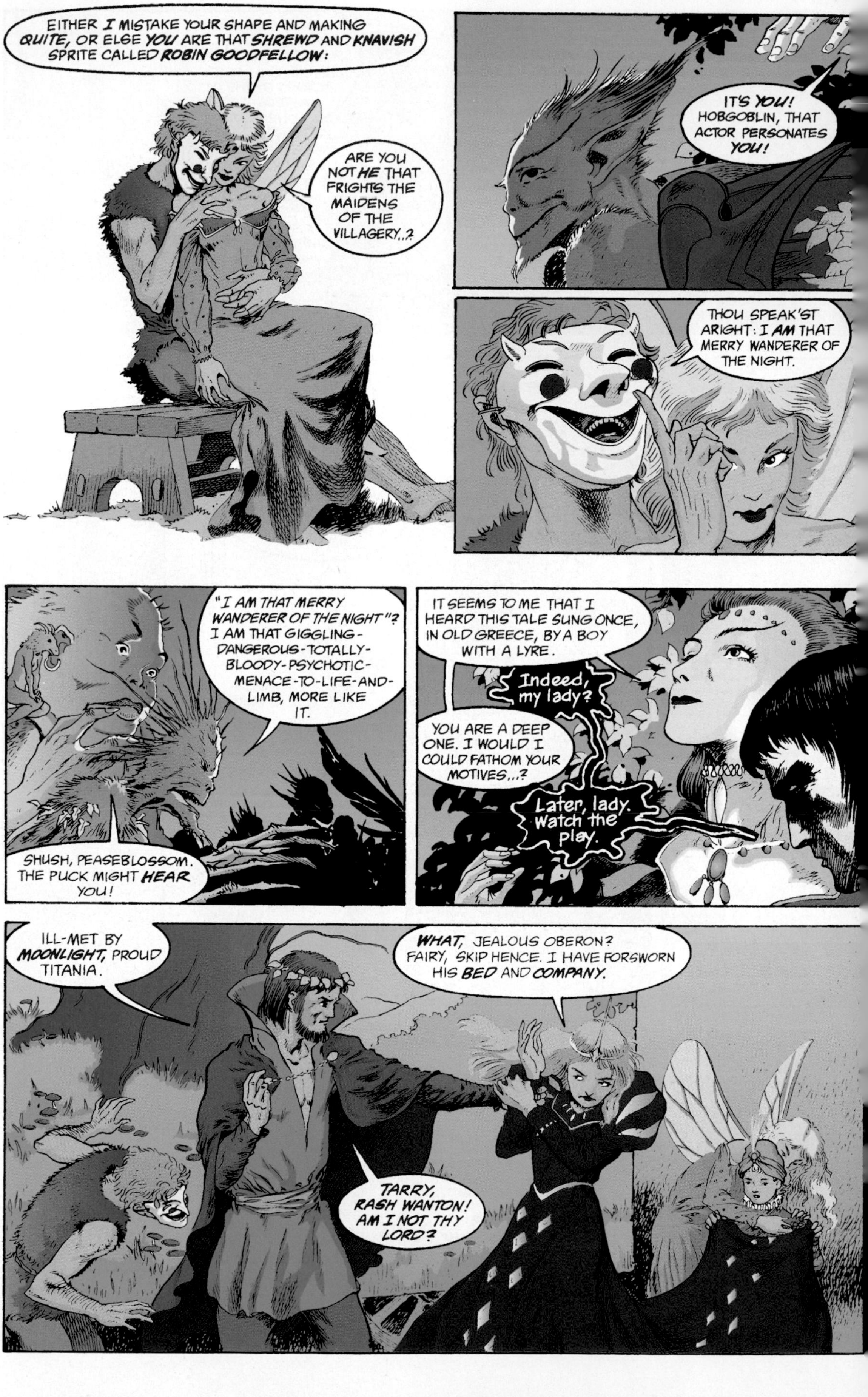
EITHER I MISTAKE YOUR SHAPE AND MAKING QUITE, OR ELSE YOU ARE THAT SHREWD AND KNAVISH SPRITE CALLED ROBIN GOODFELLOW:
ARE YOU NOT HE THAT FRIGHTS THE MAIDENS OF THE VILLAGERY...?
IT'S YOU! HOBGOBLIN, THAT ACTOR PERSONATES YOU!
THOU SPEAK'ST ARIGHT: I AM THAT MERRY WANDERER OF THE NIGHT.
"I AM THAT MERRY WANDERER OF THE NIGHT"? I AM THAT GIGGLING-DANGEROUS-TOTALLY-BLOODY-PSYCHOTIC-MENACE-TO-LIFE-AND-LIMB, MORE LIKE IT.
SHUSH, PEASEBLOSSOM. THE PUCK MIGHT HEAR YOU!
IT SEEMS TO ME THAT I HEARD THIS TALE SUNG ONCE, IN OLD GREECE, BY A BOY WITH A LYRE.
Indeed, my lady?
YOU ARE A DEEP ONE. I WOULD I COULD FATHOM YOUR MOTIVES...?
Later, lady. Watch the play.
ILL-MET BY MOONLIGHT, PROUD TITANIA.
WHAT, JEALOUS OBERON? FAIRY, SKIP HENCE. I HAVE FORSWORN HIS BED AND COMPANY.
TARRY, RASH WANTON! AM I NOT THY LORD?

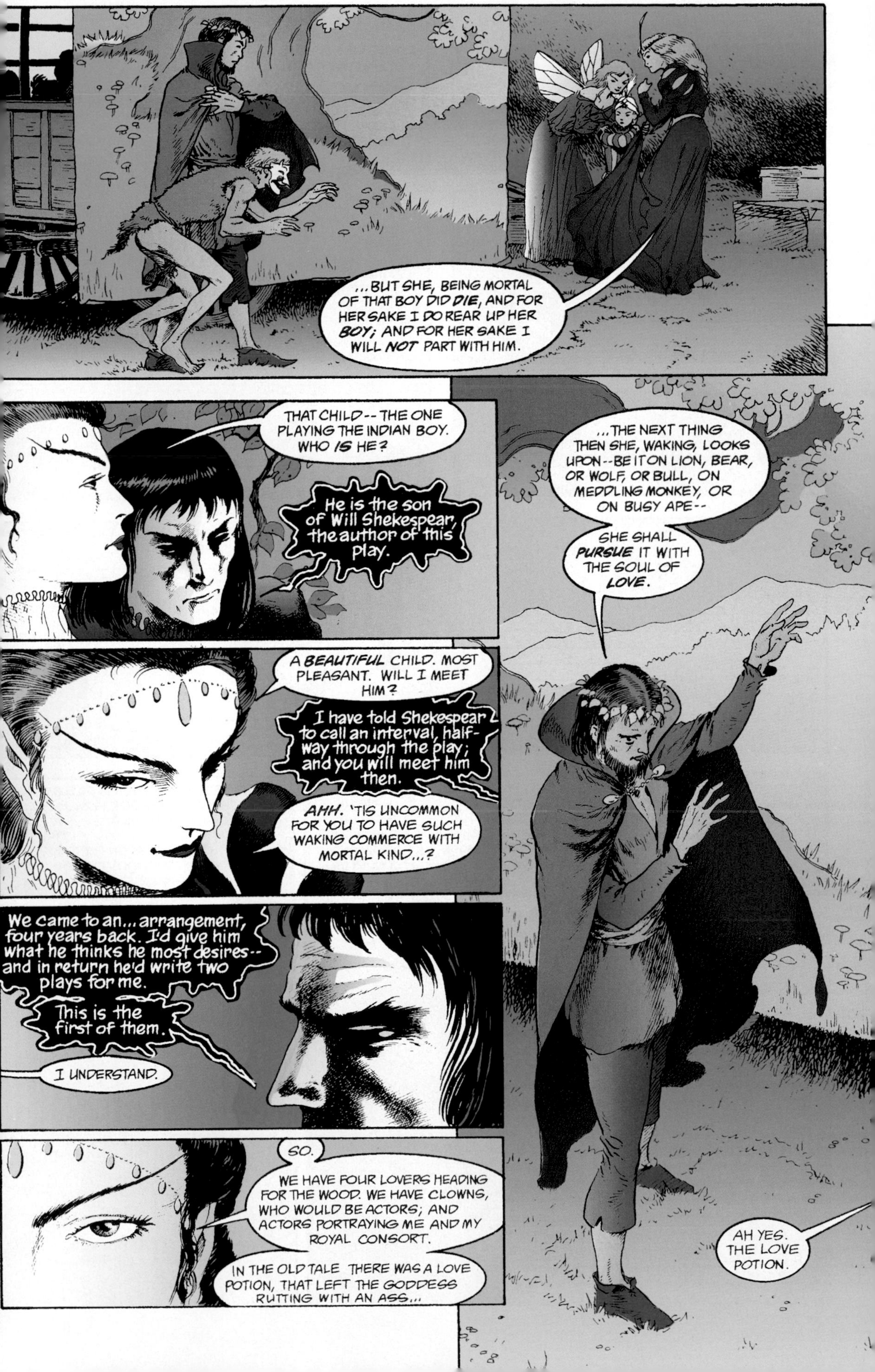
...BUT SHE, BEING MORTAL OF THAT BOY DID DIE, AND FOR HER SAKE I DO REAR UP HER BOY; AND FOR HER SAKE I WILL NOT PART WITH HIM.
THAT CHILD-- THE ONE PLAYING THE INDIAN BOY. WHO IS HE?
He is the son of Will Shekespear, the author of this play.
A BEAUTIFUL CHILD. MOST PLEASANT. WILL I MEET HIM?
I have told Shekespear to call an interval, half-way through the play; and you will meet him then.
AHH. 'TIS UNCOMMON FOR YOU TO HAVE SUCH WAKING COMMERCE WITH MORTAL KIND...?
We came to an... arrangement, four years back. I'd give him what he thinks he most desires-- and in return he'd write two plays for me.
This is the first of them.
I UNDERSTAND.
SO.
WE HAVE FOUR LOVERS HEADING FOR THE WOOD. WE HAVE CLOWNS, WHO WOULD BE ACTORS; AND ACTORS PORTRAYING ME AND MY ROYAL CONSORT.
IN THE OLD TALE THERE WAS A LOVE POTION, THAT LEFT THE GODDESS RUTTING WITH AN ASS...
...THE NEXT THING THEN SHE, WAKING, LOOKS UPON--BE IT ON LION, BEAR, OR WOLF, OR BULL, ON MEDDLING MONKEY, OR ON BUSY APE--
SHE SHALL PURSUE IT WITH THE SOUL OF LOVE.
AH YES. THE LOVE POTION.

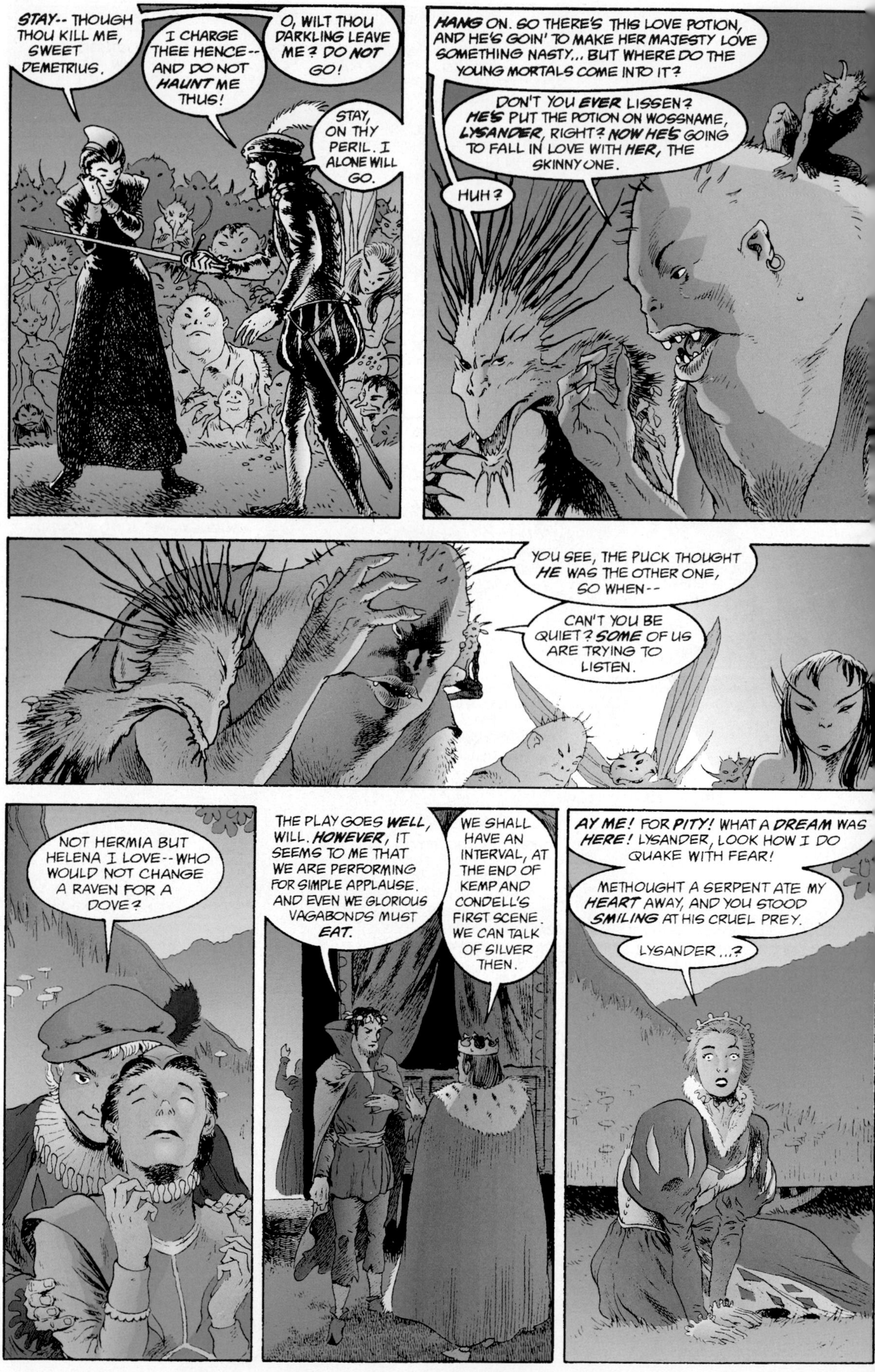
STAY-- THOUGH THOU KILL ME, SWEET DEMETRIUS.
I CHARGE THEE HENCE-- AND DO NOT HAUNT ME THUS!
O, WILT THOU DARKLING LEAVE ME? DO NOT GO!
STAY, ON THY PERIL. I ALONE WILL GO.
HANG ON. SO THERE'S THIS LOVE POTION, AND HE'S GOIN' TO MAKE HER MAJESTY LOVE SOMETHING NASTY... BUT WHERE DO THE YOUNG MORTALS COME INTO IT?
DON'T YOU EVER LISSEN? HE'S PUT THE POTION ON WOSSNAME, LYSANDER, RIGHT? NOW HE'S GOING TO FALL IN LOVE WITH HER, THE SKINNY ONE.
HUH?
YOU SEE, THE PUCK THOUGHT HE WAS THE OTHER ONE, SO WHEN--
CAN'T YOU BE QUIET? SOME OF US ARE TRYING TO LISTEN.
NOT HERMIA BUT HELENA I LOVE--WHO WOULD NOT CHANGE A RAVEN FOR A DOVE?
THE PLAY GOES WELL, WILL. HOWEVER, IT SEEMS TO ME THAT WE ARE PERFORMING FOR SIMPLE APPLAUSE. AND EVEN WE GLORIOUS VAGABONDS MUST EAT.
WE SHALL HAVE AN INTERVAL, AT THE END OF KEMP AND CONDELL'S FIRST SCENE. WE CAN TALK OF SILVER THEN.
AY ME! FOR PITY! WHAT A DREAM WAS HERE! LYSANDER, LOOK HOW I DO QUAKE WITH FEAR!
METHOUGHT A SERPENT ATE MY HEART AWAY, AND YOU STOOD SMILING AT HIS CRUEL PREY.
LYSANDER...?

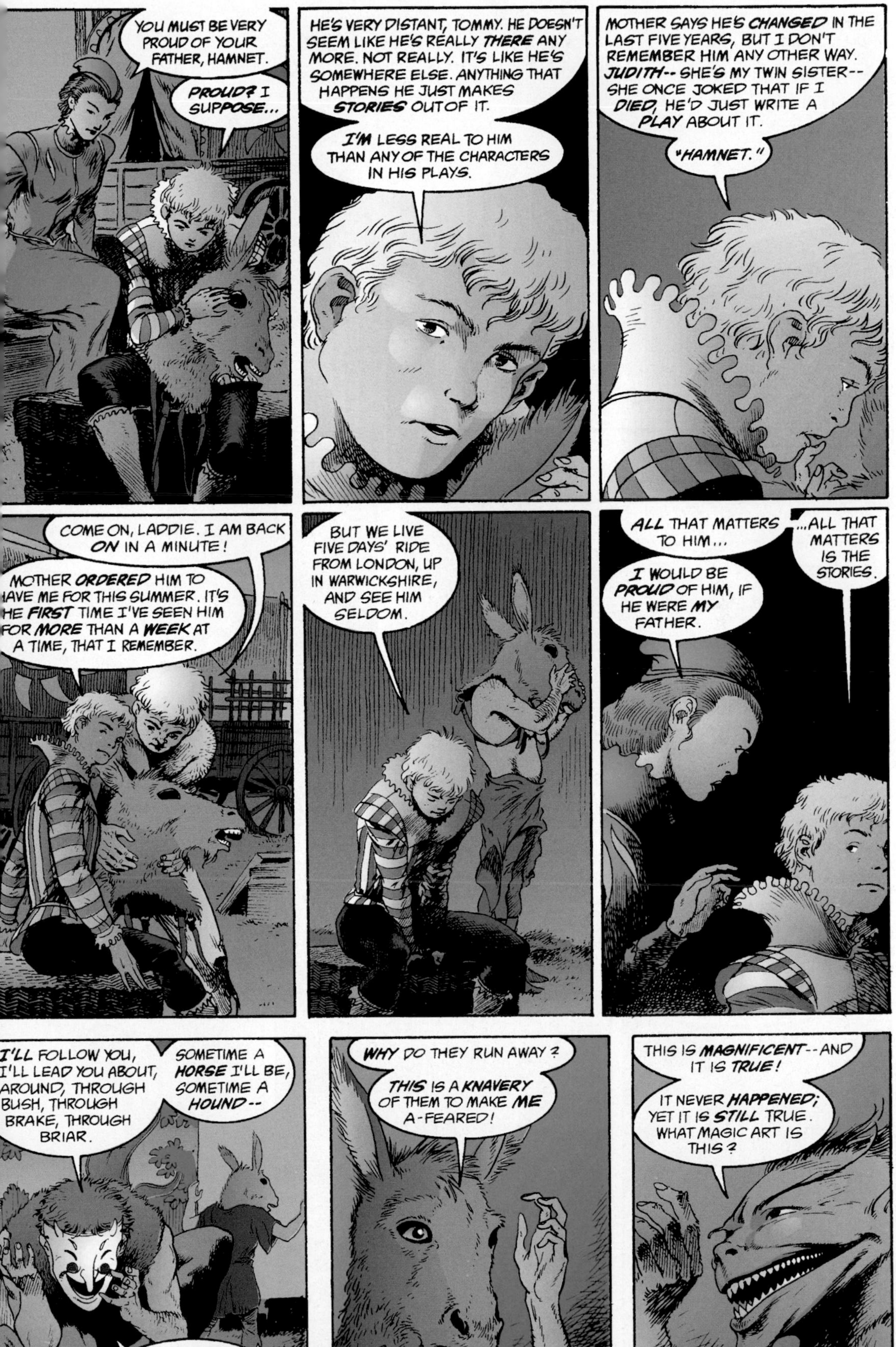
YOU MUST BE VERY PROUD OF YOUR FATHER, HAMNET.
PROUD? I SUPPOSE...
HE'S VERY DISTANT, TOMMY. HE DOESN'T SEEM LIKE HE'S REALLY THERE ANY MORE. NOT REALLY. IT'S LIKE HE'S SOMEWHERE ELSE. ANYTHING THAT HAPPENS HE JUST MAKES STORIES OUT OF IT.
I'M LESS REAL TO HIM THAN ANY OF THE CHARACTERS IN HIS PLAYS.
MOTHER SAYS HE'S CHANGED IN THE LAST FIVE YEARS, BUT I DON'T REMEMBER HIM ANY OTHER WAY. JUDITH-- SHE'S MY TWIN SISTER-- SHE ONCE JOKED THAT IF I DIED, HE'D JUST WRITE A PLAY ABOUT IT.
"HAMNET."
COME ON, LADDIE. I AM BACK ON IN A MINUTE!
MOTHER ORDERED HIM TO HAVE ME FOR THIS SUMMER. IT'S THE FIRST TIME I'VE SEEN HIM FOR MORE THAN A WEEK AT A TIME, THAT I REMEMBER.
BUT WE LIVE FIVE DAYS' RIDE FROM LONDON, UP IN WARWICKSHIRE, AND SEE HIM SELDOM.
ALL THAT MATTERS TO HIM...
...ALL THAT MATTERS IS THE STORIES.
I WOULD BE PROUD OF HIM, IF HE WERE MY FATHER.
I'LL FOLLOW YOU, I'LL LEAD YOU ABOUT, AROUND, THROUGH BUSH, THROUGH BRAKE, THROUGH BRIAR.
SOMETIME A HORSE I'LL BE, SOMETIME A HOUND--
--A HOG, A HEADLESS BEAR, SOMETIME A FIRE...
WHY DO THEY RUN AWAY?
THIS IS A KNAVERY OF THEM TO MAKE ME A-FEARED!
THIS IS MAGNIFICENT--AND IT IS TRUE!
IT NEVER HAPPENED; YET IT IS STILL TRUE. WHAT MAGIC ART IS THIS?

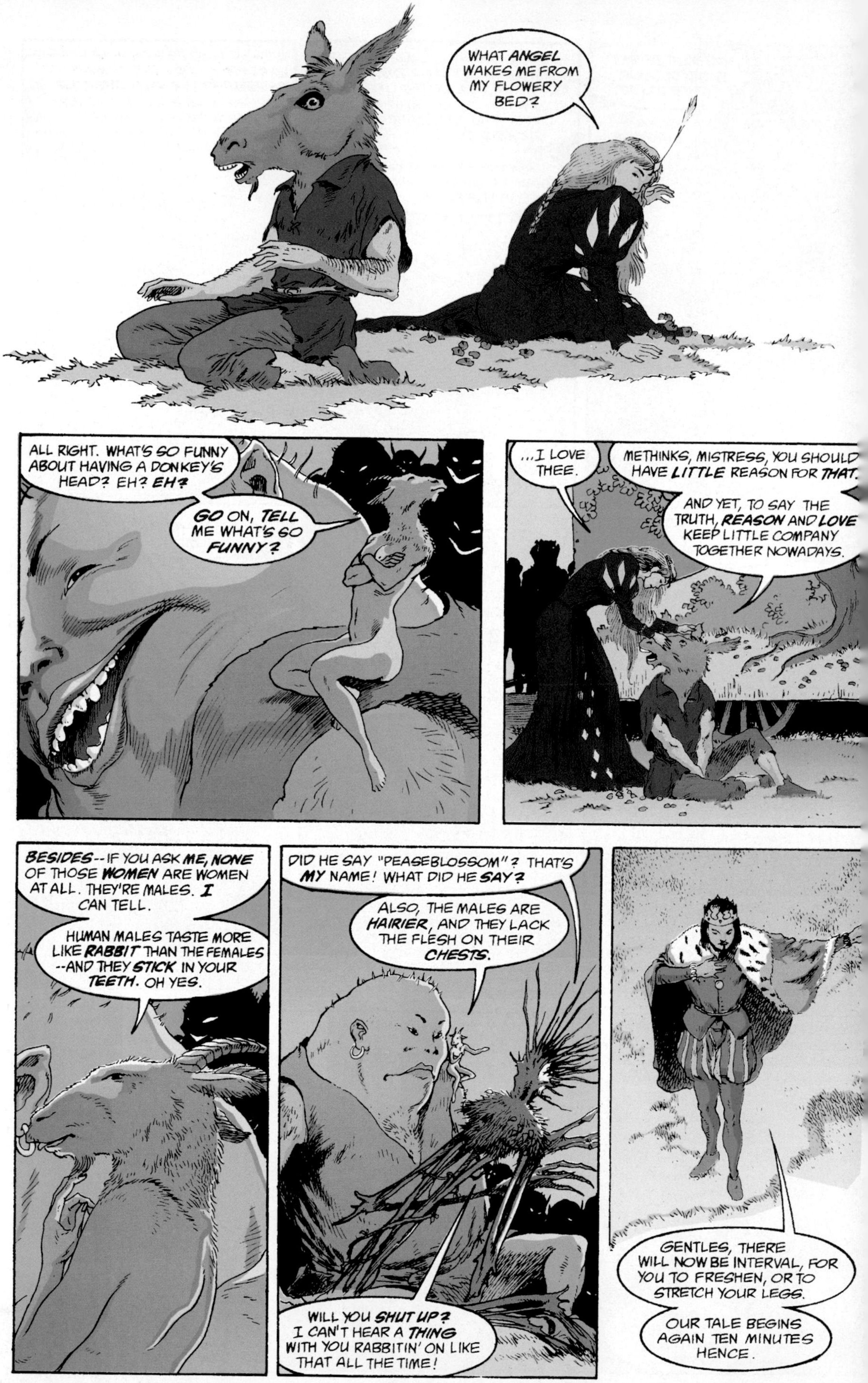
WHAT ANGEL WAKES ME FROM MY FLOWERY BED?
ALL RIGHT. WHAT'S SO FUNNY ABOUT HAVING A DONKEY'S HEAD? EH? EH?
GO ON, TELL ME WHAT'S SO FUNNY?
...I LOVE THEE.
METHINKS, MISTRESS, YOU SHOULD HAVE LITTLE REASON FOR THAT.
AND YET, TO SAY THE TRUTH, REASON AND LOVE KEEP LITTLE COMPANY TOGETHER NOWADAYS.
BESIDES--IF YOU ASK ME, NONE OF THOSE WOMEN ARE WOMEN AT ALL. THEY'RE MALES. I CAN TELL.
HUMAN MALES TASTE MORE LIKE RABBIT THAN THE FEMALES --AND THEY STICK IN YOUR TEETH. OH YES.
DID HE SAY "PEASEBLOSSOM"? THAT'S MY NAME! WHAT DID HE SAY?
ALSO, THE MALES ARE HAIRIER, AND THEY LACK THE FLESH ON THEIR CHESTS.
WILL YOU SHUT UP? I CAN'T HEAR A THING WITH YOU RABBITIN' ON LIKE THAT ALL THE TIME!
GENTLES, THERE WILL NOW BE INTERVAL, FOR YOU TO FRESHEN, OR TO STRETCH YOUR LEGS.
OUR TALE BEGINS AGAIN TEN MINUTES HENCE.

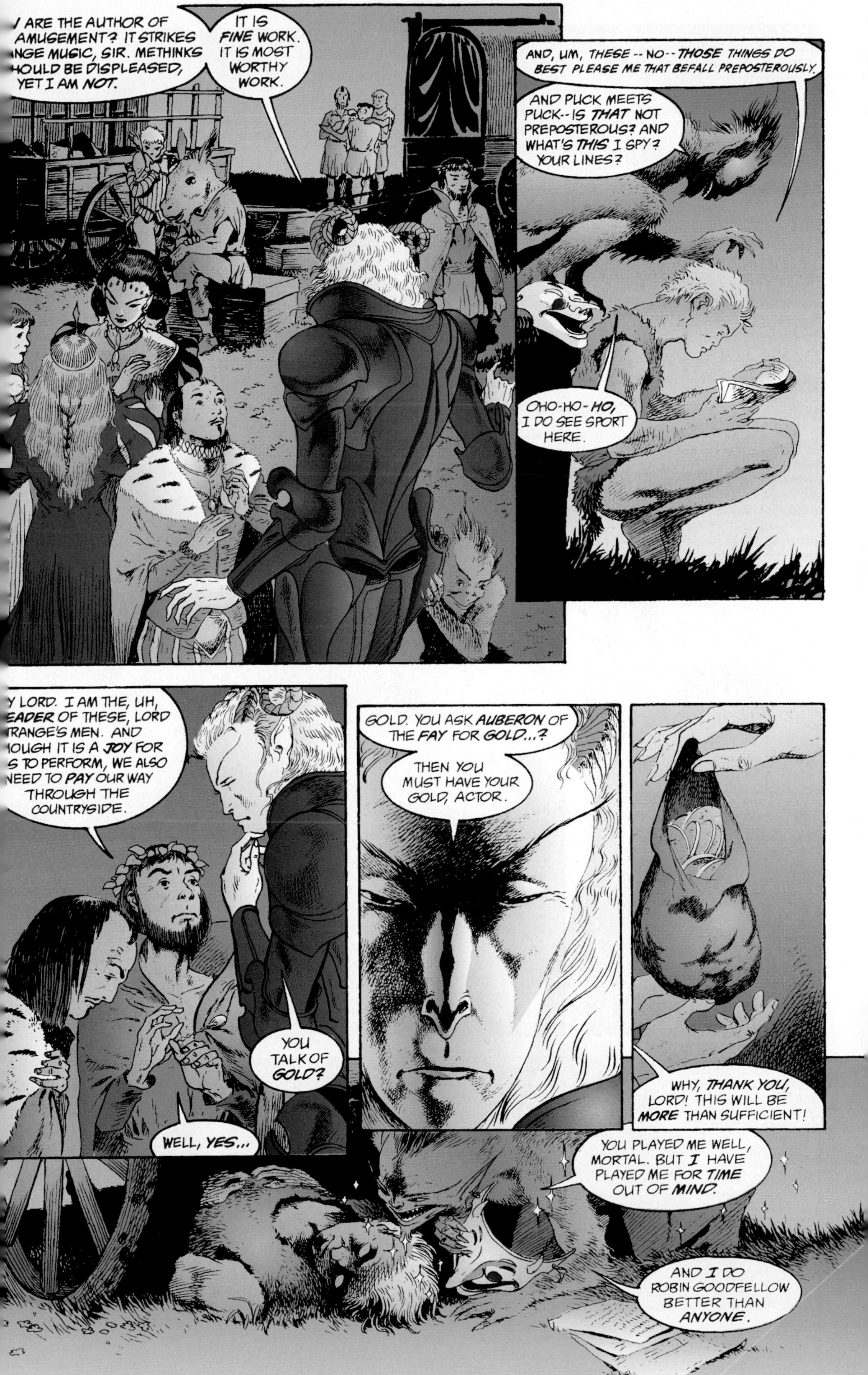
ARE THE AUTHOR OF AMUSEMENT? IT STRIKES NGE MUSIC, SIR. METHINKS HOULD BE DISPLEASED, YET I AM NOT.
IT IS FINE WORK. IT IS MOST WORTHY WORK.
AND, UM, THESE -- NO -- THOSE THINGS DO BEST PLEASE ME THAT BEFALL PREPOSTEROUSLY.
AND PUCK MEETS PUCK -- IS THAT NOT PREPOSTEROUS? AND WHAT'S THIS I SPY? YOUR LINES?
OHO-HO-HO, I DO SEE SPORT HERE.
Y LORD. I AM THE, UH, EADER OF THESE, LORD TRANGE'S MEN. AND HOUGH IT IS A JOY FOR S TO PERFORM, WE ALSO NEED TO PAY OUR WAY THROUGH THE COUNTRYSIDE.
YOU TALK OF GOLD?
WELL, YES...
GOLD. YOU ASK AUBERON OF THE FAY FOR GOLD...?
THEN YOU MUST HAVE YOUR GOLD, ACTOR.
WHY, THANK YOU, LORD! THIS WILL BE MORE THAN SUFFICIENT!
YOU PLAYED ME WELL, MORTAL. BUT I HAVE PLAYED ME FOR TIME OUT OF MIND.
AND I DO ROBIN GOODFELLOW BETTER THAN ANYONE.

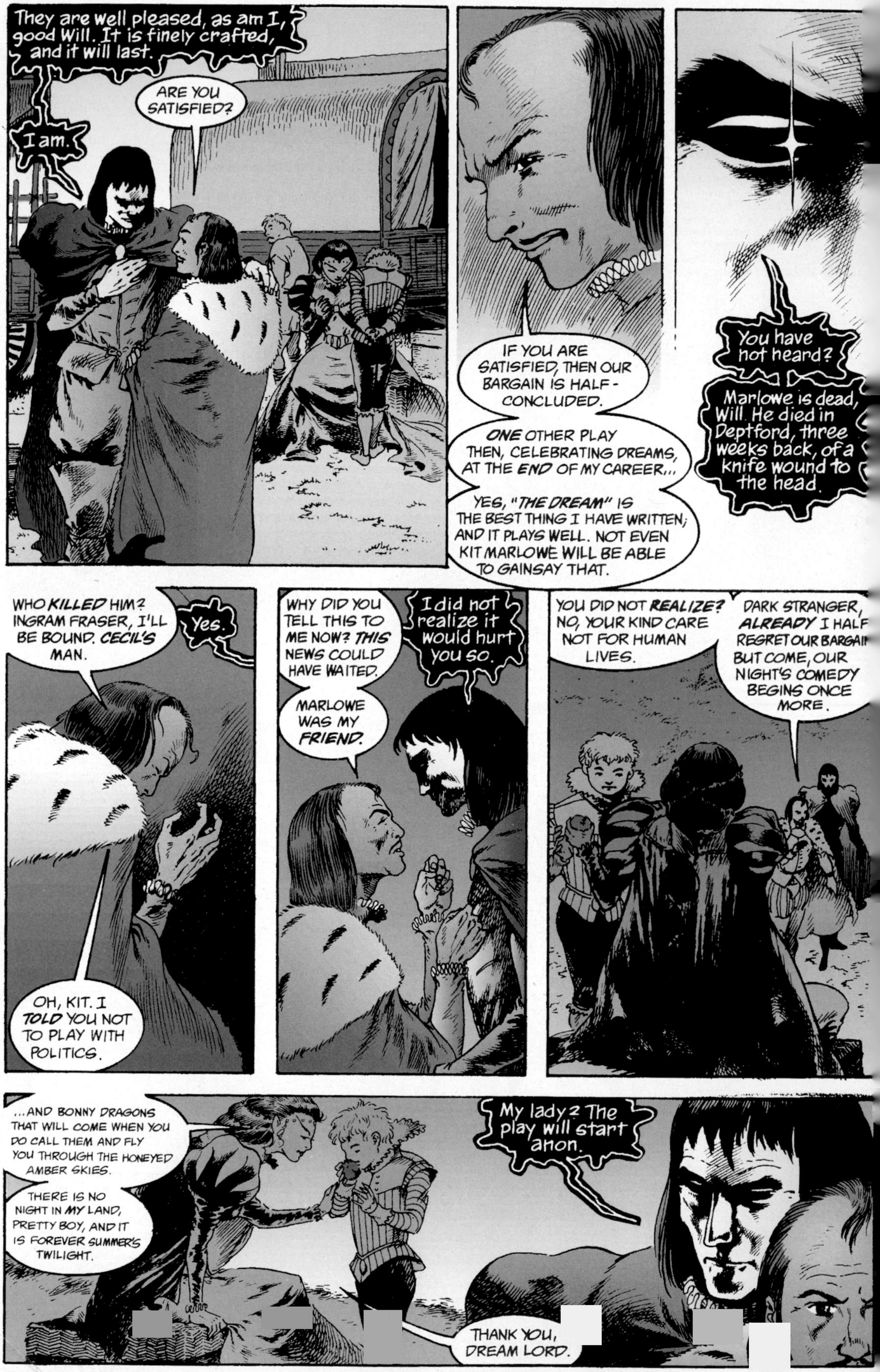
They are well pleased, as am I, good Will. It is finely crafted, and it will last.
ARE YOU SATISFIED?
I am.
IF YOU ARE SATISFIED, THEN OUR BARGAIN IS HALF-CONCLUDED.
ONE OTHER PLAY THEN, CELEBRATING DREAMS, AT THE END OF MY CAREER...
YES, "THE DREAM" IS THE BEST THING I HAVE WRITTEN; AND IT PLAYS WELL. NOT EVEN KIT MARLOWE WILL BE ABLE TO GAINSAY THAT.
You have not heard?
Marlowe is dead, Will. He died in Deptford, three weeks back, of a knife wound to the head.
WHO KILLED HIM? INGRAM FRASER, I'LL BE BOUND. CECIL'S MAN.
Yes.
OH, KIT. I TOLD YOU NOT TO PLAY WITH POLITICS.
WHY DID YOU TELL THIS TO ME NOW? THIS NEWS COULD HAVE WAITED.
I did not realize it would hurt you so.
MARLOWE WAS MY FRIEND.
YOU DID NOT REALIZE? NO, YOUR KIND CARE NOT FOR HUMAN LIVES.
DARK STRANGER, ALREADY I HALF REGRET OUR BARGAIN BUT COME, OUR NIGHT'S COMEDY BEGINS ONCE MORE.
...AND BONNY DRAGONS THAT WILL COME WHEN YOU DO CALL THEM AND FLY YOU THROUGH THE HONEYED AMBER SKIES.
THERE IS NO NIGHT IN MY LAND, PRETTY BOY, AND IT IS FOREVER SUMMER'S TWILIGHT.
My lady? The play will start anon.
THANK YOU, DREAM LORD.

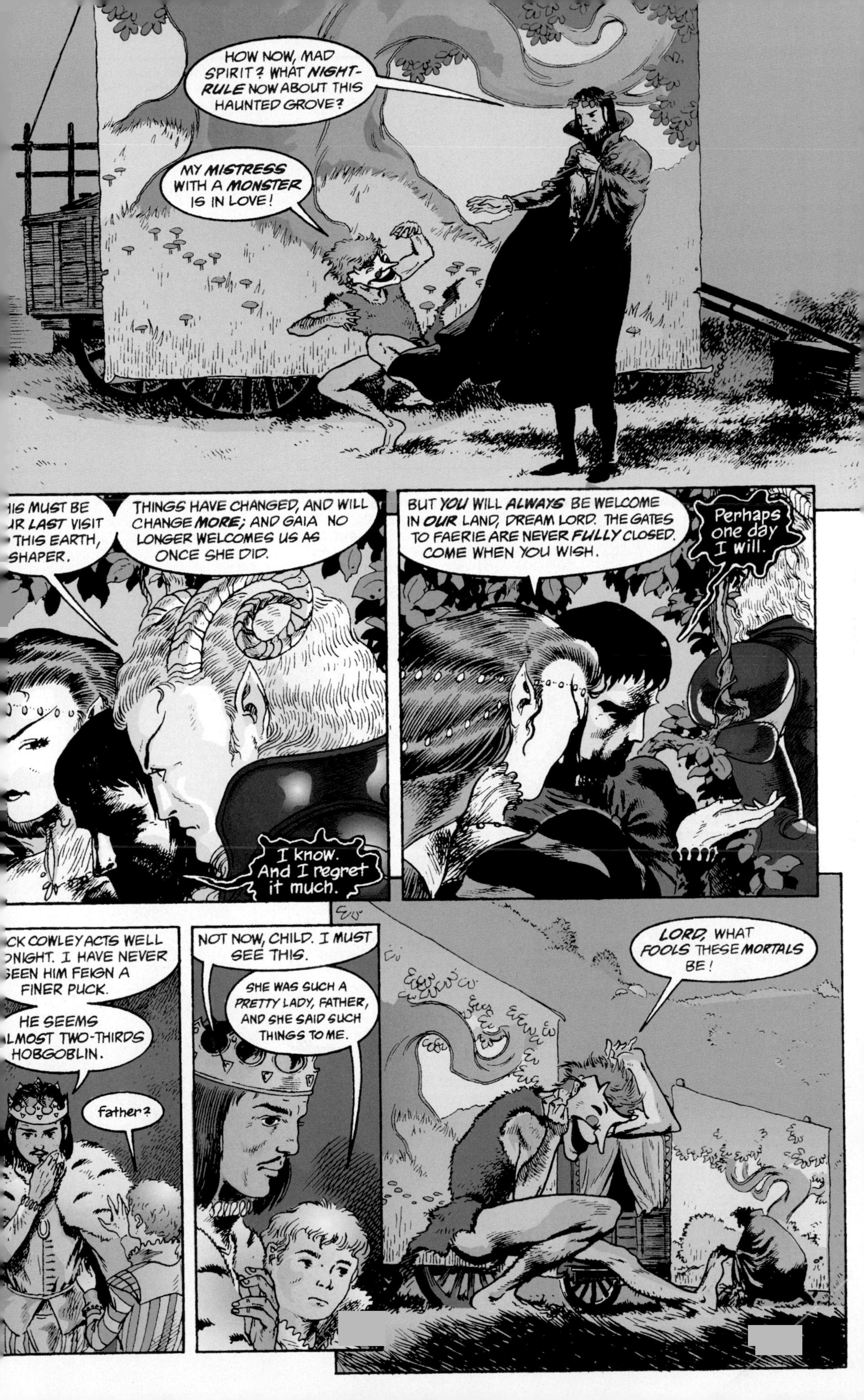
HOW NOW, MAD SPIRIT? WHAT NIGHT-RULE NOW ABOUT THIS HAUNTED GROVE?
MY MISTRESS WITH A MONSTER IS IN LOVE!
HIS MUST BE UR LAST VISIT TO THIS EARTH, SHAPER.
THINGS HAVE CHANGED, AND WILL CHANGE MORE; AND GAIA NO LONGER WELCOMES US AS ONCE SHE DID.
I know. And I regret it much.
BUT YOU WILL ALWAYS BE WELCOME IN OUR LAND, DREAM LORD. THE GATES TO FAERIE ARE NEVER FULLY CLOSED. COME WHEN YOU WISH.
Perhaps one day I will.
CK COWLEY ACTS WELL ONIGHT. I HAVE NEVER SEEN HIM FEIGN A FINER PUCK.
HE SEEMS LMOST TWO-THIRDS HOBGOBLIN.
father?
NOT NOW, CHILD. I MUST SEE THIS.
SHE WAS SUCH A PRETTY LADY, FATHER, AND SHE SAID SUCH THINGS TO ME.
LORD, WHAT FOOLS THESE MORTALS BE!

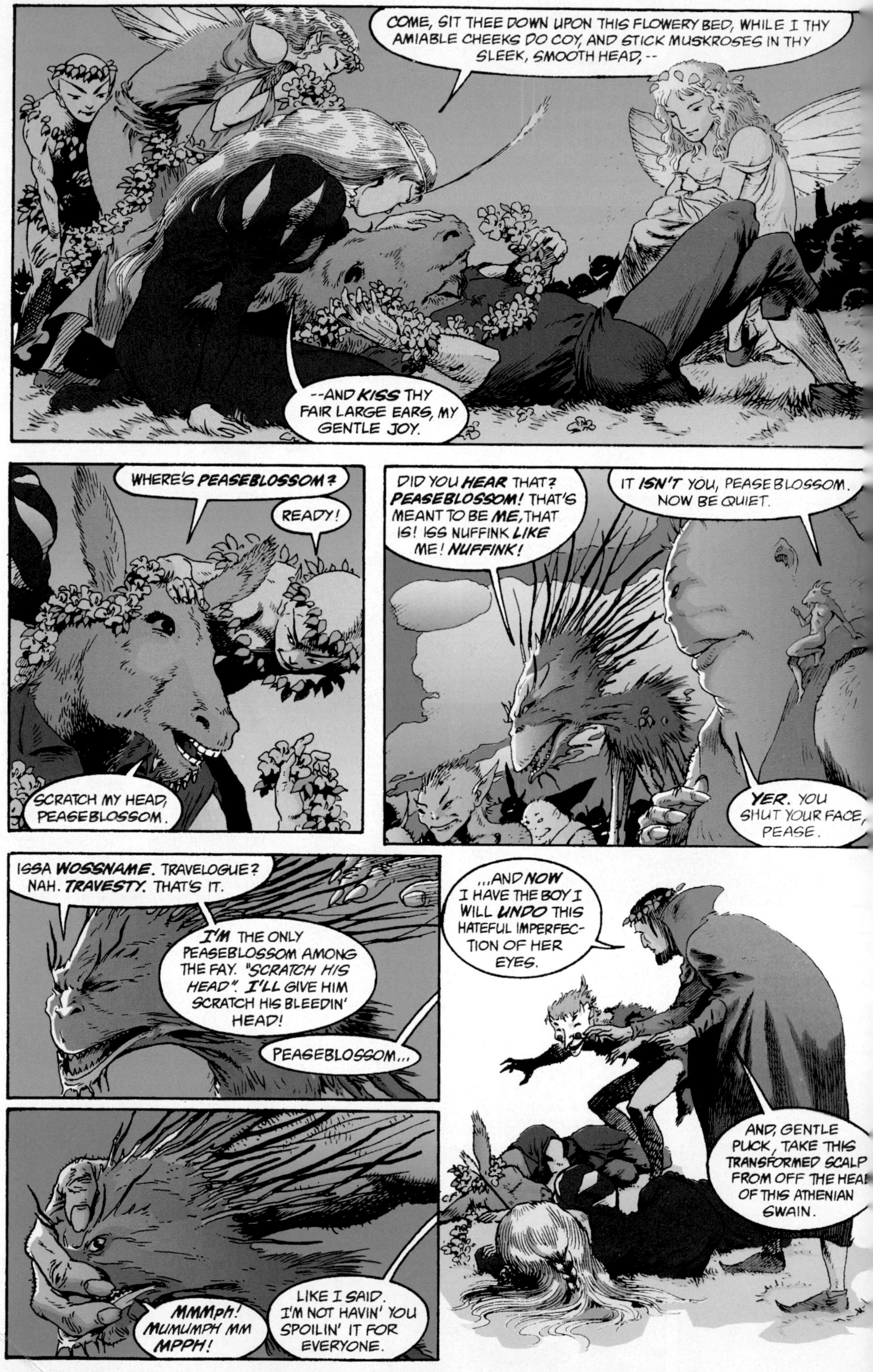
COME, SIT THEE DOWN UPON THIS FLOWERY BED, WHILE I THY AMIABLE CHEEKS DO COY, AND STICK MUSKROSES IN THY SLEEK, SMOOTH HEAD, --
--AND KISS THY FAIR LARGE EARS, MY GENTLE JOY.
WHERE'S PEASEBLOSSOM?
READY!
SCRATCH MY HEAD, PEASEBLOSSOM.
DID YOU HEAR THAT? PEASEBLOSSOM! THAT'S MEANT TO BE ME, THAT IS! ISS NUFFINK LIKE ME! NUFFINK!
IT ISN'T YOU, PEASE BLOSSOM. NOW BE QUIET.
YER. YOU SHUT YOUR FACE, PEASE.
ISSA WOSSNAME. TRAVELOGUE? NAH. TRAVESTY. THAT'S IT.
I'M THE ONLY PEASEBLOSSOM AMONG THE FAY. "SCRATCH HIS HEAD". I'LL GIVE HIM SCRATCH HIS BLEEDIN' HEAD!
PEASEBLOSSOM...
MMMph! MUMUMPH MM MPPH!
LIKE I SAID. I'M NOT HAVIN' YOU SPOILIN' IT FOR EVERYONE.
...AND NOW I HAVE THE BOY I WILL UNDO THIS HATEFUL IMPERFECTION OF HER EYES.
AND, GENTLE PUCK, TAKE THIS TRANSFORMED SCALP FROM OFF THE HEA OF THIS ATHENIAN SWAIN.

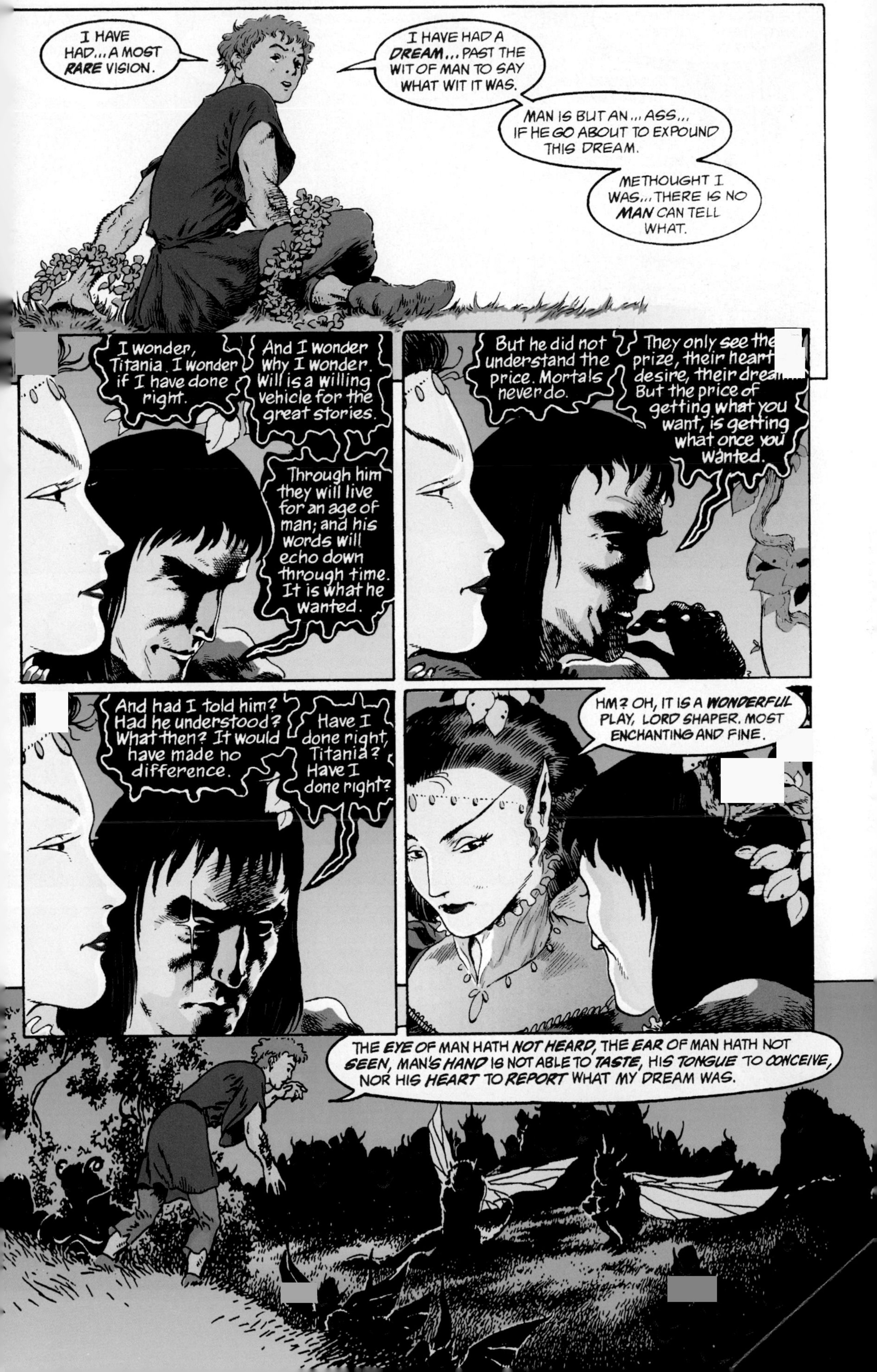
I HAVE HAD... A MOST RARE VISION.
I HAVE HAD A DREAM... PAST THE WIT OF MAN TO SAY WHAT WIT IT WAS.
MAN IS BUT AN... ASS... IF HE GO ABOUT TO EXPOUND THIS DREAM.
METHOUGHT I WAS... THERE IS NO MAN CAN TELL WHAT.
I wonder, Titania. I wonder if I have done right.
And I wonder why I wonder. Will is a willing vehicle for the great stories.
Through him they will live for an age of man; and his words will echo down through time. It is what he wanted.
But he did not understand the price. Mortals never do.
They only see the prize, their heart desire, their dream. But the price of getting what you want, is getting what once you wanted.
And had I told him? Had he understood? What then? It would have made no difference.
Have I done right, Titania? Have I done right?
HM? OH, IT IS A WONDERFUL PLAY, LORD SHAPER. MOST ENCHANTING AND FINE.
THE EYE OF MAN HATH NOT HEARD, THE EAR OF MAN HATH NOT SEEN, MAN'S HAND IS NOT ABLE TO TASTE, HIS TONGUE TO CONCEIVE, NOR HIS HEART TO REPORT WHAT MY DREAM WAS.

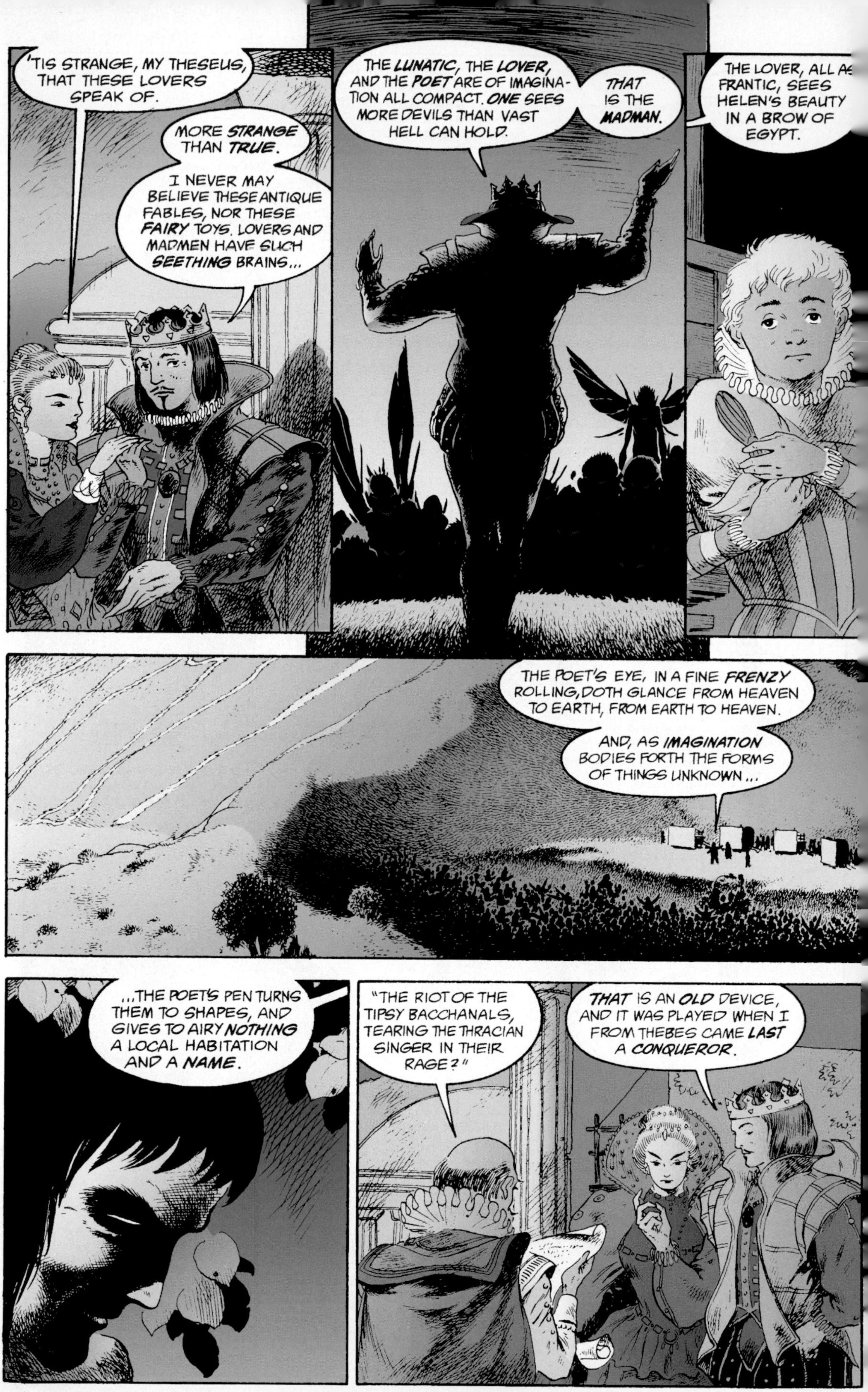
'TIS STRANGE, MY THESEUS, THAT THESE LOVERS SPEAK OF.
MORE STRANGE THAN TRUE.
I NEVER MAY BELIEVE THESE ANTIQUE FABLES, NOR THESE FAIRY TOYS. LOVERS AND MADMEN HAVE SUCH SEETHING BRAINS...
THE LUNATIC, THE LOVER, AND THE POET ARE OF IMAGINATION ALL COMPACT. ONE SEES MORE DEVILS THAN VAST HELL CAN HOLD.
THAT IS THE MADMAN.
THE LOVER, ALL AS FRANTIC, SEES HELEN'S BEAUTY IN A BROW OF EGYPT.
THE POET'S EYE, IN A FINE FRENZY ROLLING, DOTH GLANCE FROM HEAVEN TO EARTH, FROM EARTH TO HEAVEN.
AND, AS IMAGINATION BODIES FORTH THE FORMS OF THINGS UNKNOWN...
...THE POET'S PEN TURNS THEM TO SHAPES, AND GIVES TO AIRY NOTHING A LOCAL HABITATION AND A NAME.
"THE RIOT OF THE TIPSY BACCHANALS, TEARING THE THRACIAN SINGER IN THEIR RAGE?"
THAT IS AN OLD DEVICE, AND IT WAS PLAYED WHEN I FROM THEBES CAME LAST A CONQUEROR.

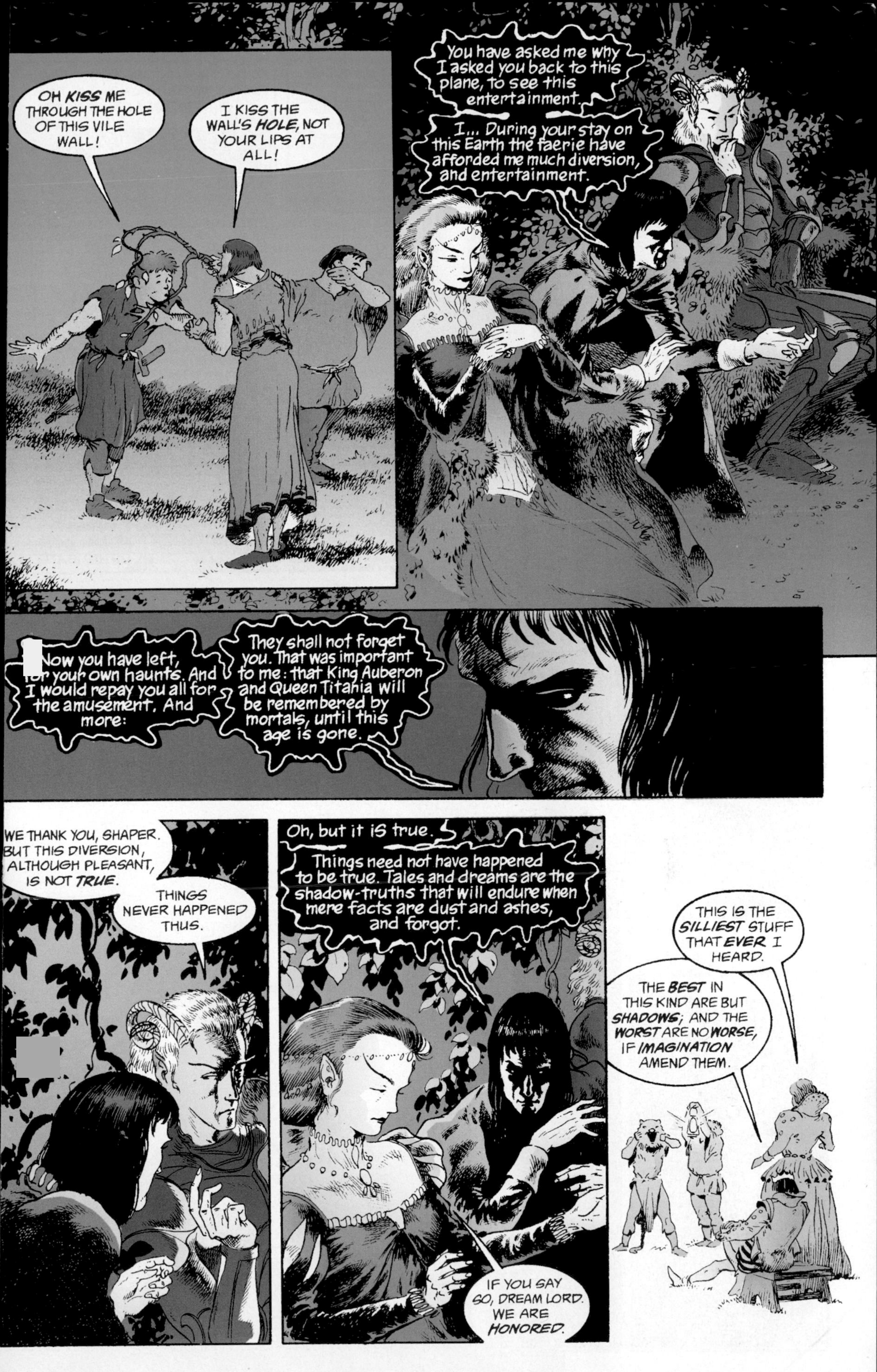
OH KISS ME THROUGH THE HOLE OF THIS VILE WALL!
I KISS THE WALL'S HOLE, NOT YOUR LIPS AT ALL!
You have asked me why I asked you back to this plane, to see this entertainment.
I... During your stay on this Earth the faerie have afforded me much diversion, and entertainment.
Now you have left, for your own haunts. And I would repay you all for the amusement. And more:
They shall not forget you. That was important to me: that King Auberon and Queen Titania will be remembered by mortals, until this age is gone.
WE THANK YOU, SHAPER. BUT THIS DIVERSION, ALTHOUGH PLEASANT, IS NOT TRUE.
THINGS NEVER HAPPENED THUS.
Oh, but it is true.
Things need not have happened to be true. Tales and dreams are the shadow-truths that will endure when mere facts are dust and ashes, and forgot.
IF YOU SAY SO, DREAM LORD. WE ARE HONORED.
THIS IS THE SILLIEST STUFF THAT EVER I HEARD.
THE BEST IN THIS KIND ARE BUT SHADOWS; AND THE WORST ARE NO WORSE, IF IMAGINATION AMEND THEM.

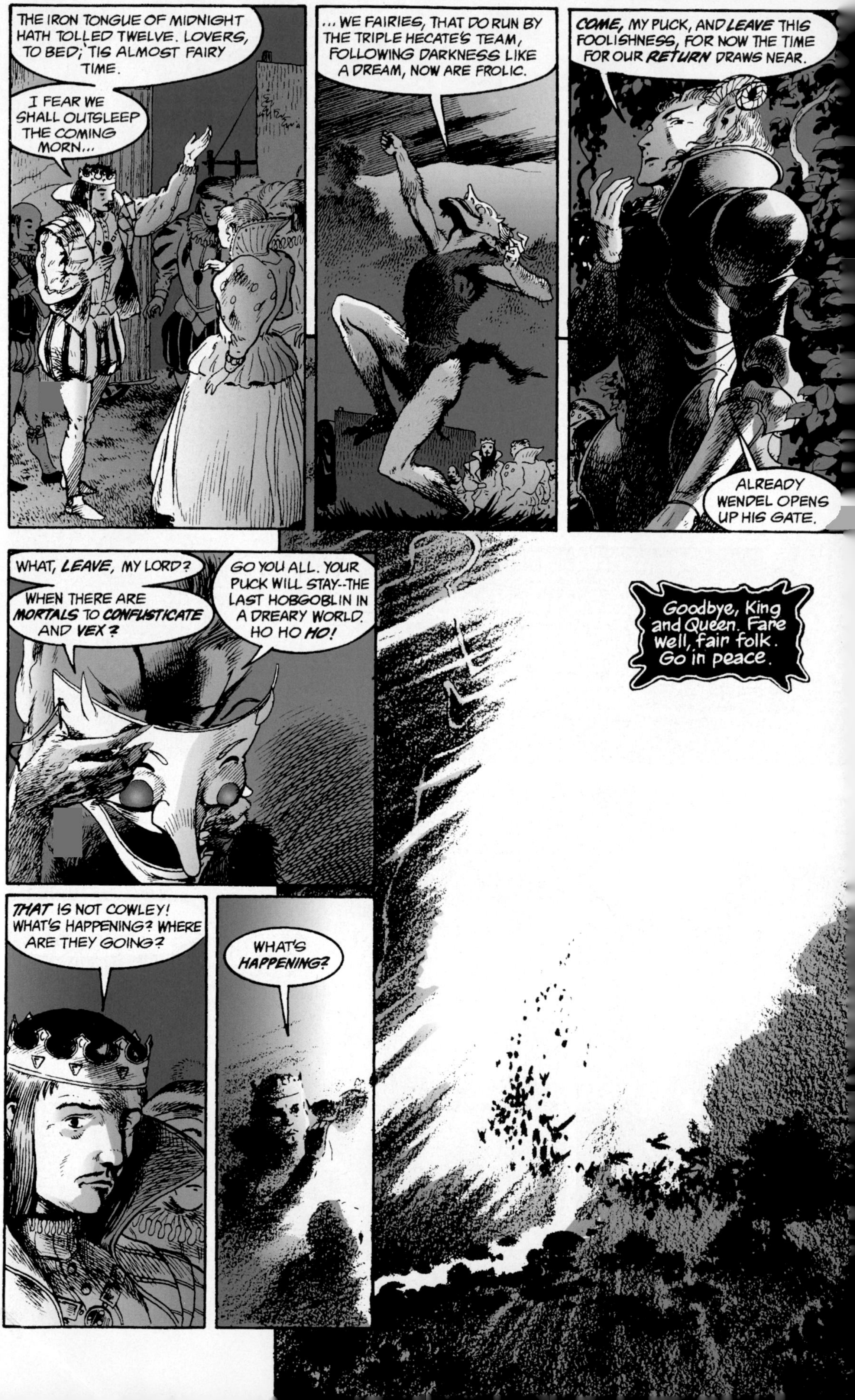
THE IRON TONGUE OF MIDNIGHT HATH TOLLED TWELVE. LOVERS, TO BED; 'TIS ALMOST FAIRY TIME.
I FEAR WE SHALL OUTSLEEP THE COMING MORN...
...WE FAIRIES, THAT DO RUN BY THE TRIPLE HECATE'S TEAM, FOLLOWING DARKNESS LIKE A DREAM, NOW ARE FROLIC.
COME, MY PUCK, AND LEAVE THIS FOOLISHNESS, FOR NOW THE TIME FOR OUR RETURN DRAWS NEAR.
ALREADY WENDEL OPENS UP HIS GATE.
WHAT, LEAVE, MY LORD?
WHEN THERE ARE MORTALS TO CONFUSTICATE AND VEX?
GO YOU ALL. YOUR PUCK WILL STAY--THE LAST HOBGOBLIN IN A DREARY WORLD. HO HO HO!
THAT IS NOT COWLEY! WHAT'S HAPPENING? WHERE ARE THEY GOING?
WHAT'S HAPPENING?
Goodbye, King and Queen. Fare well, fair folk. Go in peace.

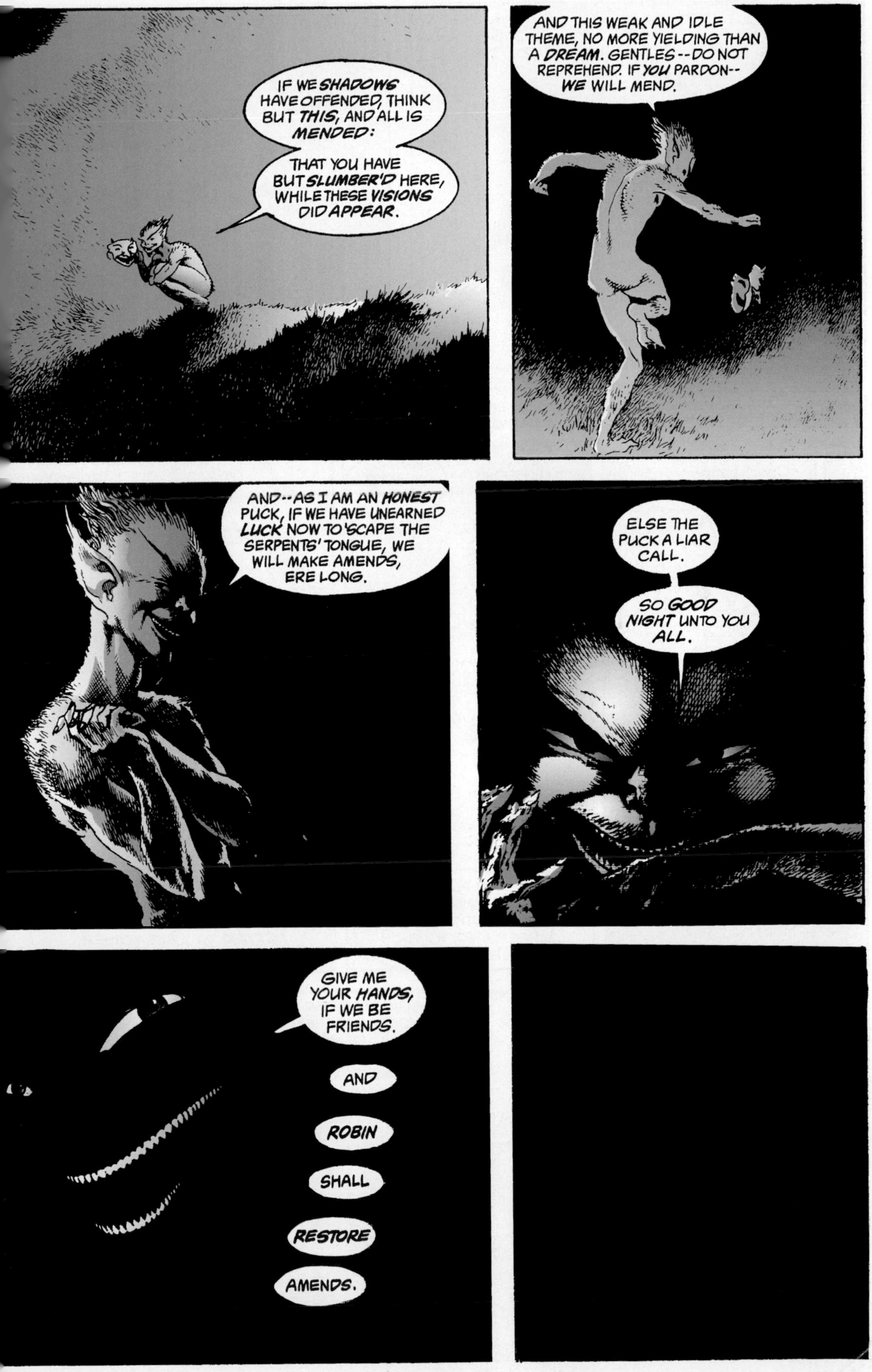

IF WE SHADOWS HAVE OFFENDED, THINK BUT THIS, AND ALL IS MENDED:
THAT YOU HAVE BUT SLUMBER'D HERE, WHILE THESE VISIONS DID APPEAR.
AND THIS WEAK AND IDLE THEME, NO MORE YIELDING THAN A DREAM. GENTLES--DO NOT REPREHEND. IF YOU PARDON--WE WILL MEND.
AND--AS I AM AN HONEST PUCK, IF WE HAVE UNEARNED LUCK NOW TO 'SCAPE THE SERPENTS' TONGUE, WE WILL MAKE AMENDS, ERE LONG.
ELSE THE PUCK A LIAR CALL.
SO GOOD NIGHT UNTO YOU ALL.
GIVE ME YOUR HANDS, IF WE BE FRIENDS.
AND
ROBIN
SHALL
RESTORE
AMENDS.

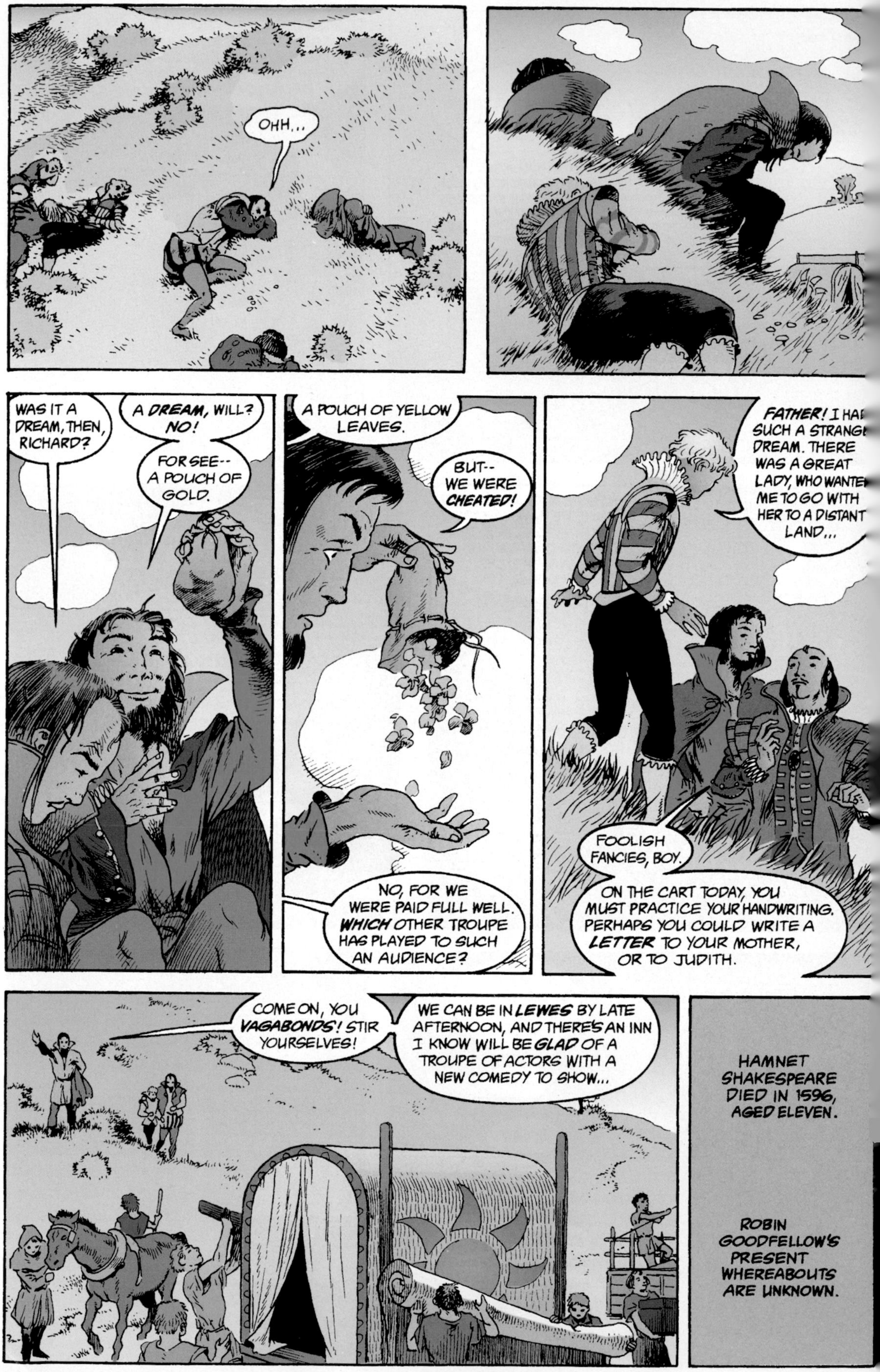
OHH...
WAS IT A DREAM, THEN, RICHARD?
A *DREAM*, WILL? *NO!*
FOR SEE-- A POUCH OF GOLD.
A POUCH OF YELLOW LEAVES.
BUT-- WE WERE *CHEATED!*
NO, FOR WE WERE PAID FULL WELL. *WHICH* OTHER TROUPE HAS PLAYED TO SUCH AN AUDIENCE?
FATHER! I HA SUCH A STRANG DREAM. THERE WAS A GREAT LADY, WHO WANTE ME TO GO WITH HER TO A DISTANT LAND...
FOOLISH FANCIES, BOY.
ON THE CART TODAY, YOU MUST PRACTICE YOUR HANDWRITING. PERHAPS YOU COULD WRITE A *LETTER* TO YOUR MOTHER, OR TO JUDITH.
COME ON, YOU *VAGABONDS!* STIR YOURSELVES!
WE CAN BE IN *LEWES* BY LATE AFTERNOON, AND THERE'S AN INN I KNOW WILL BE *GLAD* OF A TROUPE OF ACTORS WITH A NEW COMEDY TO SHOW...
HAMNET SHAKESPEARE DIED IN 1596, AGED ELEVEN.
ROBIN GOODFELLOW'S PRESENT WHEREABOUTS ARE UNKNOWN.

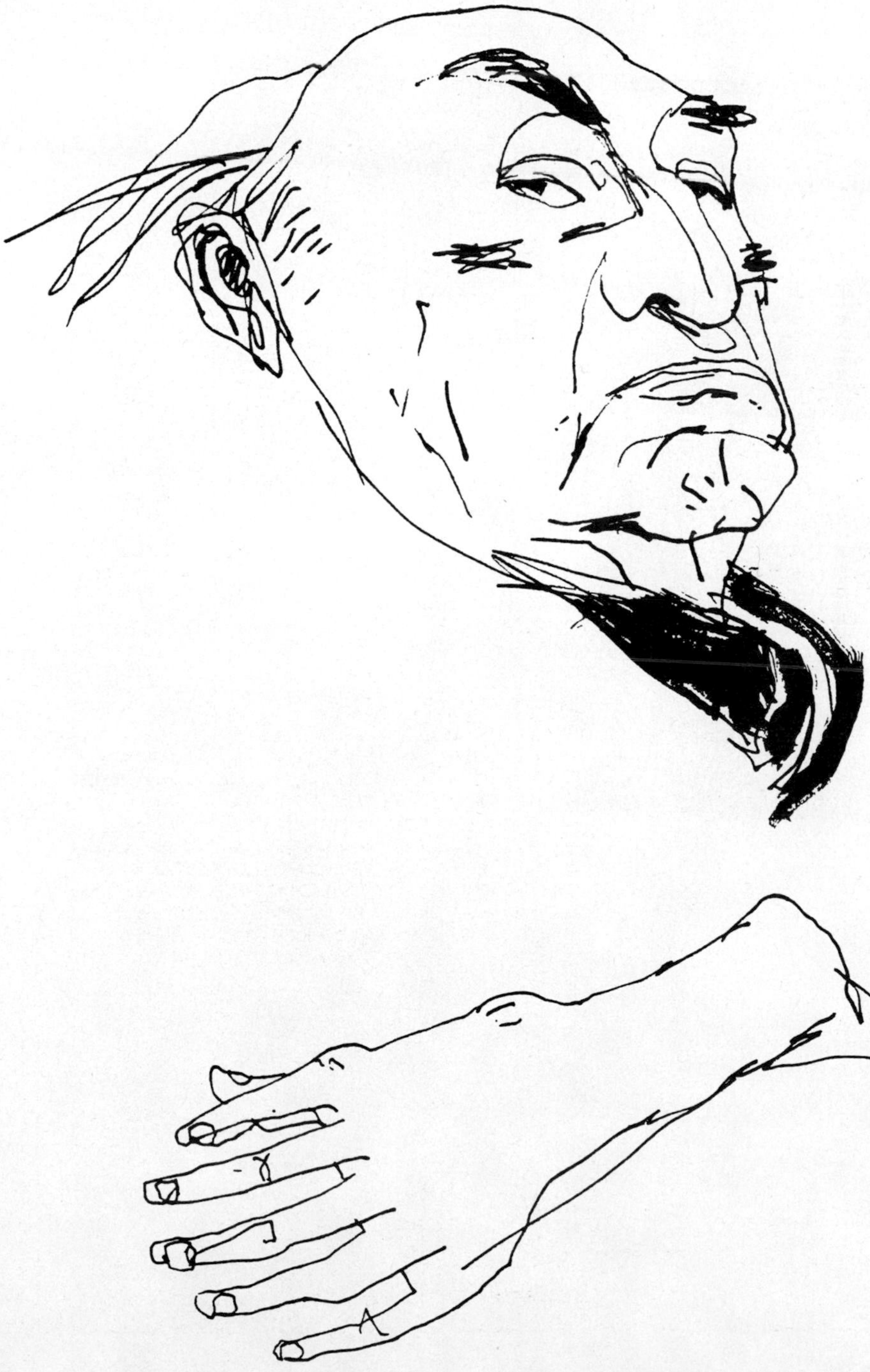

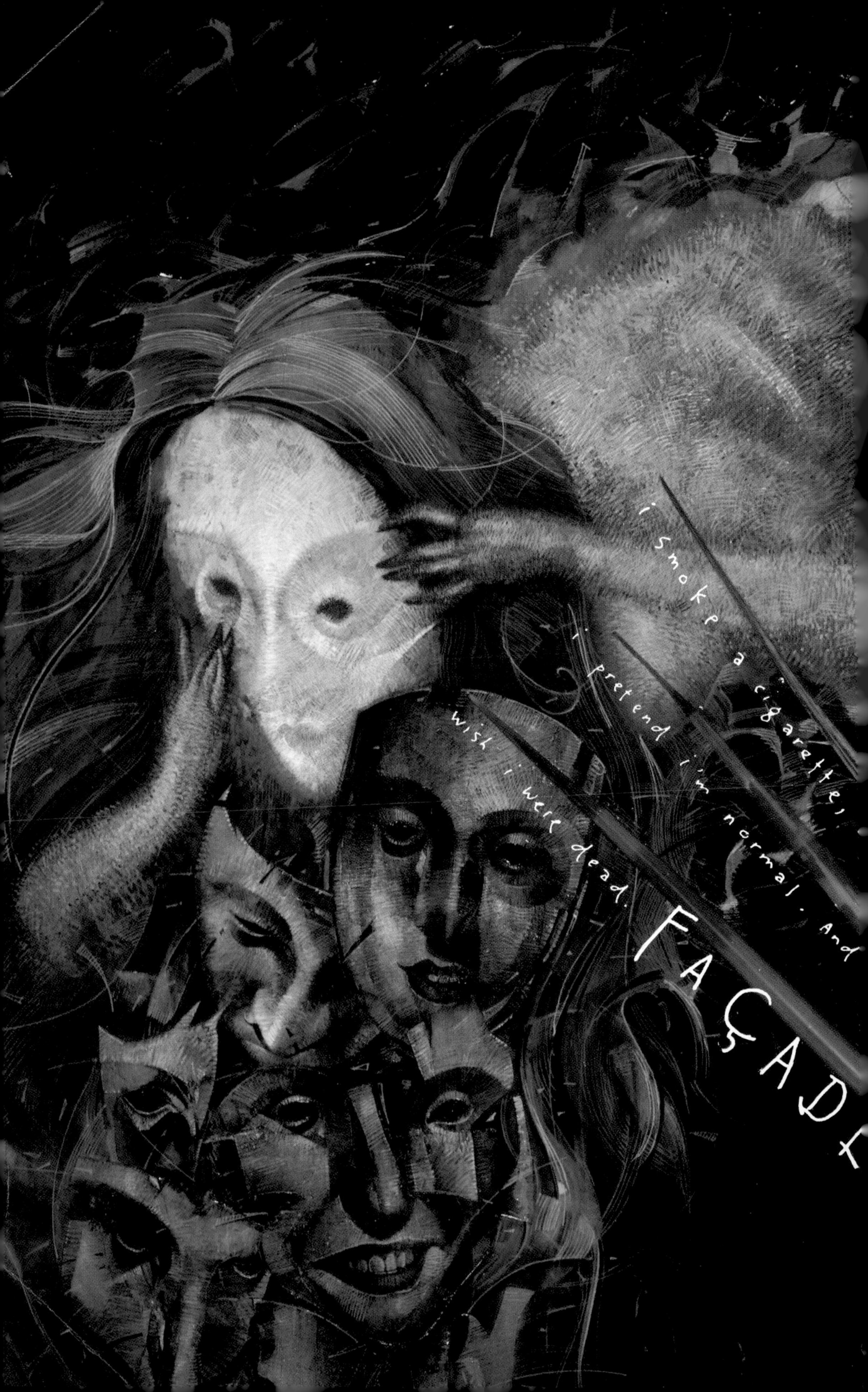
i smoke a cigarette,
i pretend i'm normal. And
wish i were dead.
FAÇADE

THEY SAY THAT CIGARETTES WILL KILL YOU, EVENTUALLY.

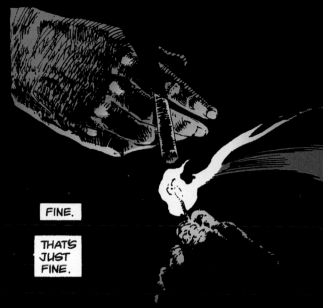

FINE.

THAT'S JUST FINE.

I ONLY WISH THEY'D DO IT *FASTER*.

I DRAW THE SMOKE INTO MY LUNGS, EXTRACT THE NICOTINE AND THE TAR. IT DOESN'T DO ANYTHING FOR ME, BUT I LIKE THE SMOKE.

I LIKE THE *ASH*. THE WAY IT *FALLS*. I LIKE BREATHING OUT THE SMOKE.

I LIKE SMOKING CIGARETTES. IT'S SOMETHING NORMAL PEOPLE DO.

I SMOKE A CIGARETTE, AND PRETEND I'M NORMAL.

AND I WISH I WAS DEAD.

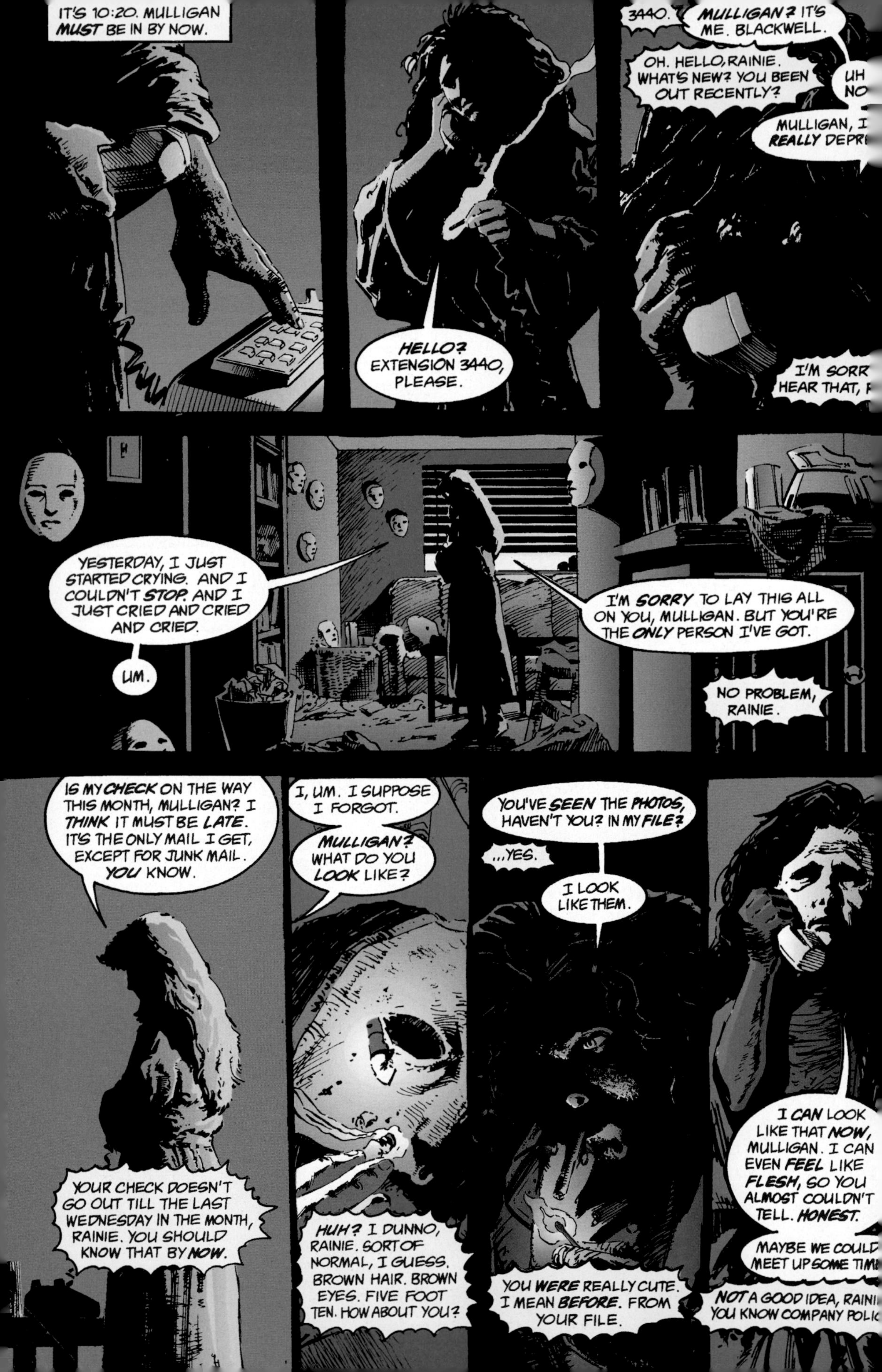
IT'S 10:20. MULLIGAN MUST BE IN BY NOW.
HELLO? EXTENSION 3440, PLEASE.
3440.
MULLIGAN? IT'S ME. BLACKWELL.
OH. HELLO, RAINIE. WHAT'S NEW? YOU BEEN OUT RECENTLY?
UH NO
MULLIGAN, I REALLY DEPR
I'M SORR HEAR THAT,
YESTERDAY, I JUST STARTED CRYING. AND I COULDN'T STOP. AND I JUST CRIED AND CRIED AND CRIED.
UM.
I'M SORRY TO LAY THIS ALL ON YOU, MULLIGAN. BUT YOU'RE THE ONLY PERSON I'VE GOT.
NO PROBLEM, RAINIE.
IS MY CHECK ON THE WAY THIS MONTH, MULLIGAN? I THINK IT MUST BE LATE. IT'S THE ONLY MAIL I GET, EXCEPT FOR JUNK MAIL. YOU KNOW.
YOUR CHECK DOESN'T GO OUT TILL THE LAST WEDNESDAY IN THE MONTH, RAINIE. YOU SHOULD KNOW THAT BY NOW.
I, UM. I SUPPOSE I FORGOT.
MULLIGAN? WHAT DO YOU LOOK LIKE?
HUH? I DUNNO, RAINIE. SORT OF NORMAL, I GUESS. BROWN HAIR. BROWN EYES. FIVE FOOT TEN. HOW ABOUT YOU?
YOU'VE SEEN THE PHOTOS, HAVEN'T YOU? IN MY FILE?
...YES.
I LOOK LIKE THEM.
YOU WERE REALLY CUTE. I MEAN BEFORE. FROM YOUR FILE.
I CAN LOOK LIKE THAT NOW, MULLIGAN. I CAN EVEN FEEL LIKE FLESH, SO YOU ALMOST COULDN'T TELL. HONEST.
MAYBE WE COULD MEET UP SOME TIM
NOT A GOOD IDEA, RAIN YOU KNOW COMPANY POLI

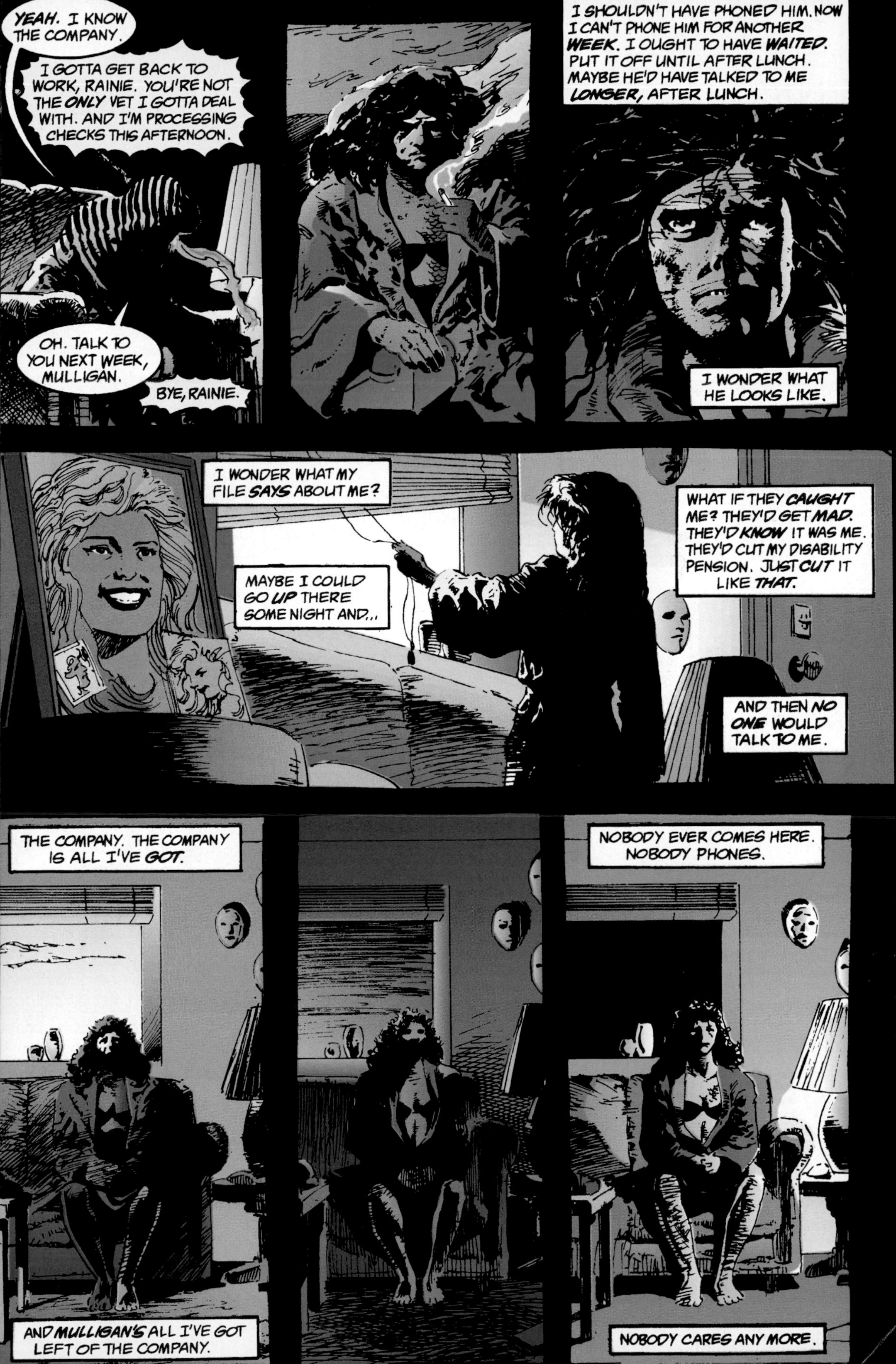
YEAH. I KNOW THE COMPANY.
I GOTTA GET BACK TO WORK, RAINIE. YOU'RE NOT THE ONLY VET I GOTTA DEAL WITH. AND I'M PROCESSING CHECKS THIS AFTERNOON.
OH. TALK TO YOU NEXT WEEK, MULLIGAN.
BYE, RAINIE.
I SHOULDN'T HAVE PHONED HIM. NOW I CAN'T PHONE HIM FOR ANOTHER WEEK. I OUGHT TO HAVE WAITED. PUT IT OFF UNTIL AFTER LUNCH. MAYBE HE'D HAVE TALKED TO ME LONGER, AFTER LUNCH.
I WONDER WHAT HE LOOKS LIKE.
I WONDER WHAT MY FILE SAYS ABOUT ME?
MAYBE I COULD GO UP THERE SOME NIGHT AND,,,
WHAT IF THEY CAUGHT ME? THEY'D GET MAD. THEY'D KNOW IT WAS ME. THEY'D CUT MY DISABILITY PENSION. JUST CUT IT LIKE THAT.
AND THEN NO ONE WOULD TALK TO ME.
THE COMPANY. THE COMPANY IS ALL I'VE GOT.
AND MULLIGAN'S ALL I'VE GOT LEFT OF THE COMPANY.
NOBODY EVER COMES HERE. NOBODY PHONES.
NOBODY CARES ANY MORE.

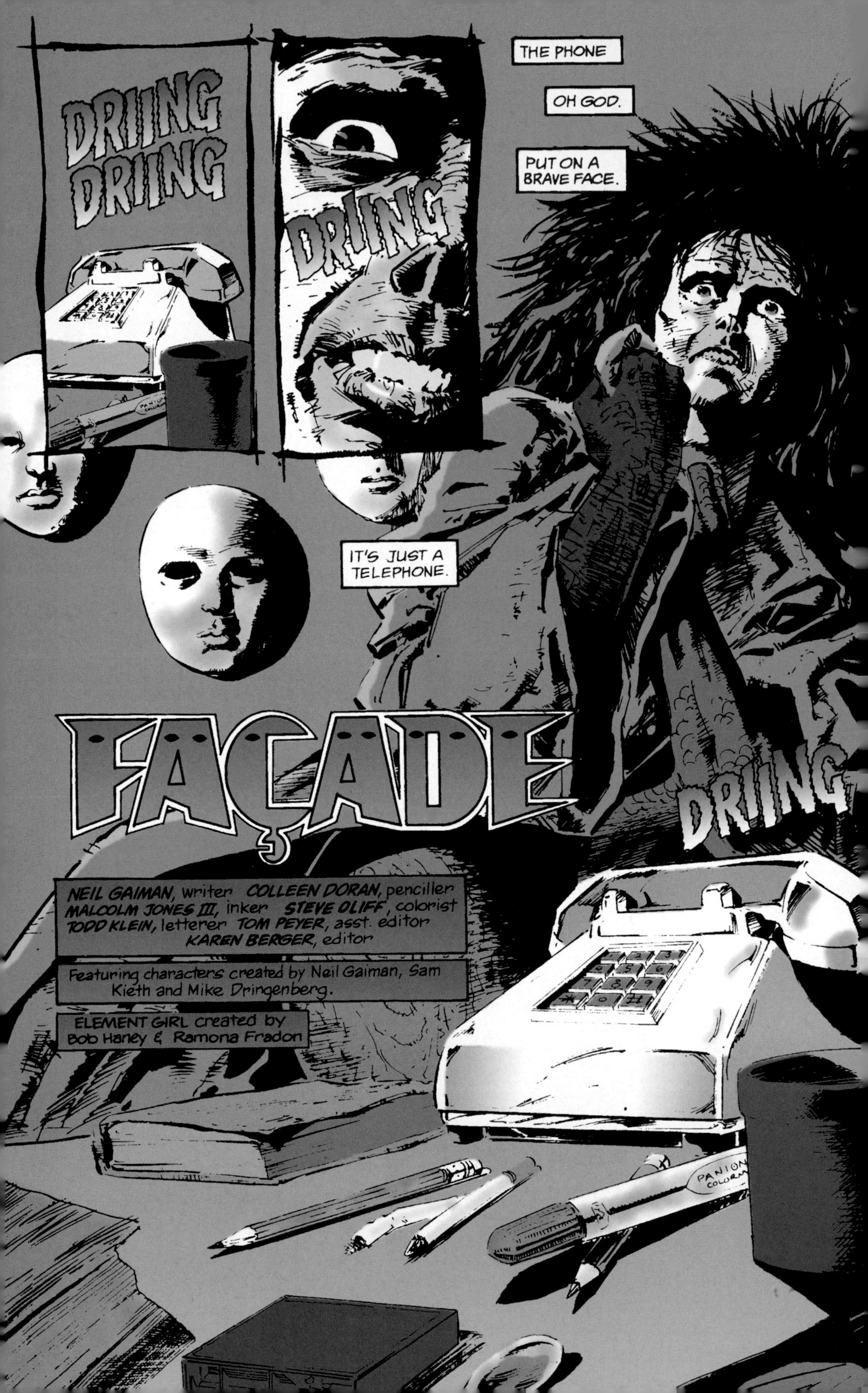
DRIING
DRING
DRING
THE PHONE
OH GOD.
PUT ON A BRAVE FACE.
IT'S JUST A TELEPHONE.
FAÇADE
DRING
NEIL GAIMAN, writer COLLEEN DORAN, penciller
MALCOLM JONES III, inker STEVE OLIFF, colorist
TODD KLEIN, letterer TOM PEYER, asst. editor
KAREN BERGER, editor
Featuring characters created by Neil Gaiman, Sam Kieth and Mike Dringenberg.
ELEMENT GIRL created by Bob Haney & Ramona Fradon

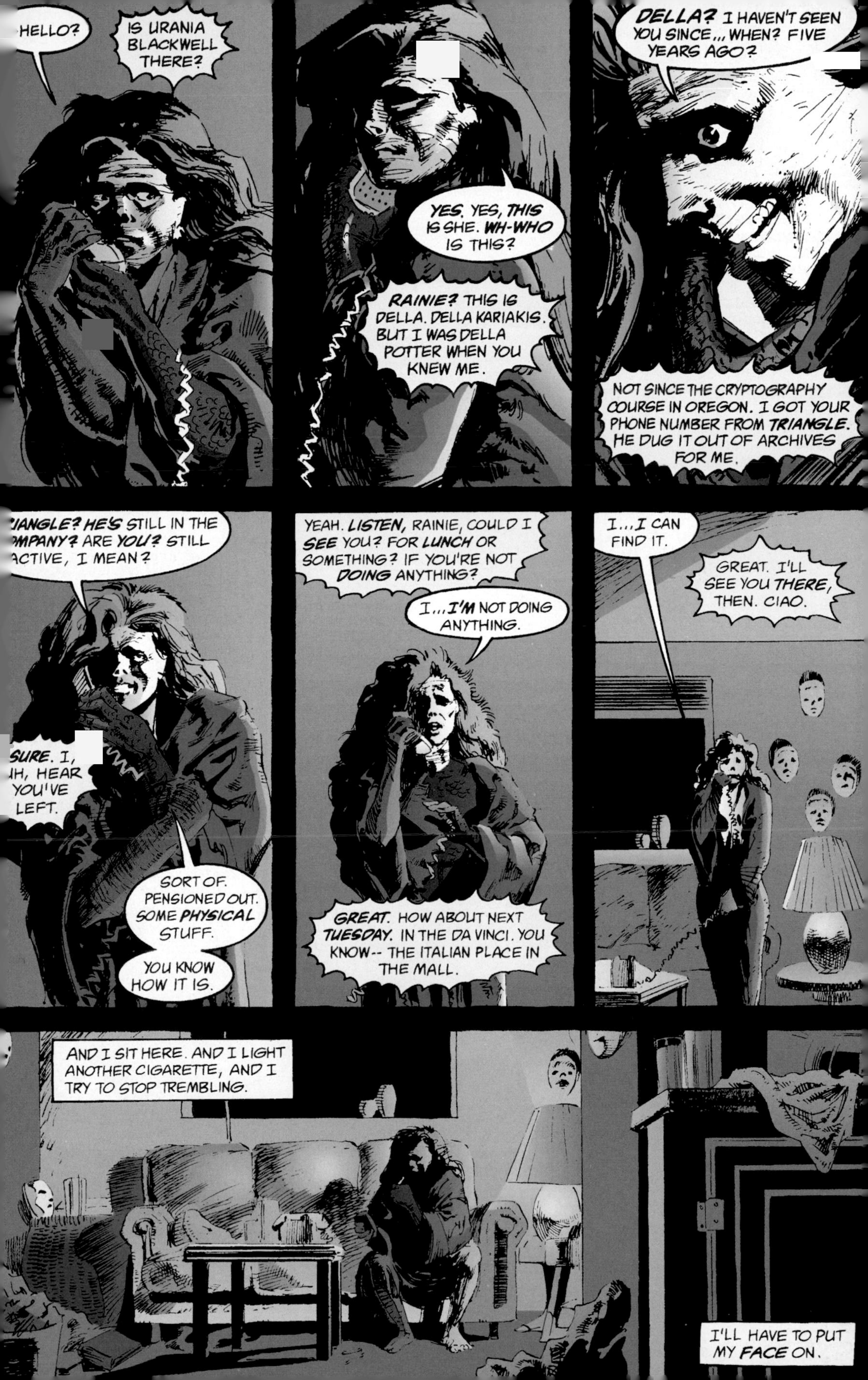
HELLO?
IS URANIA BLACKWELL THERE?
YES, YES, THIS IS SHE. WH-WHO IS THIS?
RAINIE? THIS IS DELLA. DELLA KARIAKIS. BUT I WAS DELLA POTTER WHEN YOU KNEW ME.
DELLA? I HAVEN'T SEEN YOU SINCE... WHEN? FIVE YEARS AGO?
NOT SINCE THE CRYPTOGRAPHY COURSE IN OREGON. I GOT YOUR PHONE NUMBER FROM TRIANGLE. HE DUG IT OUT OF ARCHIVES FOR ME.
IANGLE? HE'S STILL IN THE MPANY? ARE YOU? STILL ACTIVE, I MEAN?
SURE. I, H, HEAR YOU'VE LEFT.
SORT OF. PENSIONED OUT. SOME PHYSICAL STUFF.
YOU KNOW HOW IT IS.
YEAH. LISTEN, RAINIE, COULD I SEE YOU? FOR LUNCH OR SOMETHING? IF YOU'RE NOT DOING ANYTHING?
I... I'M NOT DOING ANYTHING.
GREAT. HOW ABOUT NEXT TUESDAY. IN THE DA VINCI. YOU KNOW-- THE ITALIAN PLACE IN THE MALL.
I... I CAN FIND IT.
GREAT. I'LL SEE YOU THERE, THEN. CIAO.
AND I SIT HERE. AND I LIGHT ANOTHER CIGARETTE, AND I TRY TO STOP TREMBLING.
I'LL HAVE TO PUT MY FACE ON.

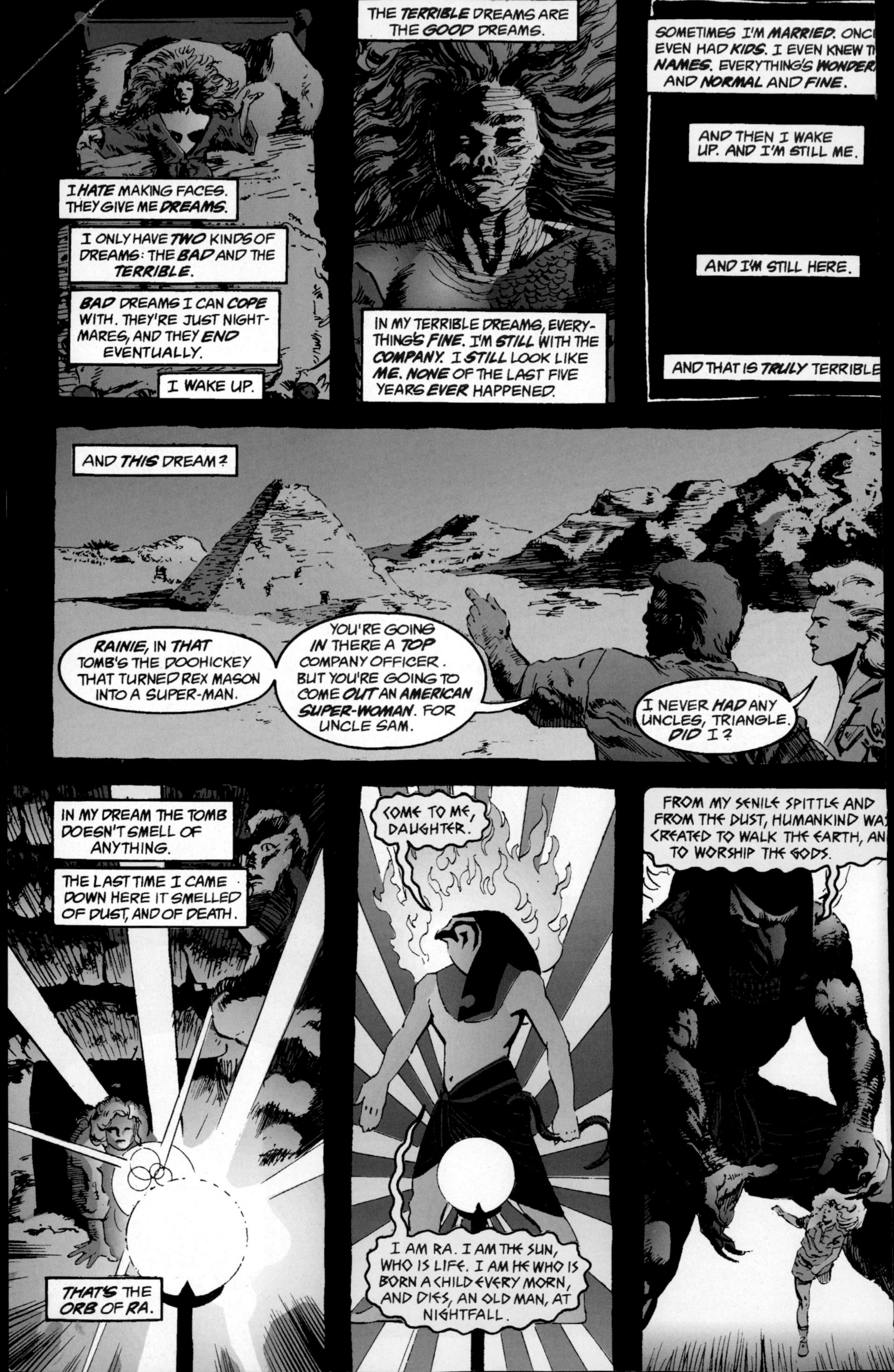
I HATE MAKING FACES. THEY GIVE ME DREAMS.
I ONLY HAVE TWO KINDS OF DREAMS: THE BAD AND THE TERRIBLE.
BAD DREAMS I CAN COPE WITH. THEY'RE JUST NIGHT-MARES, AND THEY END EVENTUALLY.
I WAKE UP.
THE TERRIBLE DREAMS ARE THE GOOD DREAMS.
IN MY TERRIBLE DREAMS, EVERY-THING'S FINE. I'M STILL WITH THE COMPANY. I STILL LOOK LIKE ME. NONE OF THE LAST FIVE YEARS EVER HAPPENED.
SOMETIMES I'M MARRIED. ONC EVEN HAD KIDS. I EVEN KNEW T NAMES. EVERYTHING'S WONDER AND NORMAL AND FINE.
AND THEN I WAKE UP. AND I'M STILL ME.
AND I'M STILL HERE.
AND THAT IS TRULY TERRIBLE
AND THIS DREAM?
RAINIE, IN THAT TOMB'S THE DOOHICKEY THAT TURNED REX MASON INTO A SUPER-MAN.
YOU'RE GOING IN THERE A TOP COMPANY OFFICER. BUT YOU'RE GOING TO COME OUT AN AMERICAN SUPER-WOMAN. FOR UNCLE SAM.
I NEVER HAD ANY UNCLES, TRIANGLE. DID I?
IN MY DREAM THE TOMB DOESN'T SMELL OF ANYTHING.
THE LAST TIME I CAME DOWN HERE IT SMELLED OF DUST, AND OF DEATH.
THAT'S THE ORB OF RA.
COME TO ME, DAUGHTER.
I AM RA. I AM THE SUN, WHO IS LIFE. I AM HE WHO IS BORN A CHILD EVERY MORN, AND DIES, AN OLD MAN, AT NIGHTFALL.
FROM MY SENILE SPITTLE AND FROM THE DUST, HUMANKIND WA CREATED TO WALK THE EARTH, AN TO WORSHIP THE GODS.

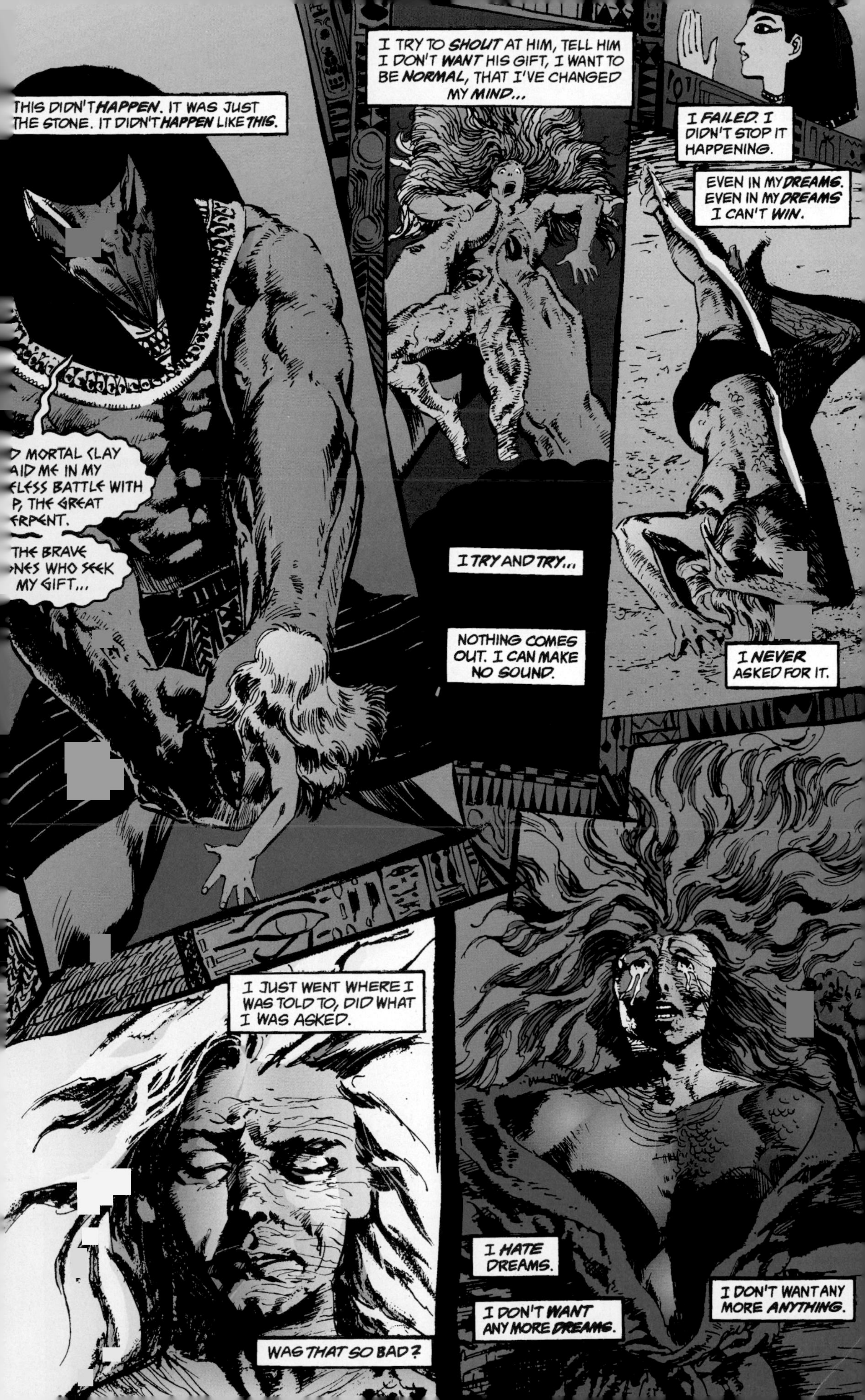
THIS DIDN'T HAPPEN. IT WAS JUST THE STONE. IT DIDN'T HAPPEN LIKE THIS.
D MORTAL CLAY AID ME IN MY ELESS BATTLE WITH P, THE GREAT ERPENT.
THE BRAVE NES WHO SEEK MY GIFT...
I TRY TO SHOUT AT HIM, TELL HIM I DON'T WANT HIS GIFT, I WANT TO BE NORMAL, THAT I'VE CHANGED MY MIND...
I TRY AND TRY...
NOTHING COMES OUT. I CAN MAKE NO SOUND.
I FAILED. I DIDN'T STOP IT HAPPENING.
EVEN IN MY DREAMS. EVEN IN MY DREAMS I CAN'T WIN.
I NEVER ASKED FOR IT.
I JUST WENT WHERE I WAS TOLD TO, DID WHAT I WAS ASKED.
WAS THAT SO BAD?
I HATE DREAMS.
I DON'T WANT ANY MORE DREAMS.
I DON'T WANT ANY MORE ANYTHING.

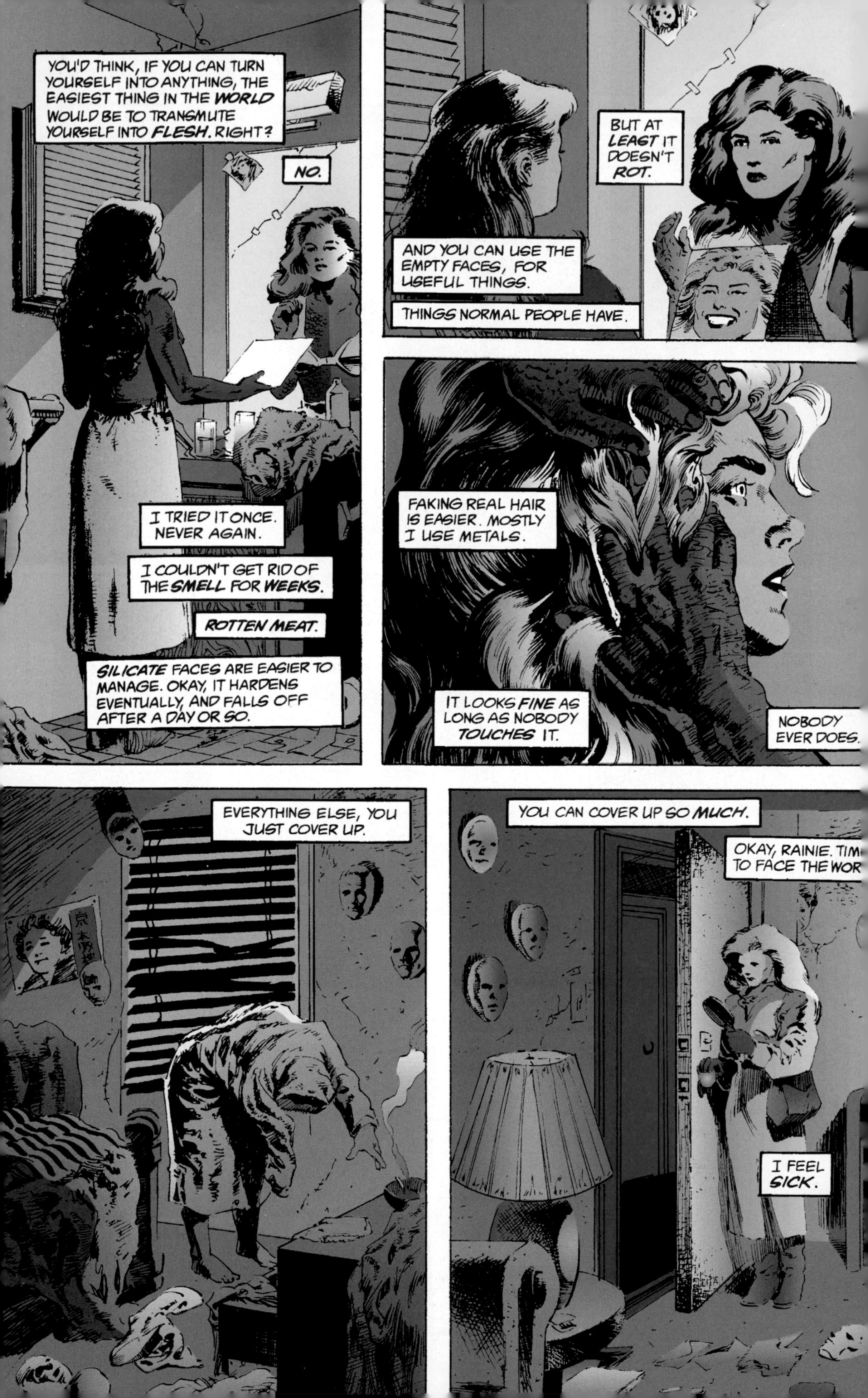
YOU'D THINK, IF YOU CAN TURN YOURSELF INTO ANYTHING, THE EASIEST THING IN THE WORLD WOULD BE TO TRANSMUTE YOURSELF INTO FLESH. RIGHT?
NO.
I TRIED IT ONCE. NEVER AGAIN.
I COULDN'T GET RID OF THE SMELL FOR WEEKS.
ROTTEN MEAT.
SILICATE FACES ARE EASIER TO MANAGE. OKAY, IT HARDENS EVENTUALLY, AND FALLS OFF AFTER A DAY OR SO.
AND YOU CAN USE THE EMPTY FACES, FOR USEFUL THINGS.
THINGS NORMAL PEOPLE HAVE.
BUT AT LEAST IT DOESN'T ROT.
FAKING REAL HAIR IS EASIER. MOSTLY I USE METALS.
IT LOOKS FINE AS LONG AS NOBODY TOUCHES IT.
NOBODY EVER DOES.
EVERYTHING ELSE, YOU JUST COVER UP.
YOU CAN COVER UP SO MUCH.
OKAY, RAINIE. TIM
TO FACE THE WOR
I FEEL SICK.

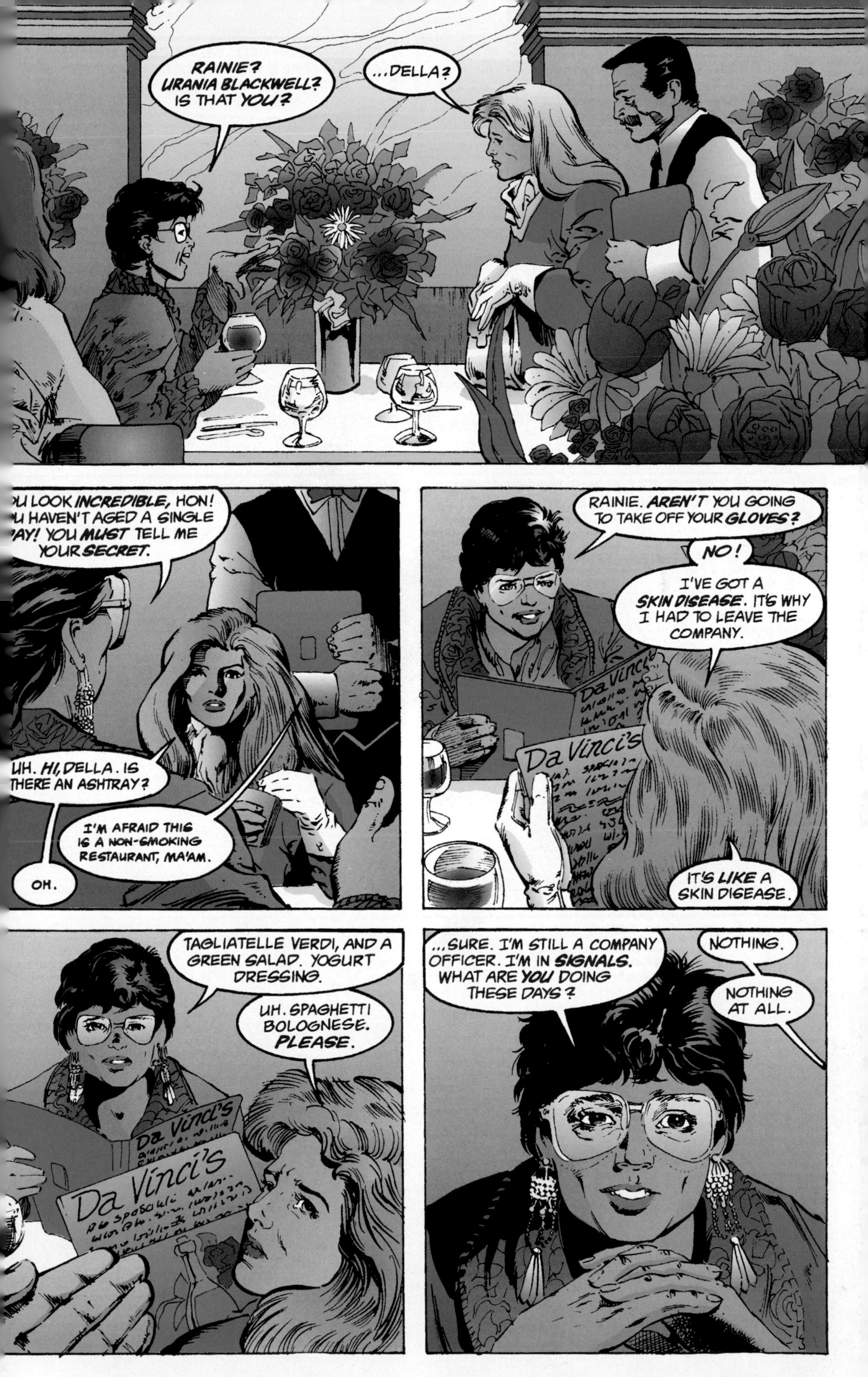
RAINIE? URANIA BLACKWELL? IS THAT YOU?
...DELLA?
OU LOOK INCREDIBLE, HON! OU HAVEN'T AGED A SINGLE AY! YOU MUST TELL ME YOUR SECRET.
UH. HI, DELLA. IS THERE AN ASHTRAY?
I'M AFRAID THIS IS A NON-SMOKING RESTAURANT, MA'AM.
OH.
RAINIE. AREN'T YOU GOING TO TAKE OFF YOUR GLOVES?
NO!
I'VE GOT A SKIN DISEASE. IT'S WHY I HAD TO LEAVE THE COMPANY.
Da Vinci's
Da Vinci's
IT'S LIKE A SKIN DISEASE.
TAGLIATELLE VERDI, AND A GREEN SALAD. YOGURT DRESSING.
UH. SPAGHETTI BOLOGNESE. PLEASE.
Da Vinci's
Da Vinci's
...SURE. I'M STILL A COMPANY OFFICER. I'M IN SIGNALS. WHAT ARE YOU DOING THESE DAYS?
NOTHING.
NOTHING AT ALL.

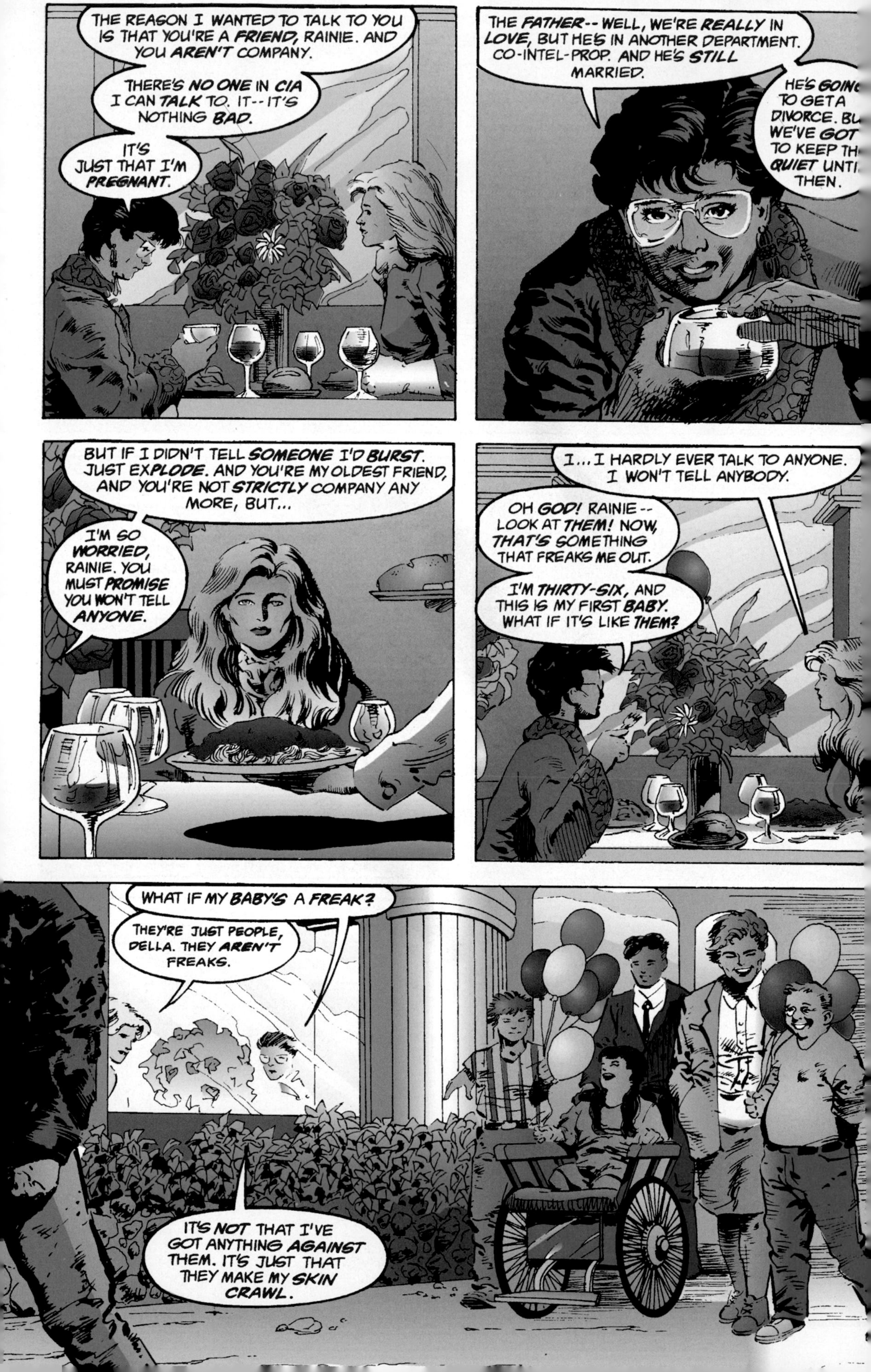
THE REASON I WANTED TO TALK TO YOU IS THAT YOU'RE A FRIEND, RAINIE. AND YOU AREN'T COMPANY.
THERE'S NO ONE IN CIA I CAN TALK TO. IT-- IT'S NOTHING BAD.
IT'S JUST THAT I'M PREGNANT.
THE FATHER-- WELL, WE'RE REALLY IN LOVE, BUT HE'S IN ANOTHER DEPARTMENT. CO-INTEL-PROP. AND HE'S STILL MARRIED.
HE'S GOING TO GET A DIVORCE. BU WE'VE GOT TO KEEP TH QUIET UNTI THEN.
BUT IF I DIDN'T TELL SOMEONE I'D BURST. JUST EXPLODE. AND YOU'RE MY OLDEST FRIEND, AND YOU'RE NOT STRICTLY COMPANY ANY MORE, BUT...
I'M SO WORRIED, RAINIE. YOU MUST PROMISE YOU WON'T TELL ANYONE.
I... I HARDLY EVER TALK TO ANYONE. I WON'T TELL ANYBODY.
OH GOD! RAINIE -- LOOK AT THEM! NOW, THAT'S SOMETHING THAT FREAKS ME OUT.
I'M THIRTY-SIX, AND THIS IS MY FIRST BABY. WHAT IF IT'S LIKE THEM?
WHAT IF MY BABY'S A FREAK?
THEY'RE JUST PEOPLE, DELLA. THEY AREN'T FREAKS.
IT'S NOT THAT I'VE GOT ANYTHING AGAINST THEM. IT'S JUST THAT THEY MAKE MY SKIN CRAWL.

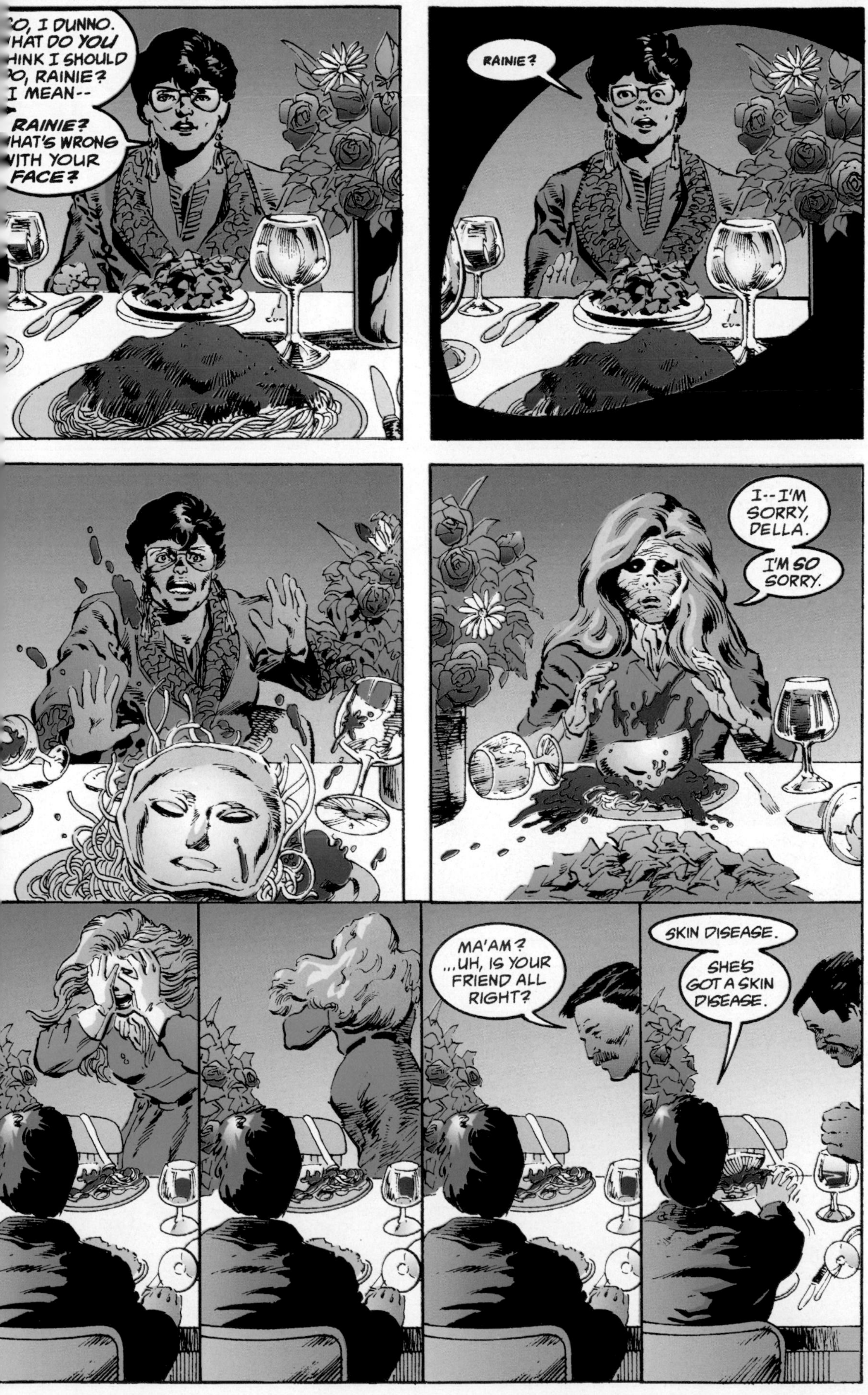
SO, I DUNNO. WHAT DO YOU THINK I SHOULD DO, RAINIE? I MEAN--
RAINIE? WHAT'S WRONG WITH YOUR FACE?
RAINIE?
I--I'M SORRY, DELLA.
I'M SO SORRY.
MA'AM? ...UH, IS YOUR FRIEND ALL RIGHT?
SKIN DISEASE.
SHE'S GOT A SKIN DISEASE.

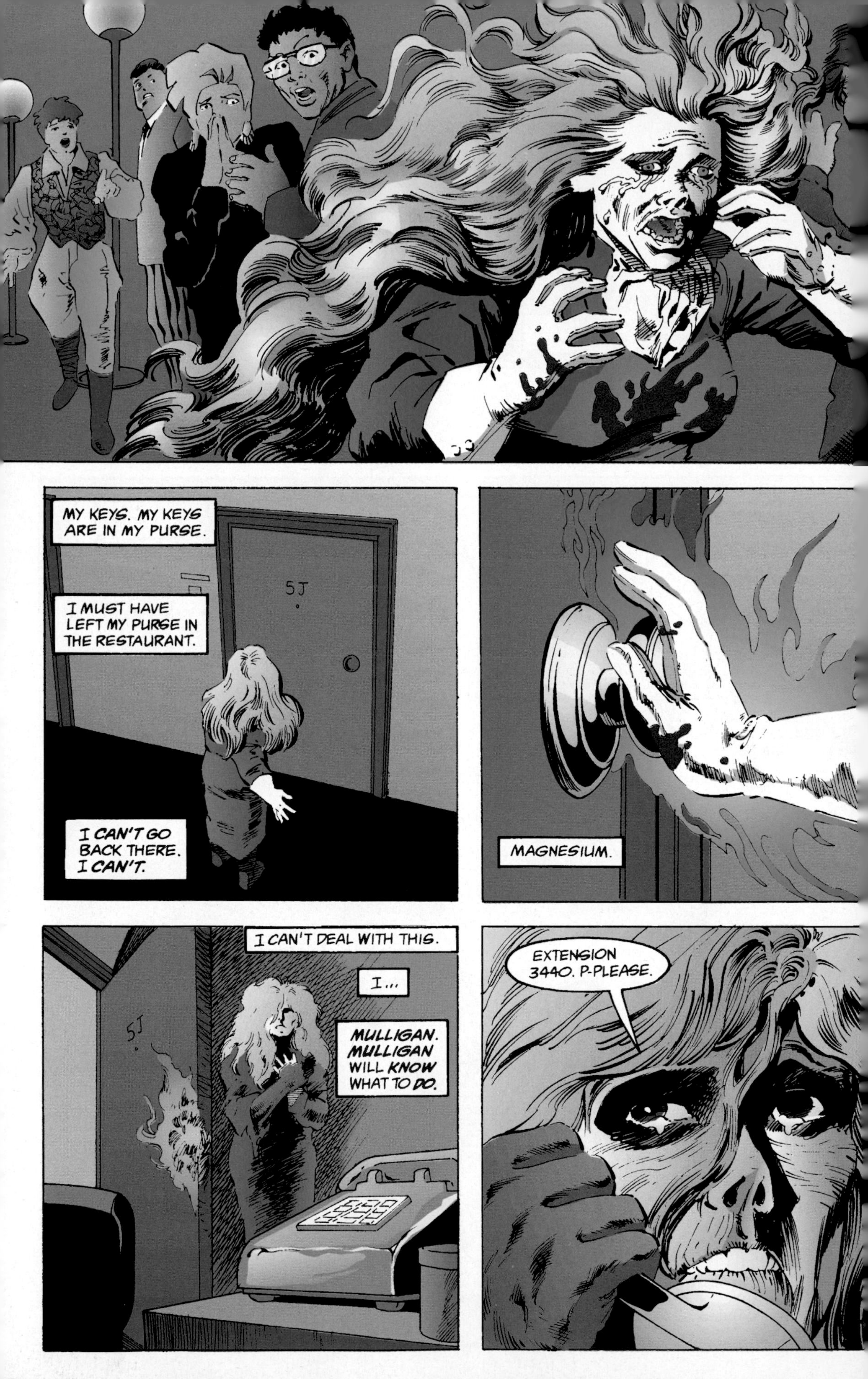
MY KEYS. MY KEYS ARE IN MY PURSE.
5J
I MUST HAVE LEFT MY PURSE IN THE RESTAURANT.
I CAN'T GO BACK THERE. I CAN'T.
MAGNESIUM.
I CAN'T DEAL WITH THIS.
I...
MULLIGAN. MULLIGAN WILL KNOW WHAT TO DO.
5J
EXTENSION 3440. P-PLEASE.

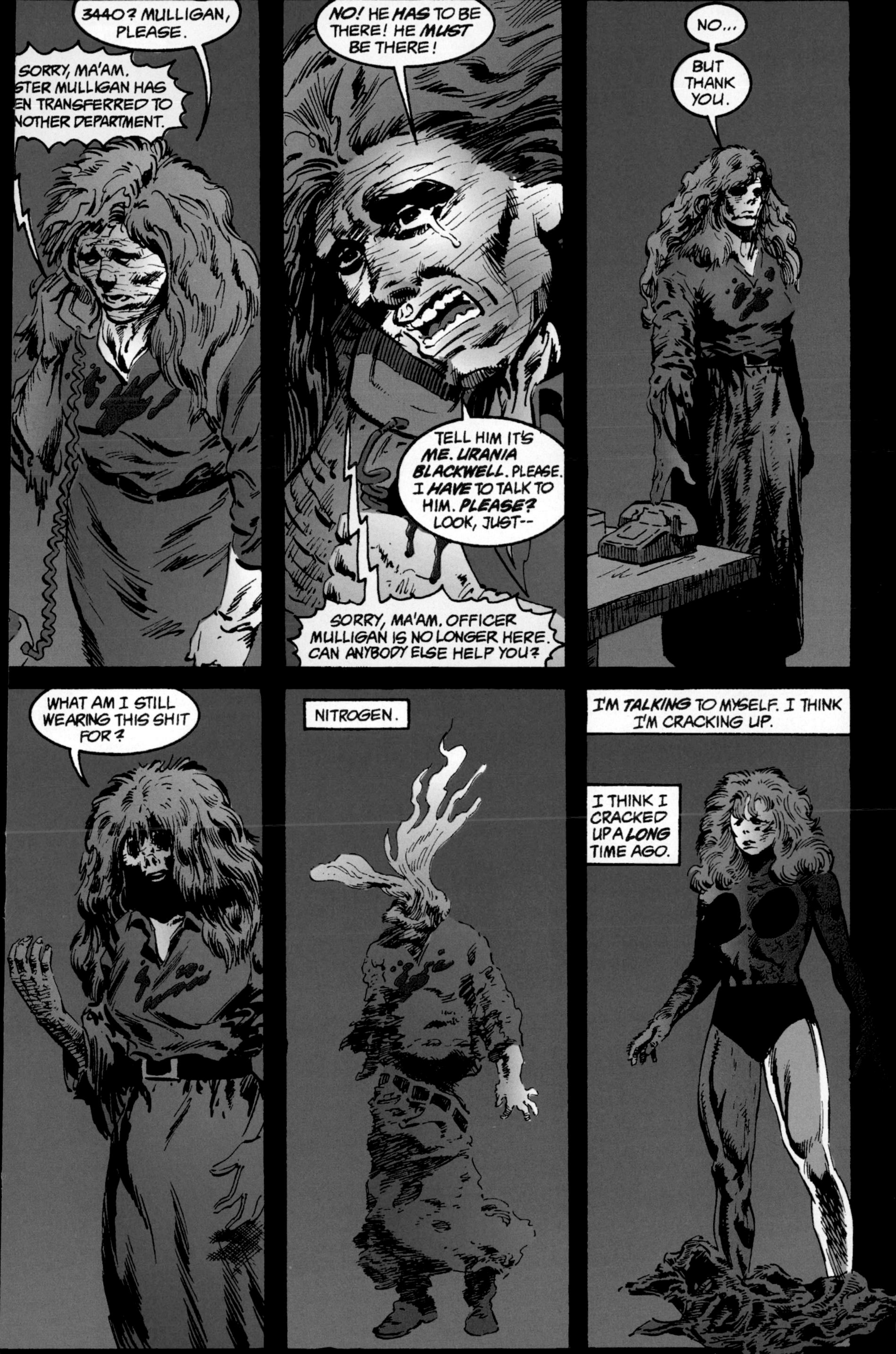
3440? MULLIGAN, PLEASE.
SORRY, MA'AM. ...STER MULLIGAN HAS ...EN TRANSFERRED TO ...NOTHER DEPARTMENT.
NO! HE HAS TO BE THERE! HE MUST BE THERE!
TELL HIM IT'S ME. URANIA BLACKWELL. PLEASE. I HAVE TO TALK TO HIM. PLEASE? LOOK, JUST--
SORRY, MA'AM. OFFICER MULLIGAN IS NO LONGER HERE. CAN ANYBODY ELSE HELP YOU?
NO...
BUT THANK YOU.
WHAT AM I STILL WEARING THIS SHIT FOR?
NITROGEN.
I'M TALKING TO MYSELF. I THINK I'M CRACKING UP.
I THINK I CRACKED UP A LONG TIME AGO.

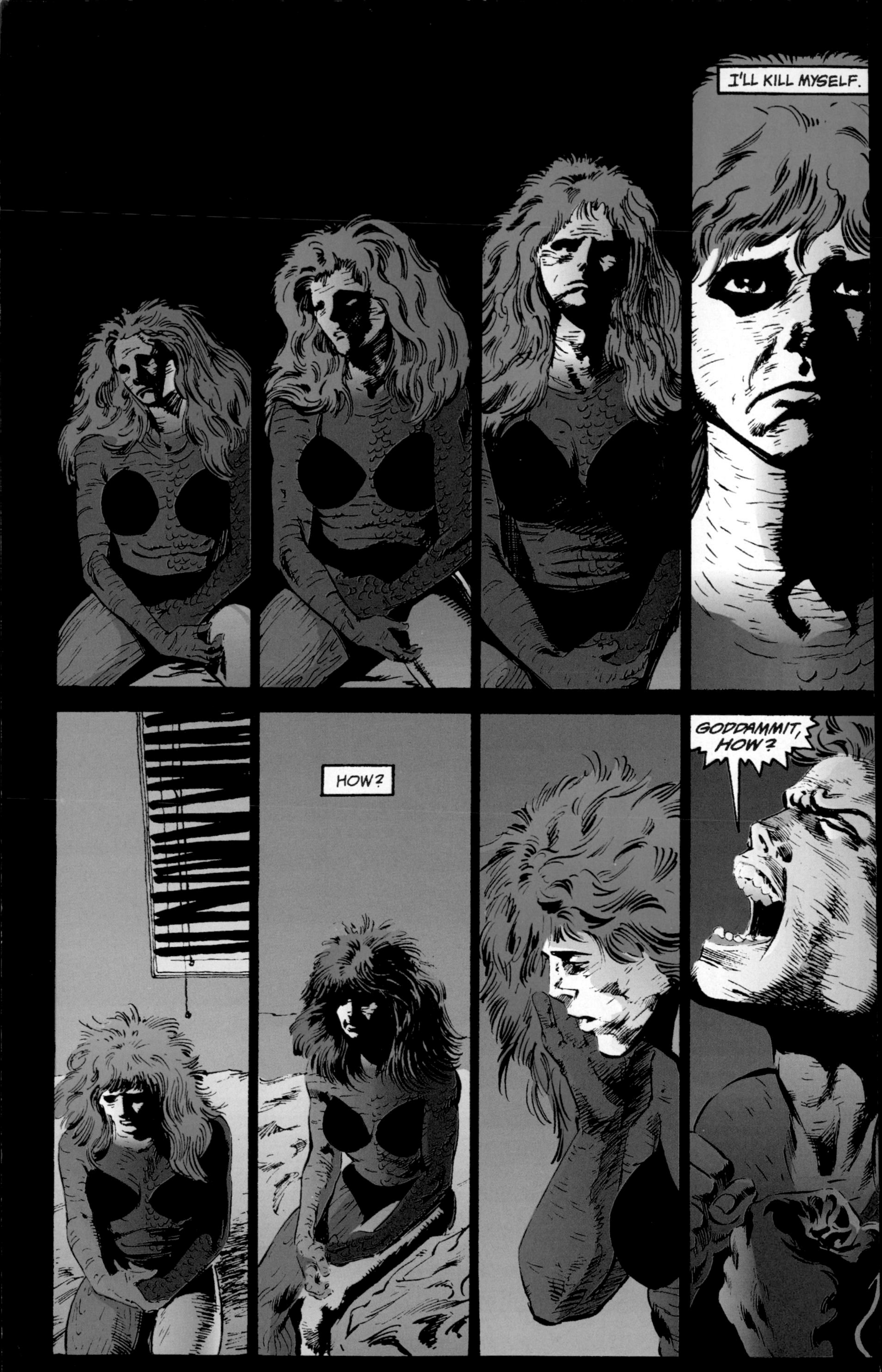
I'LL KILL MYSELF.
HOW?
GODDAMMIT, HOW?

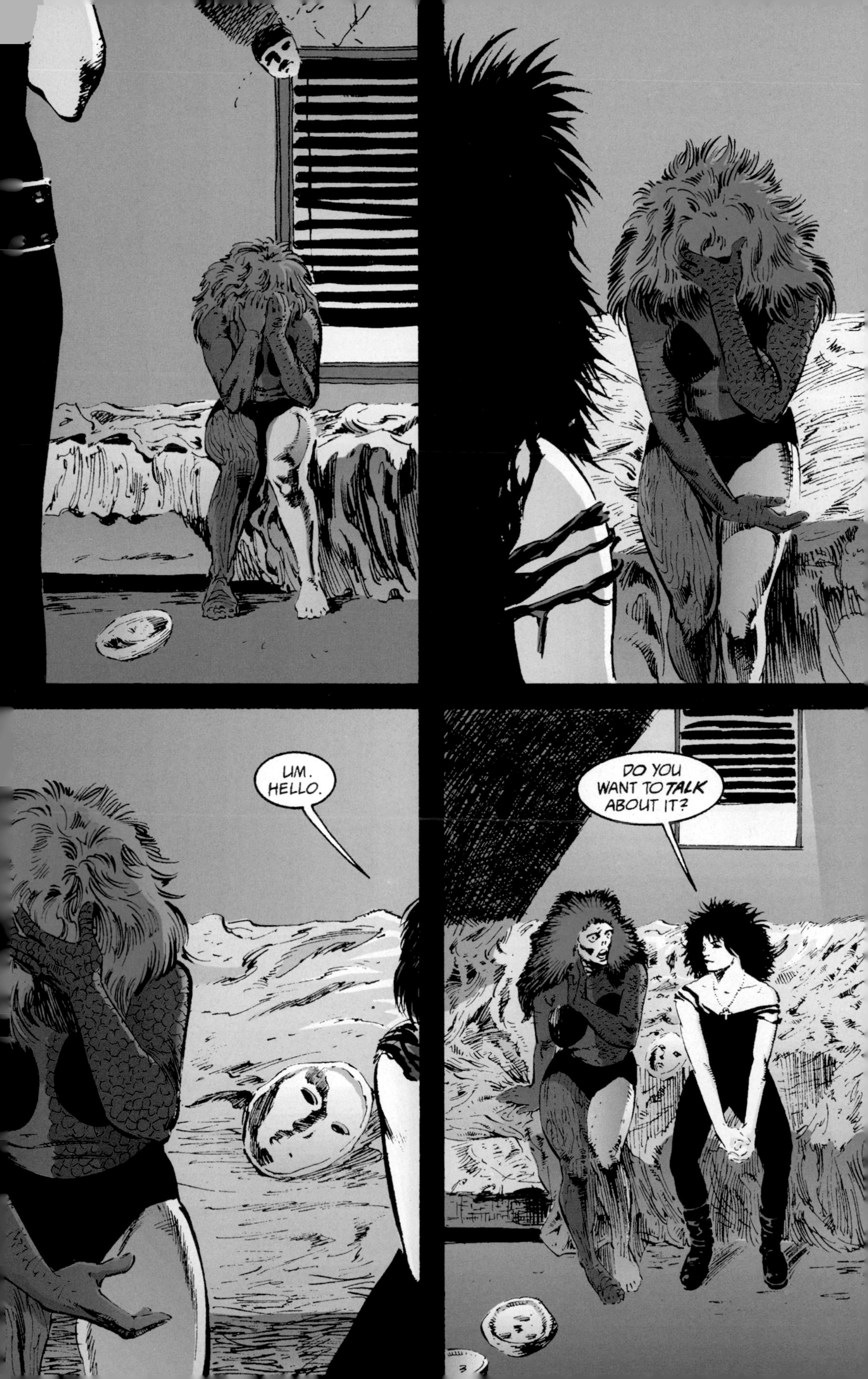
UM. HELLO.
DO YOU WANT TO **TALK** ABOUT IT?

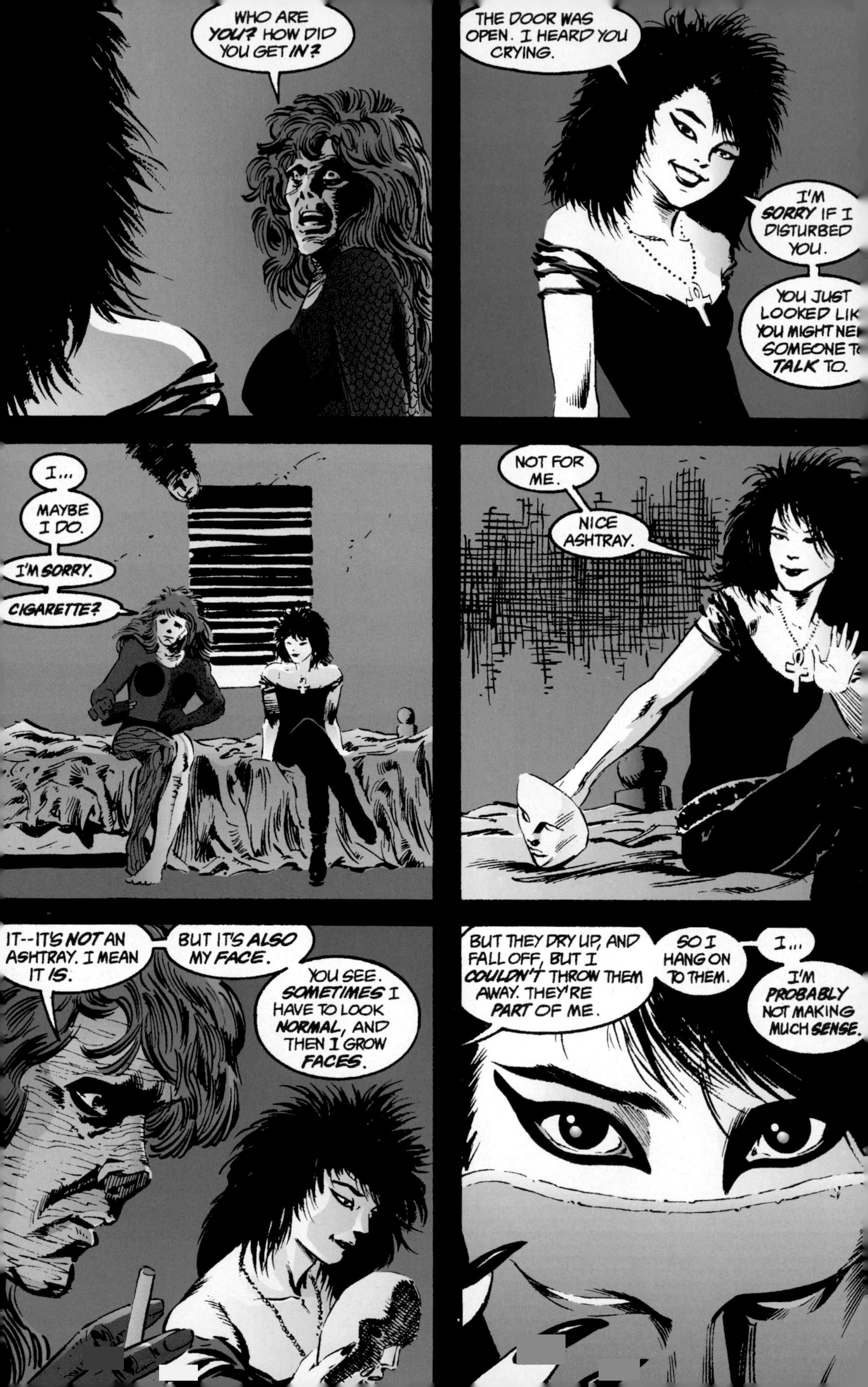
WHO ARE YOU? HOW DID YOU GET IN?
THE DOOR WAS OPEN. I HEARD YOU CRYING.
I'M SORRY IF I DISTURBED YOU.
YOU JUST LOOKED LIK YOU MIGHT NE SOMEONE T TALK TO.
I...
MAYBE I DO.
I'M SORRY.
CIGARETTE?
NOT FOR ME.
NICE ASHTRAY.
IT--IT'S NOT AN ASHTRAY. I MEAN IT IS.
BUT IT'S ALSO MY FACE.
YOU SEE. SOMETIMES I HAVE TO LOOK NORMAL, AND THEN I GROW FACES.
BUT THEY DRY UP, AND FALL OFF, BUT I COULDN'T THROW THEM AWAY. THEY'RE PART OF ME.
SO I HANG ON TO THEM.
I...
I'M PROBABLY NOT MAKING MUCH SENSE.

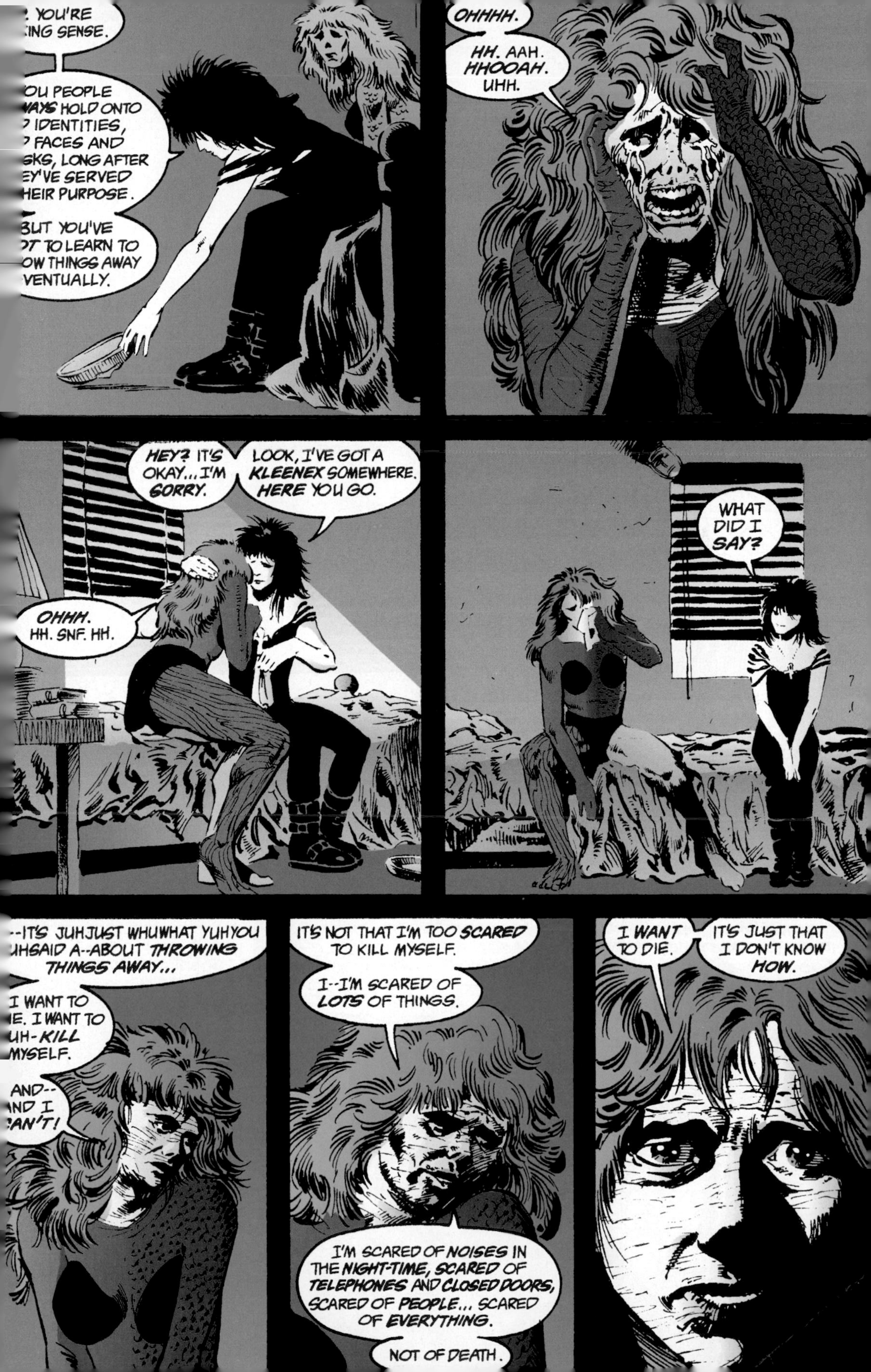
R. YOU'RE KING SENSE.
OU PEOPLE WAYS HOLD ONTO IDENTITIES, FACES AND SKS, LONG AFTER EY'VE SERVED HEIR PURPOSE.
BUT YOU'VE OT TO LEARN TO OW THINGS AWAY EVENTUALLY.
OHHHH.
HH. AAH. HHOOAH. UHH.
HEY? IT'S OKAY... I'M SORRY.
LOOK, I'VE GOT A KLEENEX SOMEWHERE. HERE YOU GO.
OHHH. HH. SNF. HH.
WHAT DID I SAY?
--IT'S JUHJUST WHUWHAT YUHYOU UHSAID A--ABOUT THROWING THINGS AWAY...
I WANT TO IE. I WANT TO UH-KILL MYSELF.
AND-- ND I AN'T!
IT'S NOT THAT I'M TOO SCARED TO KILL MYSELF.
I--I'M SCARED OF LOTS OF THINGS.
I'M SCARED OF NOISES IN THE NIGHT-TIME, SCARED OF TELEPHONES AND CLOSED DOORS, SCARED OF PEOPLE... SCARED OF EVERYTHING.
NOT OF DEATH.
I WANT TO DIE.
IT'S JUST THAT I DON'T KNOW HOW.

I'VE BEEN THINKING ABOUT IT FOR SO LONG, NOW. I CAN'T SLASH MY WRISTS--I DON'T HAVE ANY *BLOOD.*

WHEN I WAS AT HIGH SCHOOL, A KID SHUT HIMSELF IN A GARAGE, TOOK SLEEPING PILLS, CLIMBED IN THE CAR AND TURNED THE IGNITION.

"I CAN'T DO *THAT.* CARBON MONOXIDE'S JUST ANOTHER GAS, TO ME.

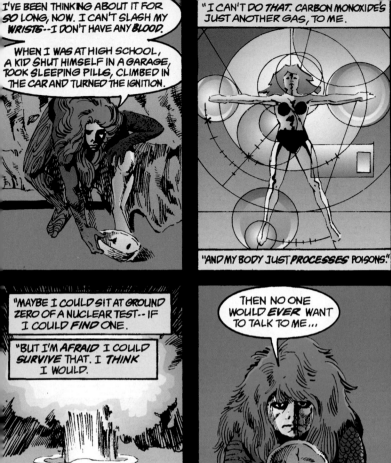

"AND MY BODY JUST *PROCESSES* POISONS."

I CAN'T *SHOOT* MYSELF. A BULLET WOULDN'T DO ANY *REAL* DAMAGE.

SO THEN I GET MORE EXTREME.

"MAYBE I COULD SIT AT GROUND ZERO OF A NUCLEAR TEST-- IF I COULD *FIND* ONE.

"BUT I'M AFRAID I COULD *SURVIVE* THAT. I *THINK* I WOULD.

"PERHAPS I'D BE RADIOACTIVE FOR ALWAYS...BUT I'D *SURVIVE.*"

THEN NO ONE WOULD *EVER* WANT TO TALK TO ME...

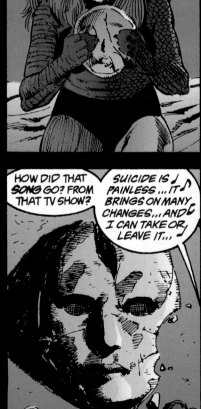

"I THOUGHT ABOUT TRANS-MUTING MYSELF TO FREE OXYGEN RADICALS AND JUST MELDING WITH THE *AIR.* OR WITH ADDED HYDROGEN, I COULD BECOME *WATER* AND JOIN MYSELF WITH THE SEA.

"BUT I'D PROBABLY *STILL* BE *CONSCIOUS.* JUST *SPREAD* OUT ALL OVER THE *WORLD.*"

I WANT IT TO *STOP.* I DON'T *KNOW* HOW TO *STOP* IT.

HOW DID THAT *SONG* GO? FROM THAT TV SHOW?

SUICIDE IS ♪ PAINLESS ...IT♪ BRINGS ON MANY CHANGES...AND♪ I CAN TAKE OR♪ LEAVE IT...

ISN'T IT *DUMB?* ALL OVER THE WORLD, PEOPLE RUNNING AROUND TRYING *NOT* TO *DIE?*

HANGING ON TO LIFE LIKE GRIM DEATH.

AND I *WANT* TO DIE. AND I *CAN'T.*

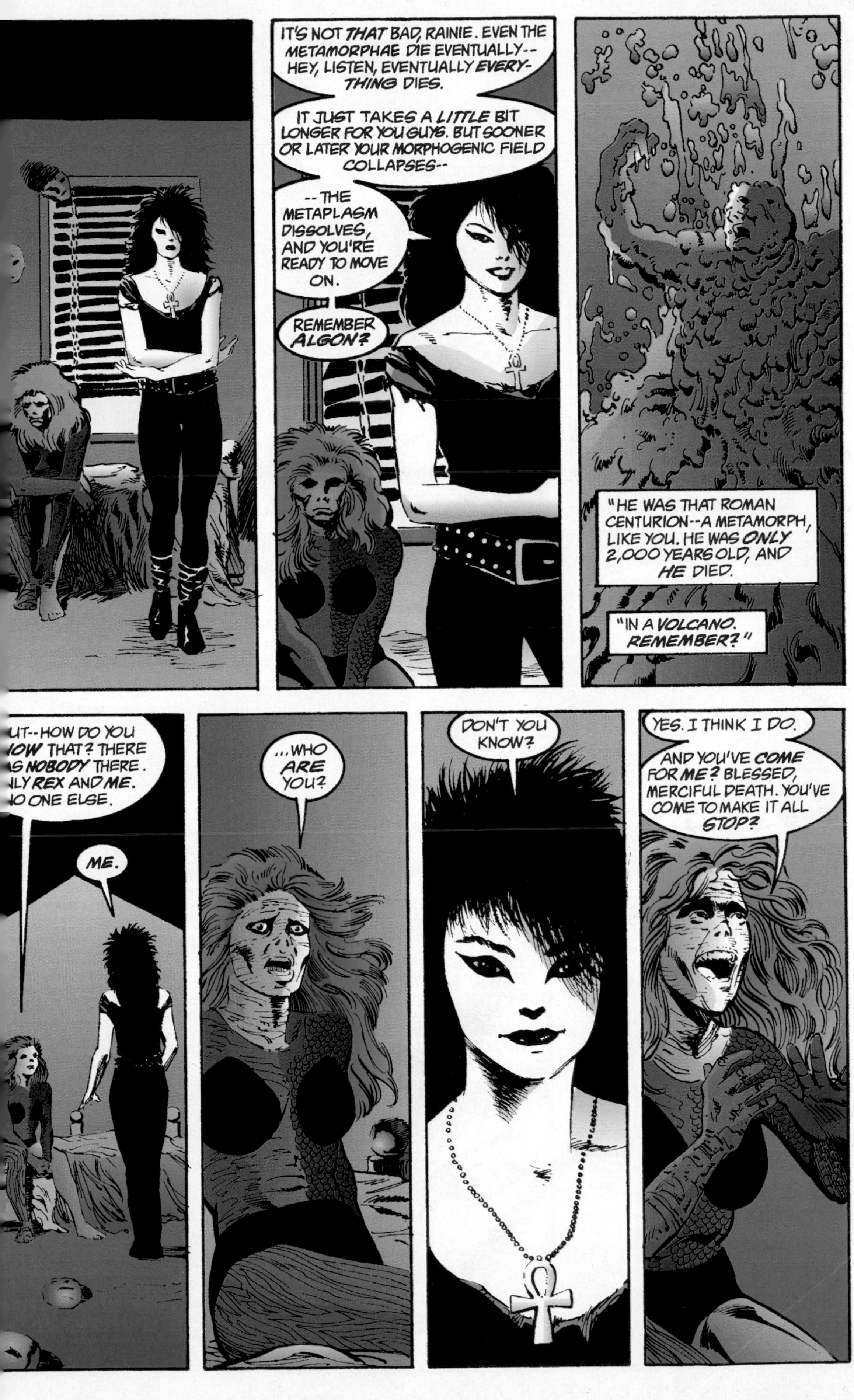
IT'S NOT THAT BAD, RAINIE. EVEN THE METAMORPHAE DIE EVENTUALLY-- HEY, LISTEN, EVENTUALLY EVERY-THING DIES.
IT JUST TAKES A LITTLE BIT LONGER FOR YOU GUYS. BUT SOONER OR LATER YOUR MORPHOGENIC FIELD COLLAPSES--
--THE METAPLASM DISSOLVES, AND YOU'RE READY TO MOVE ON.
REMEMBER ALGON?
"HE WAS THAT ROMAN CENTURION--A METAMORPH, LIKE YOU. HE WAS ONLY 2,000 YEARS OLD, AND HE DIED.
"IN A VOLCANO. REMEMBER?"
UT--HOW DO YOU NOW THAT? THERE AS NOBODY THERE. NLY REX AND ME. O ONE ELSE.
ME.
...WHO ARE YOU?
DON'T YOU KNOW?
YES. I THINK I DO.
AND YOU'VE COME FOR ME? BLESSED, MERCIFUL DEATH. YOU'VE COME TO MAKE IT ALL STOP?

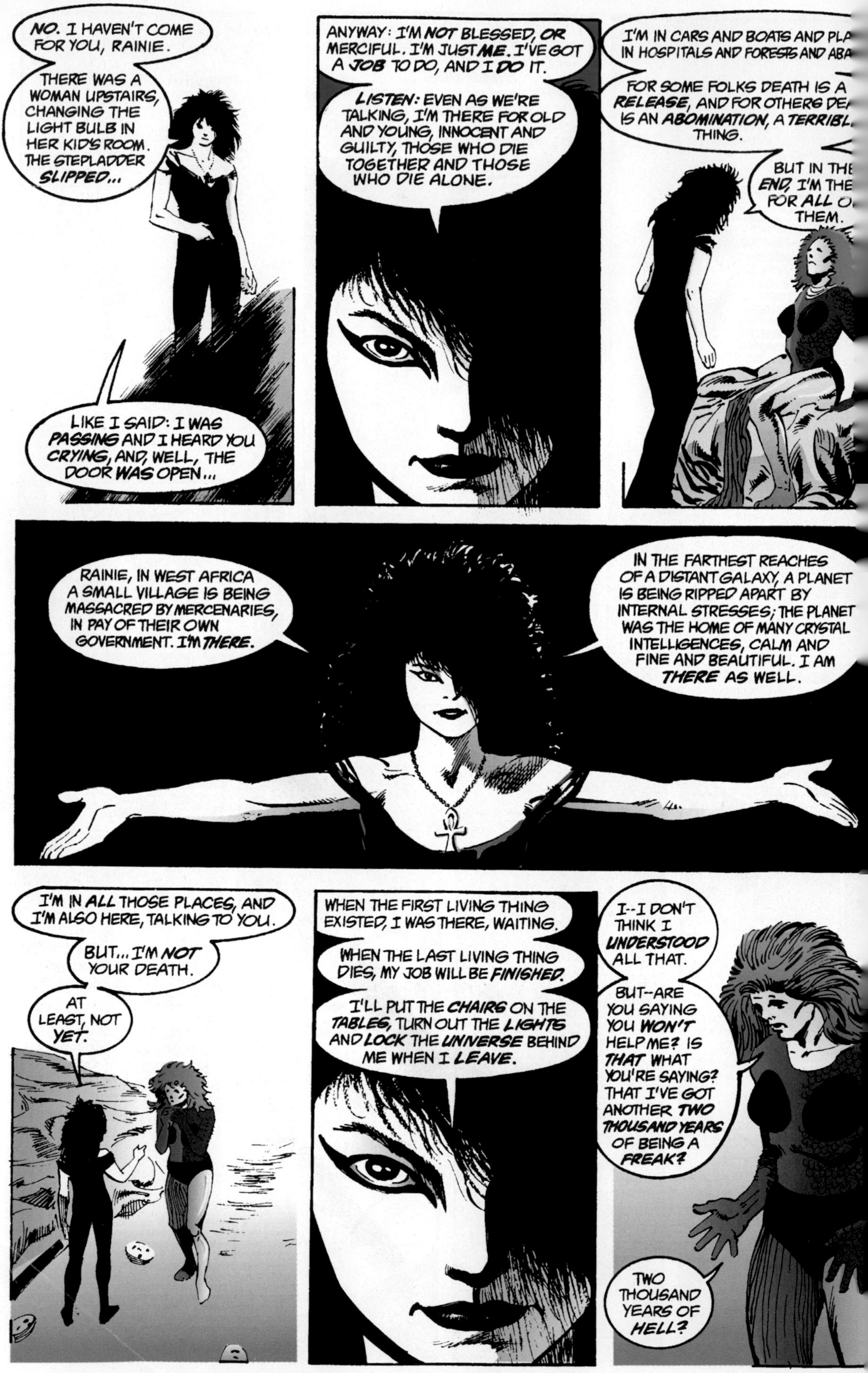

NO. I HAVEN'T COME FOR YOU, RAINIE.
THERE WAS A WOMAN UPSTAIRS, CHANGING THE LIGHT BULB IN HER KID'S ROOM. THE STEPLADDER SLIPPED...
LIKE I SAID: I WAS PASSING AND I HEARD YOU CRYING, AND, WELL, THE DOOR WAS OPEN...
ANYWAY: I'M NOT BLESSED, OR MERCIFUL. I'M JUST ME. I'VE GOT A JOB TO DO, AND I DO IT.
LISTEN: EVEN AS WE'RE TALKING, I'M THERE FOR OLD AND YOUNG, INNOCENT AND GUILTY, THOSE WHO DIE TOGETHER AND THOSE WHO DIE ALONE.
I'M IN CARS AND BOATS AND PLA
IN HOSPITALS AND FORESTS AND ABA
FOR SOME FOLKS DEATH IS A RELEASE, AND FOR OTHERS DE
IS AN ABOMINATION, A TERRIBL
THING.
BUT IN THE END, I'M THE
FOR ALL O
THEM.
RAINIE, IN WEST AFRICA A SMALL VILLAGE IS BEING MASSACRED BY MERCENARIES, IN PAY OF THEIR OWN GOVERNMENT. I'M THERE.
IN THE FARTHEST REACHES OF A DISTANT GALAXY, A PLANET IS BEING RIPPED APART BY INTERNAL STRESSES; THE PLANET WAS THE HOME OF MANY CRYSTAL INTELLIGENCES, CALM AND FINE AND BEAUTIFUL. I AM THERE AS WELL.
I'M IN ALL THOSE PLACES, AND I'M ALSO HERE, TALKING TO YOU.
BUT... I'M NOT YOUR DEATH.
AT LEAST, NOT YET.
WHEN THE FIRST LIVING THING EXISTED, I WAS THERE, WAITING.
WHEN THE LAST LIVING THING DIES, MY JOB WILL BE FINISHED.
I'LL PUT THE CHAIRS ON THE TABLES, TURN OUT THE LIGHTS AND LOCK THE UNIVERSE BEHIND ME WHEN I LEAVE.
I--I DON'T THINK I UNDERSTOOD ALL THAT.
BUT--ARE YOU SAYING YOU WON'T HELP ME? IS THAT WHAT YOU'RE SAYING? THAT I'VE GOT ANOTHER TWO THOUSAND YEARS OF BEING A FREAK?
TWO THOUSAND YEARS OF HELL?

YOU MAKE YOUR OWN HELL, RAINIE.

OKAY. I'LL HELP YOU. IF THAT'S WHAT YOU WANT.

THAT'S WHAT I GET FOR GETTING INVOLVED.

YOU'LL KILL ME? TAKE MY LIFE? GIVE ME OBLIVION?

YOUR LIFE IS YOUR OWN, RAINIE. SO IS YOUR DEATH.

AND OBLIVION...? THAT'S NOT AN OPTION, I'M AFRAID.

MM. RAINIE, MYTHOLOGIES TAKE LONGER TO DIE THAN PEOPLE BELIEVE. THEY LINGER ON IN A KIND OF DREAM COUNTRY THAT AFFECTS ALL OF YOU.

WHAT DO YOU KNOW ABOUT RA?

HE WAS A SUN GOD. IN ANCIENT EGYPT.

YEAH. THAT'S RIGHT.

HE'S SEEN BETTER DAYS. HE STILL KEEPS BRINGING THE METAMORPHAE INTO EXISTENCE, EVEN THOUGH THE BATTLE YOUR KIND FOUGHT FINISHED AGES AGO.

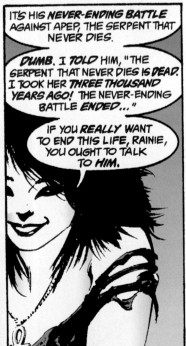

IT'S HIS NEVER-ENDING BATTLE AGAINST APEP, THE SERPENT THAT NEVER DIES.

DUMB. I TOLD HIM, "THE SERPENT THAT NEVER DIES IS DEAD. I TOOK HER THREE THOUSAND YEARS AGO! THE NEVER-ENDING BATTLE ENDED..."

IF YOU REALLY WANT TO END THIS LIFE, RAINIE, YOU OUGHT TO TALK TO HIM.

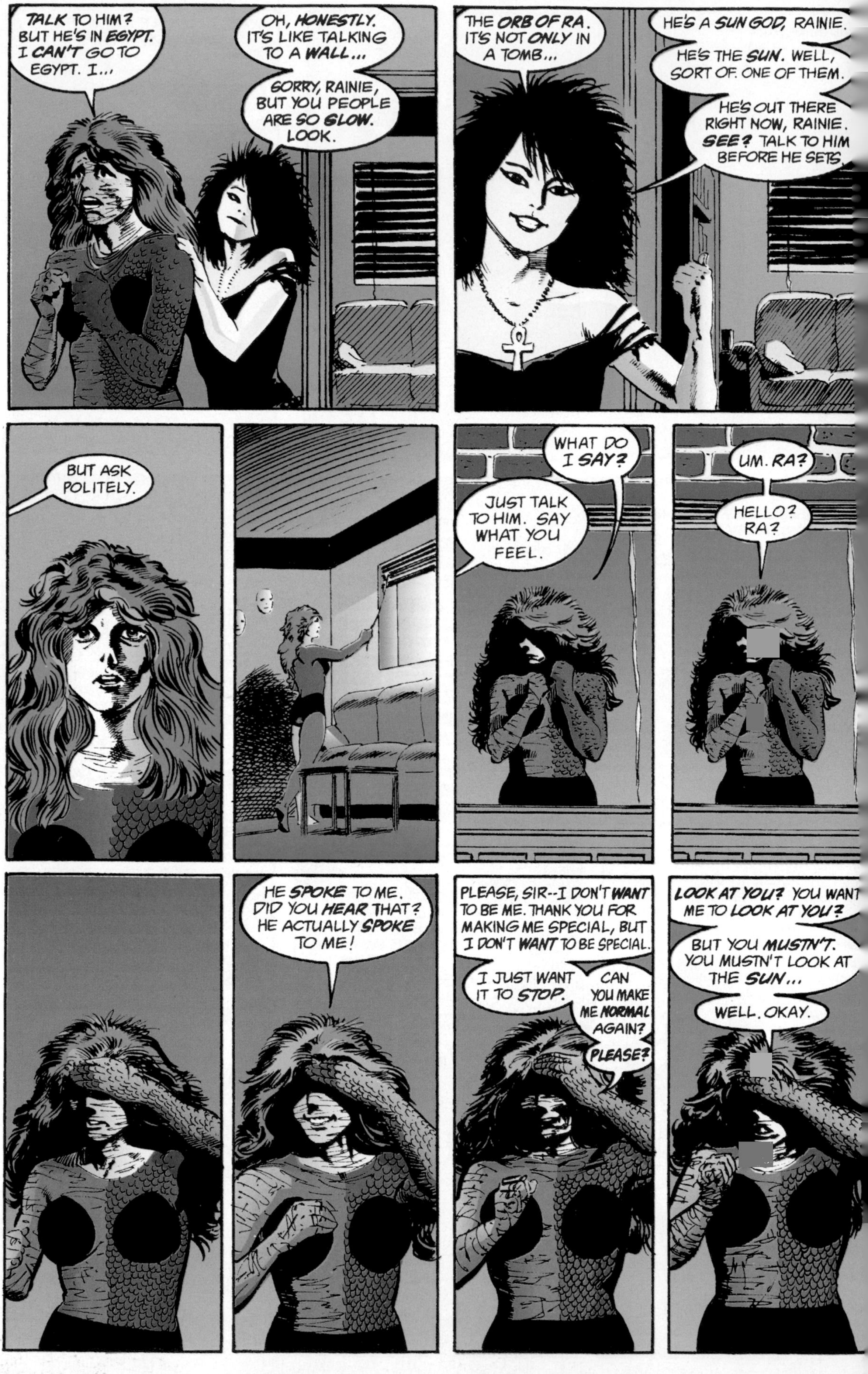
TALK TO HIM? BUT HE'S IN EGYPT. I CAN'T GO TO EGYPT. I...
OH, HONESTLY. IT'S LIKE TALKING TO A WALL...
SORRY, RAINIE, BUT YOU PEOPLE ARE SO SLOW. LOOK.
THE ORB OF RA. IT'S NOT ONLY IN A TOMB...
HE'S A SUN GOD, RAINIE.
HE'S THE SUN. WELL, SORT OF. ONE OF THEM.
HE'S OUT THERE RIGHT NOW, RAINIE. SEE? TALK TO HIM BEFORE HE SETS.
BUT ASK POLITELY.
WHAT DO I SAY?
JUST TALK TO HIM. SAY WHAT YOU FEEL.
UM. RA?
HELLO? RA?
HE SPOKE TO ME. DID YOU HEAR THAT? HE ACTUALLY SPOKE TO ME!
PLEASE, SIR--I DON'T WANT TO BE ME. THANK YOU FOR MAKING ME SPECIAL, BUT I DON'T WANT TO BE SPECIAL.
I JUST WANT IT TO STOP.
CAN YOU MAKE ME NORMAL AGAIN?
PLEASE?
LOOK AT YOU? YOU WANT ME TO LOOK AT YOU?
BUT YOU MUSTN'T. YOU MUSTN'T LOOK AT THE SUN...
WELL. OKAY.

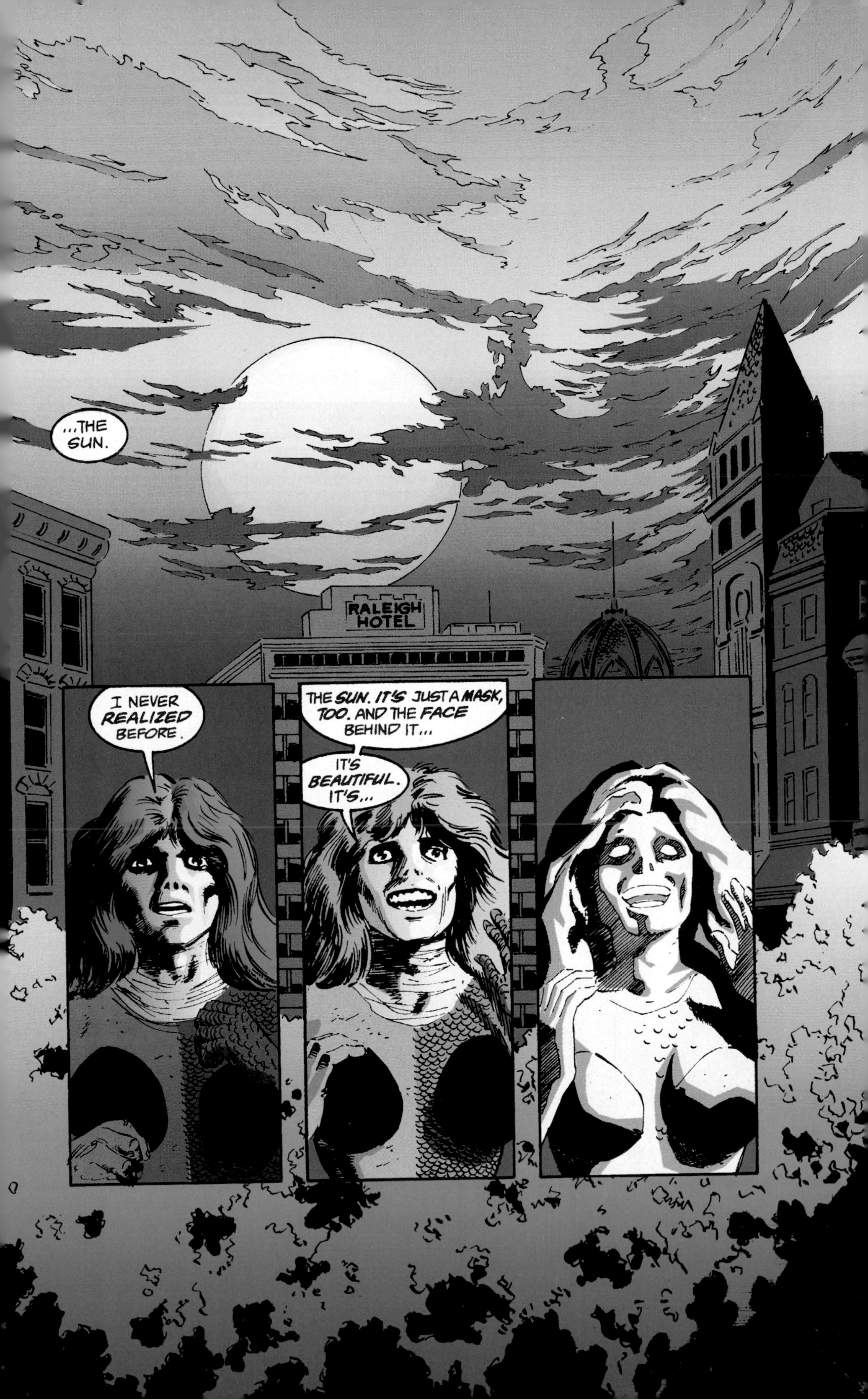
...THE SUN.
RALEIGH HOTEL
I NEVER REALIZED BEFORE.
THE SUN. IT'S JUST A MASK, TOO. AND THE FACE BEHIND IT...
IT'S BEAUTIFUL. IT'S...

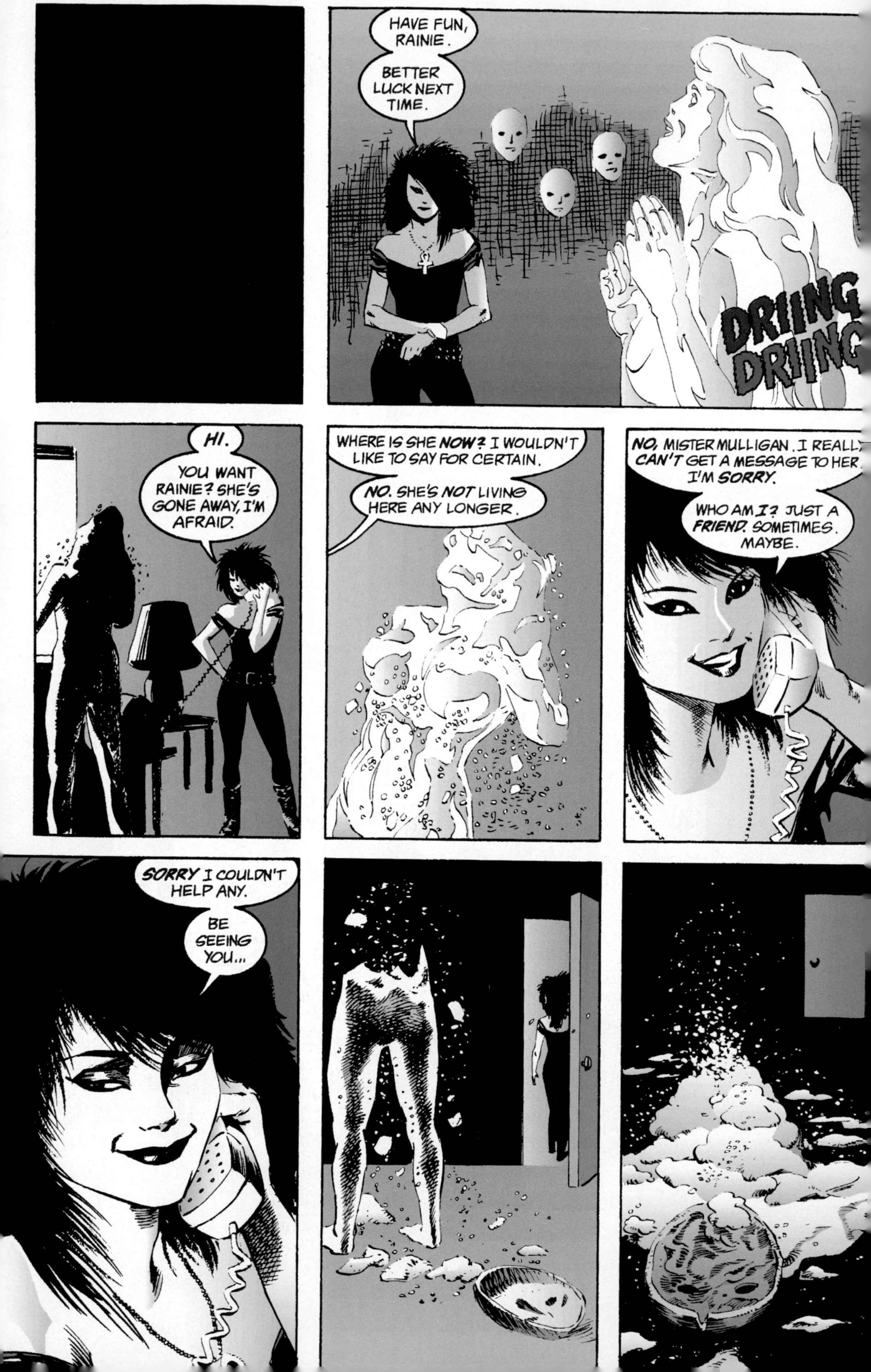
HAVE FUN, RAINIE.
BETTER LUCK NEXT TIME.
DRIING DRIING
HI.
YOU WANT RAINIE? SHE'S GONE AWAY, I'M AFRAID.
WHERE IS SHE NOW? I WOULDN'T LIKE TO SAY FOR CERTAIN.
NO. SHE'S NOT LIVING HERE ANY LONGER.
NO, MISTER MULLIGAN. I REALLY CAN'T GET A MESSAGE TO HER. I'M SORRY.
WHO AM I? JUST A FRIEND. SOMETIMES. MAYBE.
SORRY I COULDN'T HELP ANY.
BE SEEING YOU...

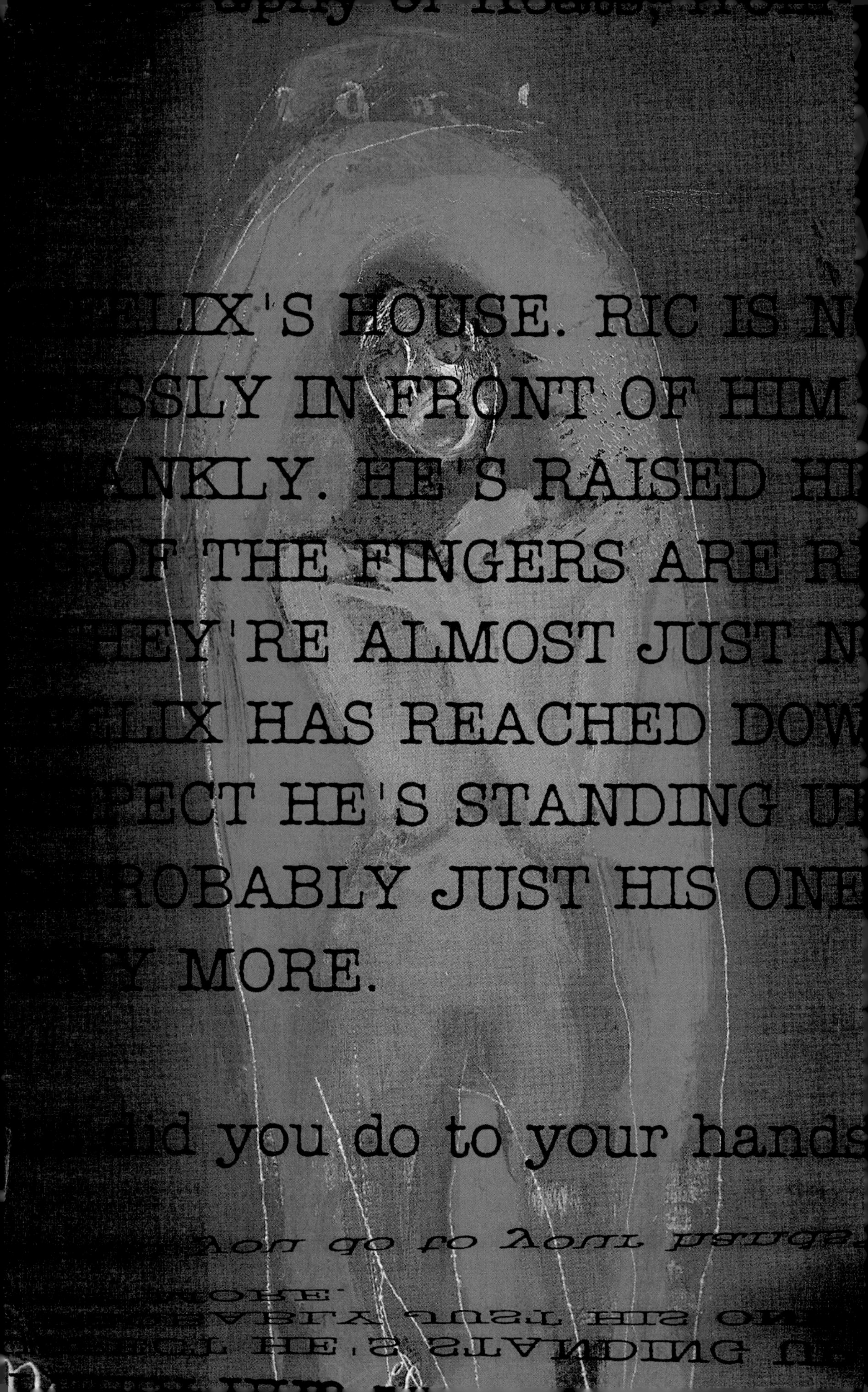
ELIX'S HOUSE. RIC IS N
SSLY IN FRONT OF HIM
ANKLY. HE'S RAISED H
OF THE FINGERS ARE R
HEY'RE ALMOST JUST N
ELIX HAS REACHED DOW
PECT HE'S STANDING U
ROBABLY JUST HIS ONE
Y MORE.
did you do to your hands

SCRIPT INTRODUCTION
by NEIL GAIMAN

Then I stripped them, scalp from
skull, and my hunting dogs fed full
And their teeth I threaded neatly
on a thong;
And I wiped my mouth and said,
"It is well that they are dead,
"For I know my work is right and
theirs were wrong."

But my Totem saw the shame;
from his ridgepole-shrine he came,
And he told me in a vision of the night:—
"There are nine and sixty ways of
constructing tribal lays,
"And every single one of them is right!"

Rudyard Kipling.
IN THE NEOLITHIC AGE. 1895

It took a little time before I could be persuaded to allow a script to be published.

For the same reason that a magician doesn't want to let you backstage when he rehearses, for the same reason you should never wander around a film set: it spoils the magic when you know how it's done.

But we all have a craving to see behind the illusion. We want to know how the magician managed to saw the lady in half without spilling blood, and put her together afterwards, apparently unharmed; we want to wander the studio back-lots and stare at the backless houses. And some of us want to know how a comic gets written.

I did.

I have always wanted to write comics. (That's not strictly true: I have always wanted to *write*, to tell stories. Comics were and are one of the media I wanted to tell stories with.)

But I could never figure it out; *how* did a writer get the story in his head onto a comics page? What did a comics script look like? What did a comics writer do?

I eventually found out, by asking someone who wrote comics (it was Alan Moore—one of the best writers ever to work in this medium) and getting him to show me what a script looked like, and how it was laid out. This he did, on one side of notebook paper.

Once I knew what a comics script looked like, the rest was easy. (No, that's not true. The rest was pretty difficult; and every story presents its own set of problems. But you know what I mean.)

Which is why I eventually agreed to allow this script to be printed. I've even added some marginal notations, and dug out from my files the folded, stapled mini-comic for this issue. (I always make a small doodled version of the comic while I'm writing, to let me know how many panels I'm putting on a page, and to suggest ideas of layout and storytelling.)

Let me throw in a warning before you begin to read the script.

This is only how *I* write a comics script. Specifically how I write SANDMAN.

There are thousands of people out in the world writing comics, and none of the others write scripts quite like this. Some just write a sequence of panel descriptions, not worrying how they'll fall on the page. Some draw doodles of what they want for an artist, with the dialogue in the margins. Sometimes the writers just suggest a plot, and then come back to it at lettering stage and write the dialogue then. Sometimes they write something closer to a movie script, just dialogue and action, and let the artists break down the story into panels.

These are all valid ways of writing a comics script. I've used a few of them myself. (But not for SANDMAN.)

A few writers put in much more detail than you'll see in this script. Some writers use far less. Some writers don't know or care who'll be drawing the story they're writing. Some do. (I do). Some artists write and draw (and often letter and colour) their own comics, and they have different ways again of writing scripts for themselves.

Which means, I suppose, that this *is* a typical comics script, insofar as every script is atypical. And it's the way I write SANDMAN.

(All the other ways of writing scripts are right, too. That's what the quotation at the top of the page is about.)

Each SANDMAN script is a letter to the artist (I drive Karen Berger, my long-suffering editor, crazy, by refusing to write a script unless I know who's going to draw it; if you write for an artist you can play to their strengths. It makes you look good); and this is a letter to Kelley Jones. (It was the first time we'd ever worked together; and working with Kelley has been fun. He's a terrific artist and a nice person.)

We picked this script to 'Calliope' for this book as probably the most interesting for a casual reader the script for 'A Midsummer Night's Dream' is longer and technically far more complex (it was much the hardest of these scripts to write), but it's also probably a lot less interesting simply to read, or so I have been assured.

To reiterate: this isn't *How To Write Comics The Neil Gaiman Way*. It's a script for 'Calliope.' It's being printed here to satisfy your curiosity (if you have any) about what a SANDMAN script looks like.

There are a number of talented people involved in the production of SANDMAN. In this issue, after Kelley pencilled it, Todd Klein lettered the comic, then Malcolm Jones inked it, going over Kelley's pencils in black ink, getting the artwork to a point at which it could be reproduced (and incidentally adding a great deal to the look of the book), Robbie Busch coloured it, and somewhere in the background Karen Berger and Tom Peyer knocked themselves out making sure that everything made sense, got from place to place on time, and that we all got paid.

If you've read 'Calliope' already, you know the story. Now you're going to see the script.

You don't have to read it, if you don't want to.

But for those of you who do, welcome backstage.

Let us show you how it was done...

Neil Gaiman

Episode 17

HI KELLEY,

WELCOME TO THE WEIRD WORLD OF SANDMAN. WHAT WE'RE DOING IS A
SERIES OF SHORT STORIES FOR FOUR OR FIVE ISSUES HERE; I'VE FINISHED THE
DOLL'S HOUSE STORYLINE, AND THERE WAS A WHILE TOWARD THE END OF
THE STORYLINE WHEN I JUST COULDN'T TAKE IT ANY MORE -- PARTLY
BECAUSE I'D KEEP GETTING NEW IDEAS FOR STORIES AND BE UNABLE TO GET
THEM IN, AND ALSO BECAUSE I WANTED TO DO A FEW TOTALLY SELF-
CONTAINED STORIES THAT I COULD GET OVER WITH IN 24 PAGES: THE WORRY
THAT I DIDN'T HAVE A CLUE HOW DOLL'S HOUSE WAS GOING TO END (WHICH I
DIDN'T, UNTIL I GOT THROUGH SANDMAN 15) WAS GETTING PRETTY NERVE-
WRACKING...

THIS IS THE FIRST OF THEM. I'M CALLING THE SHORT STORIES "DREAM
COUNTRY." INCIDENTALLY, KELLEY, I WRITE PRETTY FULL SCRIPT, FOR THE
MOST PART. HAVING SAID THAT, IT'S A GUIDE: IF YOU SEE A WAY TO IMPROVE
IT, MAKE IT WORK BETTER, THEN GO FOR IT. YOU'RE THE ARTIST, AFTER ALL.

OK -- LET'S GO.

THEY SAY THAT ON AMERICAN COP SHOWS A LOT.
....

ODD FACTS AND COINCIDENCES DEPT: SO FAR THE SANDMANS I'VE STARTED
AND THEN HAD TO RESTART, BECAUSE THEY WERE HEADING OFF IN THE
WRONG DIRECTION WERE: 2,7,12 AND NOW THIS ONE, 17. EVERY FIVE ISSUES...
....

OKAY KELLEY -- THE BAD NEWS. THE REASON WHY THIS IS PROBABLY GOING
TO BE SLIGHTLY LATE IS ALSO THE REASON THAT IT BEARS NO RESEMBLANCE
TO THE STORY I TOLD YOU ON THE PHONE. THIS IS BECAUSE I STARTED THE
ONE I TOLD YOU ABOUT, SEX AND VIOLETS, TWICE, GOT SEVEN PAGES INTO ONE
VERSION AND TEN PAGES, THE SECOND TIME, ON A TOTALLY DIFFERENT
TREATMENT, AND EACH TIME IT DIED ON THE PAGE. WHICH MEANT THAT I
BASICALLY HAD TO DECIDE WHETHER TO TRY AGAIN, OR TO STRIP THE STORY
DOWN AS FAR AS I COULD, TAKE WHAT I COULD, AND START AGAIN. I SUSPECT
AT SOME POINT I'LL COME BACK TO OLD PUCK, BUT IN THE MEANTIME WE'VE
GOT A DIFFERENT STORY ABOUT A DIFFERENT MUSE, AND ABOUT THE TWO
MEN WHO HAVE HELD HER IN THRALL, AND ABOUT THE SANDMAN, AND HIS
REVENGE ON THEM. IT'S A DARKER STORY THAN THE OTHER, CREEPIER AND
LESS COMFORTING.

THE GOOD NEWS IS THAT I'M 99% SURE IT'LL WORK THIS TIME, AND I HOPE
YOU ENJOY DRAWING IT AS MUCH YOU WOULD HAVE THE OTHER.

.....

EDITORS NOTE: The script comments that appear on the following pages,
in red and blue ink, are by Neil Gaiman and Kelley Jones, respectively.

Calliope.

Page 1 panel 1

WE ARE LOOKING AT THE FACE OF RICK MADOC. NO PANEL BORDER -- HE'S IN CLOSE UP, FULL FACE, LOOKING AT SOMETHING BELOW HIM WITH AN EXPRESSION OF INTERESTED DISTASTE. HE'S THIN, MID-THIRTIES, RED SHORT-CUT HAIR. NOT A CLASSICAL COMIC BOOK FACE -- HE'S GOOD-LOOKING IN A JOHN LENNONISH SORT OF WAY.

Caption - top right: May 1986.

Madoc:I don't have any idea.

Madoc:So what is it? It smells quite disgusting.

Guy Lawley M.D. found me a photo of a trichobezoar afterwards. It looked a lot like what Kelley had drawn. Guy is the only doctor I know who also writes comics from time to time, and he treats my stranger medical requests, for appropriate cancers or venereal diseases, with more respect than they perhaps deserve.

Page 1 panel 2

PULL BACK. WE'RE IN A ROOM IN MADOC'S HOUSE: HIS STUDY, BOOKSHELVES ON THE WALLS, A DESK WITH A WORD PROCESSOR ON IT. A SET OF ENCYCLOPEDIAS. FAIRLY MODERN. MAYBE SOME PAINTINGS ON THE WALL. LITTLE STATUES HERE AND THERE. THERE'S A SLIM TELEPHONE ON A TABLE IN ONE CORNER, AND, IN THE OPPOSITE CORNER OF THE ROOM, A DOOR TO THE WORLD OUTSIDE. BUT THAT'S ALL BACKGROUND, AND WE DON'T NEED TO PUSH IT HERE - DROP IT IN AS WE MOVE AROUND THE ROOM, LOOKING AT THESE PEOPLE. WE'RE LOOKING AT MADOC, WHO IS WEARING A BROWN LEATHER JACKET, TEE SHIRT AND JEANS, AND A YOUNGER MAN, IN GLASSES, A DOCTOR (ALTHOUGH NOT WEARING A WHITE COAT) FELIX GARRISON. DR GARRISON IS HOLDING SOMETHING OUT -- IT'S BLACK, LIKE A LARGE, HAIRY STONE, OR A FOSSILISED TRIBBLE COVERED IN SLIME. IT'S A TRICHINOBEZOAR -- YOU MAY BE ABLE TO FIND A REFERENCE PICTURE OF SOME KIND IN A MEDICAL DICTIONARY. THE DR LOOKS RATHER PLEASED WITH HIMSELF. IT'S EARLY EVENING IN EARLY SUMMER OR LATE SPRING.

Garrison:It's what you were asking for. It's a bezoar.

Madoc:Hang on, I thought they were like, precious stones?

Page 1 panel 3

WE'RE LOOKING AT THE GUNKY, HORRIBLE, CALCIFIED MASS, HELD IN THE DOCTOR'S HAND, IN CLOSE UP. IT LOOKS REVOLTING. MAKE IT LOOK HAIRY AND SLIMY AT THE SAME TIME: IMAGINE A CAT-SICKED-UP HAIRBALL TO THE MAX...

DR:Most of them are.

This is a trichinobezoar -- it's made of hair. I cut it out of a young woman's stomach this afternoon. Lovely long hair she had. Trouble was, she'd been sucking it, chewing it, -- swallowing the hairs.
Must've been doing it for years.

Page 1 panel 4

PULL BACK AGAIN. WE CAN SEE, CLOSE TO US, THE DR, LEANING DOWN, OR CROUCHING, GETTING A BOOK OUT OF HIS LARGE BLACK DOCTOR'S BAG. HE'S LEFT THE THING ON THE TABLE, AND RICK IS STARING AT IT IN DISGUST. POSSIBLY POKING AT IT WITH A FINGER.

Dr:Technically that's known as the Rapunzel syndrome.
Anyway, it's a bezoar. Mission accomplished.

Madoc:It's disgusting. But thanks. What do I owe you, Felix?

Page 1 panel 5

OKAY -- WE'RE LOOKING AT THE TWO OF THEM. FELIX IS HOLDING OUT A BOOK TOWARDS RICK, A LITTLE NERVOUSLY. RICK'S JUST PLEASED NOT TO HAVE TO HAVE PAID ANY MONEY FOR THIS THING. IF WE CAN SEE THE BOOK -- IT'S A HARDBACK, BY THE WAY -- IT'S CALLED THE CABARET OF DR CALIGARI, BY RICHARD MADOC.

Dr:Oh, nothing.

It would have only been incinerated, or popped into a jar for students to stare at. Just don't tell anyone where you got it.

And, um, I was wondering if you'd sign this for me?

Rick:Sure. No problem.

Page 2 panel 1

WE ARE LOOKING AT THE TITLE PAGE OF THE BOOK -- WE CAN SEE PRINTED OR TYPESET, IN BLACK, THE CABARET OF DR CALIGARI, RICK'S NAME, AND UNDERNEATH THAT, IN BLUE OVERLAY LETTERING, HANDWRITING -- POSSIBLY WE CAN SEE A PEN AT THE BOTTOM FINISHING OFF THE SIGNATURE. KELLEY, UNLESS YOU WANT TO DRAW ANY HANDS HERE, OR THE PEN, THIS IS PROBABLY ALL TODD'S PANEL.

TODD CAN DO IT, MY PENMANSHIP SUCKS. K

Book title -- black printing: The Cabaret of Dr Caligari.
By Richard Madoc.

Handwriting -- blue overlay:For Felix Garrison, with thanks, Rick Madoc.

Rick: (off): There you go.

Page 2 panel 2

FELIX, HOLDING THE BOOK AT ARMS' LENGTH, IN BOTH HANDS, READING THE INSCRIPTION. HE LOOKS REALLY PLEASED.
Felix:This is great. It's a real thrill for me, to, you know, be able to do something for one of my heroes. I loved the book. Amazing stuff.

Felix:So, um, what do you need the bezoar for?

Page 2 panel 3

WE'RE LOOKING AT RICK. HE SEEMS SLIGHTLY UNCOMFORTABLE AT THIS.

Rick:Like you were asking the other day -- where do writers get our crazy ideas? Heh.

Rick:It's research, really.

Felix:I heard you were writing a sequel to the Cabaret -- I'm really excited.

Rick:Oh. Great.

Page 2 panel 4

FOREGROUND -- THE PHONE. IN THE BACKGROUND WE CAN SEE RICK, HEADING FOR THE PHONE, AND FELIX, PICKING UP HIS BAG, AND PREPARING TO LEAVE.

Rick:Uh, that's the phone. Listen, thanks again for the thing.

Felix:No problem. I know how busy you are. I'll just let myself out, then. 'Bye.

FX: Near phone, small: Breep breep.

Page 2 panel 5

KEEP THE PHONE IN THE SAME POSITION IT WAS BEFORE, BUT RICK IS NOW IN THE FOREGROUND, AND HE'S PICKED UP THE PHONE. IS TALKING INTO IT. POSSIBLY WE CAN SEE FELIX GOING OUT THE DOOR INTO THE STREET, OR POSSIBLY HE SIMPLY ISN'T IN THE ROOM ANY LONGER.

Rick:Hello? Richard Madoc speaking.

Phone:Rick? It's Harry. Listen, we have to talk. Your publishers were onto me again today.

Rick:Oh. Hi Harry.

Page 2 panel 6

SIMILAR SHOT, ONLY RICK LOOKS REALLY MISERABLE, UNCOMFORTABLE, SHIFTY. AS IF HE DOESN'T WANT THIS CONVERSATION.

Phone:Listen, the novel's almost nine months overdue, and they're threatening to cause trouble. You're in breach of contract, Rick.

Phone:Is it finished yet?

Rick:Nearly finished.

Phone:Well, how much have you got to go?

Page 2 panel 7

SIMILAR SHOT, ONLY WE'VE GRADUALLY CLOSED IN ON RICK. HE
LOOKS LIKE HE'S LYING.

Rick:It's almost finished, Harry. You can't rush these things. Another
couple of weeks, maybe, okay?

Listen, I'm really busy. I'll get back to you.

Rick:Okay?

Page 3 panel 1

THREE PANELS ON THE TOP TIER. PULL BACK, SO WE'RE LOOKING AT
THE WHOLE OFFICE. RICK'S PUT THE PHONE DOWN. HE'S LOOKING AT
IT, WITH HIS ARMS FOLDED.

Rick:How much of the novel have I written? Honestly?

Page 3 panel 2

HE'S PICKING UP THE BEZOAR, THE HAIRBALL, CAREFULLY, AND
DISTASTEFULLY, AND IS DROPPING IT INTO A PLASTIC SHOPPING BAG.

Rick:Nothing.

Page 3 panel 3

RICK'S GOING OUT THE DOOR, CARRYING THE SHOPPING BAG. HE
LOOKS SLUMPED, LESS HYPER.

Rick:Not a word.

Page 3 panel 4

WE'RE OUTSIDE FOR THE FIRST TIME. LONG PANEL ACROSS THE
MIDDLE OF THE PAGE. IT'S SUNSET, AND THE SKY IS LIT WITH A MESS
OF REDS AND ORANGES. RICK MADOC IS WALKING DOWN A LONDON
STREET, HIS BACK TO US, CARRYING THE PLASTIC SHOPPING BAG. I'LL
GET YOU PHOTOREFERENCE ON THE KIND OF STREETS WE'RE LOOKING
AT HERE: CHELSEA-ISH AREA, WHICH PROBABLY MEANS NOTHING TO
YOU, BUT YEARS AGO WHEN I WAS A CHILD, IT WAS WHERE THE
PUNKS STARTED UP, ON THE KING'S ROAD, AND I ONCE HAD A
GIRLFRIEND WHO LIVED OVER A BANK JUST OFF THE KING'S ROAD. I
MERELY TELL YOU THIS TO ADD ATMOSPHERE TO AN OTHERWISE DRY
AND UNEXCITING PANEL DESCRIPTION. THE STREET IS PRETTY MUCH
DESERTED. I DOUBT WE CAN SILHOUETTE HIM AGAINST THE SKYLINE,
UNLESS HE'S ACTUALLY WALKING BESIDE THE THAMES HERE --
ANYWAY, I'LL TAKE A PILE OF PHOTOS AND YOU CAN TAKE YOUR PICK

[handwritten note: I spent a fun afternoon wandering around Chelsea and the Embankment photographing reference]

WHERE YOU PUT HIM. MAKE IT MOODY, THOUGH. LONG, EXPRESSIONIST
SHADOWS. THE STREET SHOULD BE DIRTY, NEWSPAPER BLOWING DOWN IT.

No dialogue.

Page 3 panel 5

BOTTOM TIER -- THREE PANELS. HE'S STANDING IN A DOORWAY, PRESSING THE
ENTRYPHONE BUTTON: THERE'S ONLY ONE BUTTON, AND WE CAN ASSUME
THAT WHOEVER OWNS THIS PLACE, A TERRACED RED-BRICK GOTHIC
MONSTROSITY JUST LIKE ALL THE OTHERS ON THE STREET, LIVES THERE
ALONE. ALL THE OTHERS WERE TURNED INTO APARTMENTS THIRTY YEARS
EARLIER AND FORTY PEOPLE LIVE WHERE FIVE DID IN THE EARLIER YEARS OF
THE CENTURY.
Entryphone: (jagged or square)Who is it?

Rick:Richard Madoc, to see Erasmus Fry.

Entryphone:I'll be straight down.

Page 3 panel 6

SAME SORT OF SHOT. SHIFT AROUND SLIGHTLY, SO WE'RE LOOKING HEAD ON
TO THE DOOR, AND RICK HAS HIS BACK TO US. THE DOOR HAS BEEN OPENED
ABOUT AN INCH, AND WE CAN SEE AN OLD EYE STARING OUT OF THE
DARKNESS AT US. ACTUALLY, TO GET THIS TO WORK, I THINK WE'LL HAVE TO
COME IN FOR A CLOSE-UP. WE CAN SEE THE CHAIN ON THE DOOR IS STILL IN
PLACE.

Erasmus:Are you alone?

Rick:Yes. It's just me. I've got it.

Erasmus:Well, come in, dear boy. Come in.

Page 3 panel 7

THE DOOR IS COMPLETELY OPEN NOW. AN ELDERLY MAN IS STANDING THERE,
LOOKING A LITTLE NERVOUS. HIS NAME IS ERASMUS FRY. REALLY IT IS. HE'S
WEARING A TARTAN CHECK DRESSING GOWN, AND TROUSERS AND CARPET
SLIPPERS. HE'S GOT AN OLD-FASHIONED WHITE SHIRT ON, NOT TUCKED INTO
HIS TROUSERS, AND A DUSTING OF WHITE STUBBLE ON HIS CHIN, OF THE KIND
THAT INDICATES THAT HE CAN'T BE BOTHERED TO SHAVE. HE'S GOT A SHOCK
OF WHITE HAIR, AND AN OLD FACE THAT'S STILL STRONG; LIKE AN ELDERLY
SHERLOCK HOLMES. HE'S A FAMOUS NOVELIST AND PLAYWRIGHT, OR HE WAS,
THIRTY YEARS AGO.

PURE BRIDE OF FRANKENSTIEN

Erasmus:I'm not sorry that I'm not dressed for visitors. When you get to my age,
you don't give a toss what you look like. Heh.

Erasmus:Don't just stand there. Come in.

Page 4 panel 1

NOW, WE'RE IN ERASMUS FRY'S HOUSE FOR THE NEXT FOUR PAGES, AND IT'S
CLAUSTROPHOBIC AND CRAMPED -- LONG, DIMLY LIT CORRIDORS, CRAMMED
WITH OLD STATUARY AND PHOTOGRAPHS AND BOOKS. BLACK PANEL BORDERS
TO BLEED FROM HERE UNTIL THE END OF PAGE SEVEN. THREE PANELS ON THE
TOP TIER. THEY'RE IN THE HALLWAY. IT'S DARK AND GLOOMY, WITH LARGE
OLD PHOTOGRAPHS HANGING ON THE WALLS. THE OLD MAN IS SHUFFLING
DOWN THE CORRIDOR WITH THE YOUNGER MAN, TALLER, BEHIND HIM. THE
HALLWAY IS ALSO SET WITH MIRRORS, REFLECTING THE FACES OF THE MEN.
ERASMUS IS NOT A NICE OLD MAN.

Erasmus:How are you, M'boy? Written anything profound and stirring recently?

Rick:You know I haven't, Mister Fry.

Erasmus:No. We'll go into my study, and you can show me my present.

page 4 panel 2

THEY'RE NOW IN THE OLD MAN'S STUDY. THE OLD MAN IS STANDING UP AND
POURING TWO GLASSES OF SHERRY FROM A CUT-GLASS DECANTER. WHEN WE
SEE IT, THE STUDY IS EXPENSIVELY FURNISHED, DOMINATED BY A LARGE
BLACK- AND -WHITE PHOTOGRAPH OF ERASMUS AGED ABOUT TWENTY. EMPTY
FIREPLACE. IT'S ALL DUSTY. IT LOOKS LIKE IT HASN'T BEEN CLEANED OR
TIDIED FOR YEARS. THERE ARE A COUPLE OF ARMCHAIRS IN THERE, AND A
DESK. RICK IS ABOUT TO SIT IN AN ARMCHAIR. HE'S STILL HOLDING THE
PLASTIC BAG.

Erasmus:Ah -- an excuse for a sherry.

Erasmus:Cheap stuff, of course. I'm not wasting the good stuff on a little shit like
you.

Page 4 panel 3

ERASMUS, SITTING IN THE ARMCHAIR, RAISING THE GLASS OF SHERRY TO HIS
LIPS. HE'S ABOUT TO GIVE A LECTURE TO RICK. HE'S PROBABLY RAISING ONE
FINGER, OR LEANING HIS CHIN ON ONE HAND. HE'S NOT SMILING. HE LOOKS
VERY COMFORTABLE.

Erasmus: Let me tell you about Bezoars. Word comes from the Persian. Pad-zahr.
It means counter-poison. Antidote. Mainly found in the stomachs of goats and
gazelles.

— DESCRIPTION IN PARACELSUS BOOK

Page 4 panel 4
AGAIN, RUN THIS ACROSS THE MIDDLE OF THE PAGE. THE TWO OF THEM
SITTING IN ARMCHAIRS, OPPOSITE EACH OTHER: THE YOUNG MAN, ANTSY,
SCARED, NERVOUS; THE OLD MAN, COMFORTABLE, POWERFUL. RICK HAS PUT
HIS SHERRY DOWN ON THE FLOOR, ISN'T DRINKING IT. WE CAN SEE
BOOKSHELVES ACROSS THE WAY -- POSSIBLY A CHESS SET IN ONE CORNER.
THEY'RE IN THE LOWER HALF OF THE PANEL, LEAVING PLENTY OF ROOM FOR
THE HUGE WORD BALLOONS.

Erasmus:Once believed to possess mystic powers: they can remedy poison, make the sick well. Edward IV survived the effects of a poisoned wound, due solely to a bezoar in his possession.

Queen Elizabeth the First had a bezoar set in gold, with unicorn's horn, given to her by John Dee, her spy and magician.

Page 4 panel 5

THREE PANELS ON THE BOTTOM TIER. WE'RE LOOKING AT RICK -- HE'S SITTING THERE LISTENING TO THIS STUFF, GETTING MORE AND MORE IRRITATED -- HE'S PROBABLY LOOKING UPWARDS, BORED AND NERVOUS. NEARLY EXASPERATED. THE BACK OF THE ARMCHAIR FRAMES HIS HEAD.

Erasmus (off):For the common people, apothecaries would lend out bezoars at extortionate rates, for a week, or a fortnight...

Page 4 panel 6

SAME SHOT, BUT RICK'S HALF-STOOD UP, PUSHING HIMSELF UP WITH HIS ARMS AT HIS SIDE. HE LOOKS UPSET, IRRITATED, ANGRY.

Rick:Will you shut up?

I haven't written a word in a year -- nothing I haven't thrown away! Do you know what that's like?

Rick:When it's just you, and a blank sheet of paper?

Page 4 panel 7

MOVE IN ON RICK. HIS FACE IS SHADOWY, AND PAINED. IT'S LIKE HE'S BARING HIS SOUL HERE.

Rick:When you can't think of a single thing worth saying, a single character that people could believe in, a single story that hasn't been told a thousand times before...

Page 5 panel 1

THE OLD MAN HAS STOOD UP, IS LOOKING DOWN SHARPLY. HE'S REACHING OUT HIS HAND.

Erasmus:Of course I know what it's like. Don't be a fool, boy.

Erasmus:Let me see my present.

Page 5 panel 2

THE OLD MAN HOLDING UP THE BEZOAR, ADMIRING IT ON HIS OPEN HAND. HE'S IN LECTURE MODE AGAIN.

Erasmus:Oh yes. Rapunzel, let down your hairball. A genuine trichinobezoar. The smell comes from the partly digested particles of food, trapped in--

Erasmus:I'm sorry. I'm lecturing again. An old writer with no-one else to talk to gets fond of the sound of his own voice...

Page 5 panel 3

ERASMUS AND RICK ARE BOTH STANDING UP, NOW. ERASMUS HAS EXTENDED AN ARM, IS USHERING RICK OUT OF THE ROOM.

Erasmus:I will put the bezoar with the rest of them.

I suppose that you want her, now.

Did you bring any clothes?

Rick:Clothes? I didn't know I...

Erasmus:Never mind. I have an old coat you may use.

Page 5 panel 4

THEY'RE WALKING UP STAIRS, NOW, A NARROW, DARK STAIRWAY, HUNG WITH BOOK-COVERS AND PLAYBILLS, ALL WITH THE NAME ERASMUS FRY ON THEM, IN LARGE LETTERS. I DON'T KNOW IF WE CAN SEE ANY TITLES IN THIS OR THE NEXT PANELS, BUT THEY'RE THINGS LIKE A STRANGER IN EDEN OR HALL OF SHADOWS OR HERE COMES A CANDLE, THINGS THAT SOUND LIKE FAMOUS NOVELS OF THIRTY YEARS AGO. RICK IS NERVOUS, ERASMUS KNOWS EXACTLY WHERE HE'S GOING.

Erasmus:I caught her on Mount Helicon, you know. 1927. Greece. I was 27. I'll be 87 next year.

She was bathing in a spring, and I caught her and bound her with Moly -- sorcerer's garlic, as it's sometimes called -- and with certain rituals.

Page 5 panel 5

THEY'RE AT THE TOP OF THE STAIRS, WALKING DOWN A NARROW CORRIDOR. IF YOU WANT TO MESS WITH THE ANGLES, SO THE INSIDE SEEMS SUBTLY WRONG, THEN BE MY GUEST. IT'S REALLY DARK. WE OUGHT TO BE ABLE TO SEE THEM, BUT IT'S VERY GLOOMY AND ILL-LIT, ERASMUS HAS PULLED OUT A KEY, WHICH HE'S HOLDING IN FRONT OF HIM. I SUSPECT THEY'RE WALKING TOWARDS US. ERASMUS IS IN THE FRONT, OF COURSE.

Erasmus:The hardest part was getting her back to England.

Erasmus:They say one ought to woo her kind, but I must say I found force most efficacious...

After all, I got the fame and the glory. I created the novels, the poems, the plays...

Page 5 panel 6

THEY'RE STANDING IN FRONT OF A DOOR. ERASMUS HAS PUT THE KEY
INTO THE LOCK, AND IS TURNING THE KEY. ONE BARE BULB DANGLES
FROM A FRAYED FLEX, LIGHTING THE HALLWAY, JUST. I MEAN, IT'S
ABOUT A FIFTEEN WATT BULB, BUT IT'S A BULB.

Erasmus:I don't need her anymore, Madoc. And you do.

Here she is.

AND THEN WE GO OVER THE PAGE TO SEE WHAT'S IN THE ROOM...

PAGE 6 PANEL 1

SPLASH PAGE. DARK BORDER AROUND THE PAGE. WE'RE LOOKING
STRAIGHT THROUGH THE OPEN DOOR -- POSSIBLY THE PANEL BORDER
IS THE DOORWAY. AND WE'RE LOOKING AT IS APPARENTLY A THIN,
FIFTEEN-YEAR OR POSSIBLY JUST-SIXTEEN OLD GIRL. SHE'S STANDING
THERE STARING AT US. SHE HAS A BEAUTIFUL FACE, WITH DEEP
CHEEKBONES -- SHE'S A GODDESS AFTER ALL -- AND A THIN BODY: SHE
LOOKS AS IF SHE'S BEEN STARVED FOR A COUPLE OF WEEKS. WE CAN
SEE THE OUTLINE OF HER HIPBONES, AND NOT QUITE COUNT HER RIBS.
SHE'S NAKED. SHE LOOKS VERY VULNERABLE -- THIS IS THE
VULNERABILITY OF NAKEDNESS; IF YOU'VE EVER SEEN ANY PHOTOS
OF FAMINE VICTIMS, OR CONCENTRATION CAMP VICTIMS, THERE'S A
POINT AT WHICH NAKEDNESS TOTALLY CEASES TO TITILLATE, INSTEAD
JUST AROUSES FEELINGS OF PITY. (BILL SIENKIEWICZ CAUGHT IT
PERFECTLY IN THE MENTAL HOSPITAL SEQUENCES IN ELEKTRA:
ASSASSIN #1.) EITHER SHE HAS HER HANDS ON HER OPPOSITE
SHOULDERS, HUGGING HERSELF, OR SHE'S COVERING HER BREASTS
WITH ONE ARM, AND REACHING DOWN WITH HER OTHER HAND,
COVERING HER PUBIC AREA WITH A HAND. IT'S NOT FALSE MODESTY --
IT'S A WISH TO PROTECT HERSELF FROM. SHE DOESN'T LOOK SCARED --
NERVOUS, PERHAPS, OR UNHAPPY MORE LIKE. SHE ALSO HAS MASSES
OF SHAGGY BLONDISH HAIR, DOWN TO THE SMALL OF HER BACK. THE
KEY HERE IS VULNERABILITY -- THIS SHOULDN'T LOOK TITILLATING,
IT'S NOT A HUBBA HUBBA KIND OF NAKED WOMAN SHOT; IT'S ONE
THAT IT ALMOST HURTS TO LOOK AT. TEAR THEIR HEARTS OUT,
KELLEY. SHE'S LIT BY THE MUTED BULB IN THE HALL. DIMLY BEHIND
HER WE MIGHT BE ABLE TO MAKE OUT A CHEAP CAMP BED WITH A
THIN BLANKET ON IT. AT THE BOTTOM OF THE PANEL, PREFERABLY IN
THE KIND OF LETTERING WE HAD FOR THE TITLE OF #7, IS THE TITLE.

Erasmus (off, left): Her name's Calliope.

Title: Calliope.

And Credits.
At the bottom of the page, Sandman (logo) characters created by Gaiman,
Kieth and Dringenberg.

Kelley drew Calliope as really really skinny, with horribly protruding ribs. Karen felt that this was too extreme, and when Malcolm inked it he made her a little less skinny...

-10-

Page 7 panel 1

(JUST A BRIEF APOLOGY -- I'M AFRAID ERASMUS TALKS AN AWFUL LOT, AND
MAKES SURE HE TAKES THE LONGEST POSSIBLE ROUTE THROUGH ANY
SENTENCE. I TRY TO KEEP HIM SHORT-WINDED, BUT HE DOES RATHER TEND TO
OVERLOAD ANY PANELS HE'S IN WITH WORDS. OH WELL --AT LEAST THIS IS HIS
LAST PAGE ON STAGE, AS IT WERE... IF NECESSARY YOU COULD SLIP THIS
PANEL ONTO THE BOTTOM RIGHT HAND CORNER OF THE SPLASH PAGE, BUT I
THINK IT'LL WORK BETTER AS A SPLASH.) WE'RE LOOKING AT CALLIOPE, IN
CLOSE UP. A FACE SHOT, SHADOWY, AS SHE STARES STRAIGHT OUT AT US.
SHE'S COME OUT OF THE ROOM, AND IS NOW IN THE HALLWAY, SO THE LIGHT
IS DIRECTLY ABOVE HER, CASTING LOW SHADOWS FROM HER NOSE AND
ACROSS HER EYES. I TEND TO IMAGINE HER AS A STARVED YOUNG BRIGITTE
BARDOT, BUT THAT'S POSSIBLY BECAUSE THERE'S A BRIGITTE BARDOT MOVIE
ON LATE NIGHT TV RIGHT NOW. SHE HAS A COMBINATION OF GRANDEUR AND
INNOCENCE, HERE, BUT OBVIOUSLY HATES ERASMUS, IS COUNTING THE DAYS
AND THE HOURS UNTIL HER IMPRISONMENT IS OVER. HE MAY HAVE HER
SPIRIT, BUT HE DOESN'T HAVE HER SOUL, AND SHE SAYS:

Calliope:What would you with me now, Erasmus? Am I now to perform for your
amusement? Is this man to be our audience?

Page 7 panel 2

ANOTHER FULL-PANEL FACE SHOT, HEAD AND SHOULDERS, THIS TIME OF
ERASMUS, PROBABLY NOT LOOKING DIRECTLY AT US, BUT OFF SLIGHTLY. HE'S
BITCHY AND OLD AND HATES EVERYTHING, ESPECIALLY HER.

Erasmus:Don't get yourself all worked up, Calliope.

No, this is Richard Madoc. He's a novelist -- or at least, he's written one extremely
successful first novel, and has found himself quite unable to write anything else.

Page 7 panel 3

NOW WE'RE LOOKING AT RICK, AGAIN FULL FACE, AS HE STARES AT US, LIPS
PRESSED CLOSE TOGETHER, STARING AT THE GIRL (AT US) HIS EXPRESSION
UNREADABLE. MAKE THESE THREE PANELS VERY SIMILAR, JUST WITH
DIFFERENT PEOPLE IN THEM, IF YOU SEE WHAT I MEAN.

Erasmus (off):Richard, this is Calliope. The youngest of the nine muses. She was
Homer's muse, so she ought to be good enough for you.

Calliope, I'm giving you to Richard. You're his now.

Page 7 panel 4

PULL BACK NOW. CLOSE TO US, ON THE RIGHT OF PANEL, HER BACK TO US, IS
CALLIOPE, AND BEYOND HER, FACING US, ARE THE OLD MAN, AND, TALLER
AND YOUNGER AND ILL-AT-EASE, MADOC. HER ARMS ARE NOW AT HER SIDES.

Calliope:But you said -- you told me, you promised that you would free me before
you died. You said I could have my freedom...

Erasmus:Put not your trust in princes, my dear.

Page 7 panel 5

BACK TO CALLIOPE. SHE'S CRYING, SILENTLY. ONE TEAR IS
TRICKLING DOWN HER FACE. SHE'S RAISED A HAND TO HER
MOUTH, BUT HER CHIN IS STILL RAISED PROUDLY.

Erasmus (off):Nor in an aging author who has never been what one
might call a shining example when it came to keeping his word...

Writers are liars, my dear. Surely you have realised that by now?

Page 7 panel 6

PULL BACK AGAIN FOR A LONG SHOT. MADOC IS PUTTING A COAT
AROUND CALLIOPE'S SHOULDERS. ERASMUS HAS TURNED HIS BACK
ON BOTH OF THEM, IS WALKING TOWARDS US.

Erasmus:Take the little cow away, Madoc. I never want to see either
of you again.

Page 7 panel 7

OUT ON THE STREET, NOW. MADOC AND CALLIOPE ARE STANDING
THERE -- SHE'S WEARING THE COAT, BUTTONED UP, AND NOTHING
UNDER IT, SO WE CAN SEE HER BARE LEGS AND FEET ON THE
HARD SIDEWALK. ERASMUS IS STANDING IN THE DOORWAY,
FACING THEM, FACING US. FOR THE ONLY TIME, HE LOOKS
VULNERABLE, INSECURE. HE LOOKS OLD.

Erasmus:However, if you ever happen to feel a spark of gratitude,
you might want to persuade some publisher to bring 'Here Comes A
Candle' back into print.

Erasmus:I was particularly proud of that one.

Page 8 panel 1

THIS IS OPPOSITE AN AD PAGE. OKAY. NOW, FOR THE FIRST TIME
WE SLIDE OUT OF REAL-TIME AND INTO AN ALMOST MONTAGE
MODE. OVER THE NEXT FEW PAGES WE'RE GOING TO COVER A FEW
YEARS IN REAL TIME. WE'RE ALSO OPENING UP HERE, SO THE
FEELING OF CLAUSTROPHOBIA, WE SHOULD HAVE GOT FROM THE
LAST FEW PAGES, SINCE WE ENTERED FRY'S HOUSE, SHOULD BE
RELIEVED. WHITE PANEL BORDERS HERE AGAIN, FOR THE FIRST
TIME SINCE PAGE 4. WE'RE LOOKING AT THE TOP, ATTIC ROOM OF
A HOUSE -- MADOC'S HOUSE, -- FROM OUTSIDE. WE CAN SEE THE
BRICKWORK, AND A WINDOW, BARRED WITH A METAL GRILLE.
THROUGH THE WINDOW WE CAN SEE, ON THE INSIDE, CALLIOPE,
LOOKING AT US SILENTLY. SHE'S NAKED AGAIN, BUT WE CAN
PROBABLY ONLY SEE HER HEAD AND BARE SHOULDERS, AND THE
SIDE OF HER ARMS.

Caption:And Madoc took Calliope back to his home, and locked her in
the topmost room, which he had prepared for her.

*WHITE INK ON BLACK
FOR FIGURE of CALLIOPE*

I changed "bare wooden floor to "musty old camp-bed" when I saw the art-work. (For obvious reasons.

Page 8 panel 2

NOW I WANT TO TRY TO GET ACROSS THE RAPE, AND THE HORROR AND THE DOMINANCE, FAIRLY SUBTLY, DOING ALL THE WORK IN THE READER'S HEAD. THE WHOLE THING SHOULD BE REALLY UNDERSTATED. WHAT WE'RE ACTUALLY LOOKING AT IN THIS PAGE ARE BARE WOODEN FLOORBOARDS. AND COMING IN FROM THE RIGHT, WE CAN SEE CALLIOPE'S LEFT ARM AND HAND, PALM UPWARD, LAYING FLAT ON THE FLOOR. COMING DOWN FROM ABOVE IS RICK'S RIGHT ARM; HIS HAND IS CLAMPED AROUND HER WRIST, HOLDING IT DOWN TO THE GROUND. THAT'S ALL WE CAN SEE.

Caption:His first action was to rape her, nervously, on the bare wooden floor. musty old camp-bed.

Caption:She's not even human, he told himself. She's thousands of years old. But her flesh was warm, and her breath was sweet, and she choked back tears like a child whenever he hurt her.

Page 8 panel 3

WE ARE NOW DOWN IN HIS STUDY, FROM PAGE ONE, AND HE'S SITTING DOWN IN THE CHAIR NEXT TO HIS WORD-PROCESSOR, SMOKING A CIGARETTE. HE LOOKS VERY PLEASED WITH HIMSELF, SMILING A LAZY SMILE, HIS FEET UP ON THE DESK. THE SMOKE FROM THE CIGARETTE DRIFTS UPWARD. HE'S NOW BAREFOOT, AND JUST WEARING JEANS AND A SINGLET.

Caption:It occurred to him momentarily that the old man might have cheated him: given him a real girl. That he, Rick Madoc, might possibly have done something wrong, even criminal...

Caption:But afterwards, relaxing in his study, something shifted inside his head.

I sent Kelley some photos I took of my work-space, to give him an idea of the kind of place I had in mind. He reproduced it embarrassingly accurately. [Although he left out the Groucho Marx statue.]

Page 8 panel 4

WE'RE NOW BEHIND THE WORD PROCESSOR. WE CAN SEE THE BACK OF HIS HEAD, PERHAPS HIS HANDS ON THE KEYBOARD. AND WE CAN SEE THE SCREEN, IN FRONT OF HIM. I'LL GIVE YOU SOME TEXT THAT COULD BE REDUCED AND PUT ON THE SCREEN -- FAILING THAT JUST MAKE IT CLEAR THAT THERE'S TEXT ON THE SCREEN. ANOTHER POSSIBILITY IS THAT WE CAN SEE HIS FACE REFLECTED IN THE SCREEN, OR PARTLY REFLECTED ON ONE SIDE OF THE SCREEN. IF WE CAN, HE'S SMILING.

Screen: CHAPTER THREE. "AND SOME IN VELVET GOWNS"

"Your face," he said to her. "What have you done to your face?"

Marion shrugged. "I wanted to look on the outside like I do on the inside," she said simply, not putting down the knife.

Caption:He switched on the word processor to write it down before it fled.

Caption:He had been writing for three hours before he surfaced enough to realise that he had begun his second novel.

Although they aren't together in this collection the ad placement in the original comic should have ensured that pages 9 and 10 were opposite each other in Sandman #17 in the original ... were facing pages...

Page 9 panel 1

OKAY, FIVE PANELS ON THE PAGE, IN THREE TIERS. TOP TIER OF THREE PANELS, THEN TWO PANELS BELOW THAT. BASICALLY IT'S A NINE-PANEL GRID. FIRST PANEL, WE'RE LOOKING AT CALLIOPE, SITTING ON THE FLOOR OF THE ATTIC ROOM, IN THE CORNER OF THE ROOM, HANDS CLASPED IN FRONT OF HER. SHE'S STILL SORT OF NAKED, BUT, ALONE, SHE'S MORE COMFORTABLE WITH HER NAKEDNESS: HAVING SAID THAT, BEAR IN MIND THAT THE MUSES (UNLIKE THE GRACES) WERE ALWAYS DEPICTED CLASSICALLY AS BEING DRESSED IN LIGHT SHIFTS: THEY WERE ALWAYS CLOTHED, SO SHE'S NOT AT EASE, NAKED. ACTUALLY, ON REFLECTION, HOW ABOUT KEEPING HER IN THE COAT THAT SHE WAS IN BEFORE, ALTHOUGH IT'S NOT ACTUALLY DONE UP: IT'S LOOSE AND OPEN, ALTHOUGH IT WOULD SHADOW HER BODY. WE'RE ABOUT FIVE FEET AWAY FROM HER.

PLAY with Angles of LAYOUT - CONTRAST CALLIOPE to emptiness of the ATTIC

Calliope:Gracious ladies, mother of the Camenae, hear my prayer.
Calliope: Melete, Mneme, Aiode, attend my supplication.

Page 9 panel 2

RIGHT, WE'RE ZOOMING IN ON HER, SO NOW WE'RE LOOKING AT HER CHEST TO HEAD HERE. SHE'S LOOKING DOWN -- HER HANDS STILL CLASPED IN FRONT OF HER. SHE'S PRAYING, AND SHE'S ALSO VERY SAD, HURTING INSIDE. SHE HAS NO HOPE THAT ANYONE WILL RESPOND.

calliope:It is I, your daughter Calliope, who calls you, as I have called you a thousand times. I...

I implore you, ladies, deliver me from this place and this time.

Page 9 panel 3

RIGHT, WE'VE GOT A FINAL CLOSE-UP ON HER FACE, FRAMED BY THE FALLING HAIR, EYES LOOKING DOWN, OR HIDDEN BY LASHES.

The panel placement meant we moved a few of these balloons around.

Calliope:To whom can I speak, in my grief? I who am laden with wretchedness.

Calliope:Ladies of Meditation, Remembrance and Song, hearken to me.

Page 9 panel 4

OKAY -- THIS ONE RUNS ALL THE WAY ACROSS THE MIDDLE TIER: LEFT TO RIGHT, WE'RE LOOKING AT MELETE, MNEME, AIODE. NOW WE'RE PLAYING WITH A RUNNING THEME IN SANDMAN, OF THE TRIPLE GODDESS. HUNTING

THROUGH MATERIAL ON THE MUSES (NINE OF THEM -- THREE TIMES
THREE) I DISCOVERED THERE WAS AN EARLIER VERSION OF THE
MUSES WHEN THERE WERE ONLY THREE -- THIS THREE -- AND IT MADE
MORE SENSE THAT THEY'D COME FROM AN EARLIER, TRIPLE VERSION
OF THE MUSES THAN THAT, AS IN OTHER VERSIONS OF THE LEGENDS,
THEY WERE THE DAUGHTERS OF ZEUS AND MNEMOSYNE (MEMORY).
CHECK OUT SANDMAN 10 PAGE 19, AND THE DAVE MCKEAN COVER TO
SANDMAN 2: THIS IS THE VERY BASIC DESIGN FOR THE THREE, BUT
HAVING SAID THAT, FEEL FREE TO DESIGN YOUR OWN VERSIONS.
BASICALLY THEY ARE ALL WEARING WHITE CLASSICAL SHIFTS:
MELETE, THE OLD HAG ON THE LEFT, LOOKS LIKE A VERY OLD
WOMAN, HER STRAGGLY HAIR LONG AND GREASY, HER ARMS THIN
AND BONY; MNEME IS BASICALLY THE FACE FROM THE COVER OF
SANDMAN 2, RATHER THAN EITHER MIKE OR SAM'S VERSIONS OF THE
CHARACTER, BUT HER HAIR IS LONGER, AND WE CAN SEE HER FIGURE
THROUGH THE SHIFT -- IT'S HUGE BREASTS AND HUGE HIPS, AS WITH
ANY OLD STATUES OF THE EARTH MOTHER: HER ARMS ARE CROSSED
ACROSS HER HIPS, HER FACE ROUND AND MOTHERLY; AND ON THE
RIGHT STANDS AIODE, TALL AND HAUGHTY, WITH MASSES AND
MASSES OF BLONDE HAIR TUMBLING AROUND HER. THE CRONE, THE
MAIDEN, THE MOTHER. BEHIND THEM WE CAN EITHER SEE DARKNESS,
OR THE BARE WALLS OF THE ATTIC ROOM. THIS IS PROBABLY WAIST
TO HEAD SHOTS, AND A FOOT OR SO ABOVE THEIR HEADS. *OLD WOMAN will Be MY NEIGHBOR*

Melete:All right. Enough, Beautiful Voice. Why do you call us?

Mneme:We feel your pain, daughter, but we cannot help you.

Aiode:You were snared upon Helicon according to the mysteries. You are
lawfully bound.

Page 9 panel 5

SMALL INSET SQUARE PANEL ON THE RIGHT -- CALLIOPE'S FACE,
TALKING URGENTLY TO THE WOMEN.

Calliope:But it is not just, my mothers. I can bear this burden no more.

Is there nothing you can do? No-one who can intercede on my behalf?

Page 9 panel 6

LONG PANEL ACROSS THE BOTTOM OF THE PAGE. THE THREE AGAIN,
ALTHOUGH NOW THEY'VE CHANGED POSITION, THE OLDER AND THE
YOUNGER HAVE SWAPPED PLACES. AND WE'VE MOVED IN CLOSER TO
THEM. THE YOUNGER ONE LOOKS SYMPATHETIC, THE MIDDLE ONE
LOOKS MOTHERLY, THE OLDER ONE LOOKS UNSYMPATHETIC.

Aiode:There are few of the Old Powers willing or able to meddle in mortal
affairs in these days, Calliope.

Mneme:Many gods have died, my daughter; while aspects of other gods
have been lost for ever.

Melete:Hehh. Only the Endless will never die -- and even they are having a difficult time of late.

Still, every little bit helps, as the old woman said when she pissed in the sea.

A genuine old English proverb, strangely enough.

Page 10 panel 1

THE WOMEN HAVE STARTED TO TALK AMONG THEMSELVES, HAVE TURNED INWARDS -- LEFT TO RIGHT THE ORDER NOW GOES MOTHER, MAIDEN, CRONE, BY THE WAY -- AND ARE DISCUSSING WHAT THEY CAN DO ABOUT THIS.

Mneme:The Endless -- now, there's a thought -- after all, the Dream-King and Calliope were close, long ago. For a short while. Weren't you, my pet?

Aiode:Not for long. And, remember, sister-self, they did not part on the best of terms.

Melete:But she did bear his cub.

That boy-child, who went to Hades for his lady-love, and died in Thrace, torn apart by the sisters of the frenzy, for his sacrilege.
Page 10 panel 2

INSET PANEL, SMALL AND SQUARE, OF CALLIOPE'S FACE -- SHE LOOKS HOPEFUL, AND DESPERATE. (NOTE, SHE NEVER APPEARS IN THE SAME PANEL AS THE 3 SISTERS).

Calliope:Not him. Not after what he did to me. He hates me for that, and I despise him. I would not accept his help.

Page 10 panel 3

PANEL ACROSS THE CENTRE TIER OF THE PAGE, CLOSE IN SO THAT WE'RE JUST LOOKING AT THE THREE FACES OF THE WOMEN, STARING DOWN AT US (OLD ONE, YOUNG ONE, MOTHER, LEFT TO RIGHT). BEAR IN MIND THAT THESE ARE NOT WOMEN BUT ARCHETYPES -- IN THIS CASE A GRECIAN VARIANT ON THE ONE-WHO-IS-THREE WE'VE SEEN BEFORE.

Melete:Foolish child. Oneiros is in no position to help you, even if he wished to -- which is unlikely, to put it mildly.

Aiode:You see, just like you, Calliope, your one-time admirer has been ensnared by mortals.

And while you are imprisoned in your tower, he is immured beneath the ground.

Mneme:I am sorry, my little one. Your prayers were wasted. There is nothing we can do for you, and nothing you can do but hope.

Page 10 panel 4

OKAY -- NOW WE GO BACK TO THREE PANELS ON THE BOTTOM TIER, LIKE THE THREE PANELS ON THE TOP OF PAGE 9. (BEAR IN MIND THAT BECAUSE OF THE AD PAGE ON PAGE 8 THESE TWO PAGES ARE OPPOSITE EACH OTHER, ALTHOUGH DON'T MAKE THEM A DOUBLE PAGE SPREAD.) CALLIOPE'S STOOD

UP. WE'RE FAIRLY CLOSE UP ON HER STANDING FIGURE. SHE'S LOOKING
TOWARDS US, ARMS OUTSTRETCHED, PALMS UPWARD, PLEADING.

Calliope: No -- please, come back, please. There must be something, there must be
someone who can free me...

Page 10 panel 5

PULL BACK FROM CALLIOPE A LITTLE FURTHER. SHE'S LOWERING HER HANDS
TO HER SIDES. SHE'S TALKING TO AN EMPTY ROOM.

Calliope:Please... Send someone... anyone...

Page 10 panel 6

OKAY, PULL BACK ALL THE WAY. CALLIOPE IS A SMALL FIGURE, HER HANDS
BY HER SIDES; WHILE WE CAN SEE ALL THE ROOM AROUND HER, AND IT'S
TOTALLY EMPTY. THE THREE WOMEN HAVE GONE.
Calliope: (small) Even Oneiros.

Page 11

I DUNNO IT'S HALF PAST FIVE IN THE MORNING, AND THE TV IS SHOWING AN
"IN-DEPTH EXAMINATION" OF THE CLOSING OF A CANADIAN RAILROAD; AT
FOUR IN THE MORNING I WAS RUNG THREE TIMES IN SUCCESSION BY SOMEONE
OR SOMETHING WHO DIDN'T SPEAK. INITIALLY I THOUGHT IT WAS JUST
SOMEONE CALLING FROM THE U.S. WITH A BAD LINE, BUT THE THIRD TIME I
THOUGHT I HEAR RUSTLING AND BREATHING. SPOOKED THE SHIT OUT OF ME, I
CAN TELL YOU. ANYWAY, I WANTED TO GET THROUGH PAGE 12 TONIGHT, BUT
I'LL BE HAPPY IF I CAN GET TO THE END OF PAGE 11. *It WASNT ME. K*

Page 11 panel 1

AT THE TOP LEFT OF THE PAGE IS CALLIOPE'S FACE, SHADOWY, INTENSE -- NOT
IN A PANEL BORDER. I SUSPECT WE'D ONLY ACTUALLY GET THE LEFT SIDE OF
HER FACE, IF SHE'S STARING STRAIGHT IN FRONT OF HER, AND GOING OFF
INTO A FLASHBACK, THE RIGHT HAND SIDE OF HER FACE WOULD MERGE WITH
THE PANEL WE'RE GOING INTO, IF YOU SEE WHAT I MEAN; SO THE LEFT SIDE
OF HER FACE, FRAMED BY HAIR, IS ALMOST PANEL BORDER. OH, WHILE I
THINK OF IT, ALTHOUGH SHE'S THIN, AND NOT 100% CLEAN, HER HAIR IS
STILL FAIRLY UNMATTED, SHE'S NOT ILL, OR ACTIVELY STARVING, OR
ANYTHING -- THIS IS BECAUSE SHE'S ONE OF THE IMMORTALS. PERHAPS SHE'S
LOOKING SLIGHTLY TO THE RIGHT.

Caption:It had been her own fault.

Caption:Spring 1927. Mount Helicon.

Caption:She had only returned for a brief time, lured perhaps by nostalgia...

Page 11 panel 2

OKAY -- SEGUE INTO THE PANEL FROM THE LAST ONE. WE'RE LOOKING
AT CALLIOPE AS SHE WAS OVER SIXTY YEARS AGO. SHE LOOKS NOW
LIKE A HAPPY FIFTEEN-YEAR-OLD BRIGITTE BARDOT. SHE'S WEARING
A WHITE CLASSICAL SHIFT, AND IS UP TO HER THIGHS IN WATER, ON A
GOLDEN, SUNNY DAY, IN GREECE. SHE LOOKS VERY YOUNG AND VERY
HAPPY. ONE IDEA MIGHT BE TO COLOUR THIS IN VERY VIVID COLOURS;
ANOTHER IDEA MIGHT BE TO DO THIS PANEL AND THE NEXT IN SEPIA --
POSSIBLY A BETTER IDEA, BECAUSE GETTING COLOURS TO APPEAR
MORE VIVID THAN THEY DO AUTOMATICALLY CAN BE A REAL BITCH.
ON THE BANK OF THE POOL IS A SCROLL.

Caption:She had laid down her scroll, and was bathing in a clear pool,
remembering the lost, golden days: when the nine were still sought and
wooed and needed...

Caption:When the music of the spheres still resonated [echoed] in mortal
souls.

Page 11 panel 3

DO THIS PANEL NEXT TO THE OTHER ONE, WITH ONLY A THIN WIGGLY
LINE BETWEEN THIS PANEL AND THE LAST. CALLIOPE'S VIEWPOINT.
WE'RE LOOKING AT A YOUNG, 27-YEAR-OLD ERASMUS FRY,
RECOGNISABLE FROM THE PHOTOS WE SAW IN HIS HOUSE, EARLIER.
HE'S WEARING A 1920S SUIT, NO HAT, HAS DARK, SLICKED-BACK
HAIR, AND IS STANDING FAIRLY CLOSE TO US (HE'S ON DRY LAND, BUT
WE'RE PROBABLY LOOKING AT HIM FROM WAIST TO HEAD), GRINNING
LIKE A WOLF. IN ONE HAND HE'S HOLDING LONG-STEMMED WILD
GARLIC FLOWERS, IN THE OTHER HE'S HOLDING A ROLLED-UP
PARCHMENT SCROLL, HOLDING IT TOWARDS US. HIS EYES ARE BRIGHT,
AND HE'S A TOTAL BASTARD.

Caption:In one hand he held Moly flowers, that had power over her kind,
and in his other hand he held her scroll.

Caption:Which one are you? He had asked her.

Caption:Calliope, she told him.

Caption:Kall-i-oh-pee, he had echoed, as if he were tasting her name.

Page 11 panel 4

ACROSS THE CENTRE OF THE PAGE IS THE SCROLL, LAID
HORIZONTALLY ACROSS -- NOT IN A PANEL BORDER: IT'S BURNING,
FLAMES LICKING UP FROM IT.

Caption:And then he smiled. Well, he said, you can call me master.

Caption:And then he burned her scroll.

-18-

Page 11 panel 5

BOTTOM TIER. THE ATTIC ROOM -- RICK HAS ENTERED. HE LOOKS REALLY
HAPPY. SHE'S STANDING THERE IN HER COAT, HER EXPRESSION SET. STARING
AT HIM. MEDIUM SHOT.

Madoc:Hey! Great news! I've finished the novel. It's called "And My Love She
Gave Me Light." Two drafts in five weeks. And it's all good stuff.

Calliope:I am pleased for you. Now will you let me go?

You can find the ancient riddle this line is taken from in Book Four of "The Books of Magic", at the end of time.

Page 11 panel 6

CLOSE IN ON THE TWO OF THEM CLOSE. HE'S PUTTING HIS ARMS AROUND HER.
SHE'S LOOKING UP AT HIM SADLY.

Madoc:Are you out of your mind? This is just the beginning. Come here, gorgeous.
Let's make two and a half minutes of squelching noises...
Calliope:Please, Madoc. Let me go. Stop forcing me to do these things.

Page 11 panel 7

LIKE PANEL ONE -- JUST MADOC'S FACE, LOOKING STRAIGHT AT US, NO PANEL
BORDER. IF YOU JUST DID THE LEFT SIDE OF CALLIOPE'S FACE AT THE TOP,
THEN JUST DO THE RIGHT SIDE OF MADOC'S FACE HERE, HIS FACE SET AND
HARD. IF HE'S SMILING, HE'S SMILING CRUELLY. IF SHE WAS LOOKING OFF TO
THE RIGHT IN THE FIRST PANEL, THEN HERE HE'S LOOKING SLIGHTLY OFF TO
THE LEFT.

Madoc:Listen. You're my possession, until I tell you that you're free. Don't
forget it.

 You're my personal muse, sweetheart. Now.

Let's party.

SHOCKING - NOT SEXUAL

Page 12

OKAY -- THIS PAGE AND THE NEXT ARE A SERIES OF QUICK HOPS, WATCHING
RICK MAKING IT UP TO THE TOP OF THE TREE. KEEP ALL THE PANEL BORDERS
HERE VERTICAL, AND KEEP THE PANELS DISTINCT FROM EACH OTHER. IT'S
BASICALLY A SIX-PANEL GRID -- THREE ON THE TOP TIER, THREE BELOW.

Page 12 panel 1

THE TOP HALF OF PAGE 12. WE'RE AT A PARTY -- IT'S A PUBLISHER'S PARTY,
WELL-LIT. PEOPLE ARE MILLING AROUND, SMALL KNOTS OF PEOPLE, SOME OF
THEM DRINKING GLASSES OF WINE. IN THE MIDDLE OF THE PARTY IS A
DISPLAY OF THE BOOK, WITH, ABOVE IT, A HUGE MOCK-UP, OF THE BOOK
COVER. IT'S CALLED "...AND MY LOVE SHE GAVE ME LIGHT," THE COVER
SHOWING A CANDLE BURNING ON A SKULL, AND, AT THE BOTTOM OF THIS, RIC
MADOC. (HE'S LOST THE K FROM HIS NAME, FOR REASONS OF COOL.) BIG

PHOTO OF HIM IN THE BACKGROUND. THERE COULD BE A FEW
BALLOONS AROUND, POSSIBLY WITH REPRODUCTIONS OF THE BOOK
COVER ON THEM. SOME OF THE PEOPLE -- MEN AND WOMEN -- ARE
REALLY WELL DRESSED, SOME ARE FASHIONABLY SLOPPY: SOME OF
THEM ARE LOOKING SIDELONG AT RICK -- HE'S THE STAR, AFTER ALL.
STANDING NEXT TO RICK, WHO'S ON THE EXTREME RIGHT, FAIRLY
NEAR TO THE BOOK DISPLAY, IS RICK. HE'S IN A GOOD SUIT, LOOKING
REASONABLY COMFORTABLE. HE'S GRINNING. NOW REMEMBER, HE'S
GOING TO GET BETTER DRESSED AND COOLER SLICKER OVER THE NEXT
PAGE OR SO, SO WE DON'T WANT TO BLOW IT ALL HERE. STANDING
NEXT TO HIM IS AN ATTRACTIVELY DRESSED YOUNG WOMAN WITH
LONG BLACK HAIR AND TOO MUCH MAKE-UP. HE'S SMOKING A
CIGARETTE. IT'S REALLY UP TO YOU HOW MANY PEOPLE YOU DRAW,
BUT TRY TO GIVE THE IMPRESSION THAT THIS A WELL-ATTENDED
LUNCH PARTY SOMEWHERE QUITE LARGE.

Caption:May 1987.

Boring psuedy type on the left (small):
Really, John, I don't see any way that a work of genre fiction could be
nominated for the Booker prize.

Another boring psuedy type next to him (small):
Well, I feel in the light of his latest novel that Madoc's work has to be
seen as transcending genre. It's as if it were written by a different man.

Someone: (small)It's a beautiful book. Quite remarkable. I mean, the sheer
richness of the material...

Woman talking to Rick:I loved your characterisation of Aileen. There
aren't enough strong women in fiction.

Rick:Actually, I do tend to regard myself as a feminist writer.

Woman:So tell me -- where do you get your ideas?

Page 12 panel 2

BOTTOM TIER -- THREE PANELS. AN EXPENSIVE GENTLEMAN'S CLUB,
DIMLY LIT. TALKING TOGETHER ARE RICK AND A PRODUCER, A TUBBY
TYPE, WITH A HUGE SHOCK OF WHITE HAIR, SMOKING A HUGE CIGAR
(SOME OF THEM DO). THEY'RE SITTING OVER A LITTLE TABLE, WITH A
COUPLE OF DRINKS ON IT.

caption:June 87.

Rick:Harvey, the only condition under which I'd be willing to do a
screenplay for you of "...And My Love," would be if I could direct it.

Harvey:Let me put this simply for you, Ric. Impossible.

Page 12 panel 3

WE'RE OUT ON A LONDON PAVEMENT AT NIGHT, WITH THE LIGHTS
TWINKLING OFF ROMANTICALLY INTO THE DISTANCE. RICK IS
WALKING WITH A BEAUTIFUL YOUNG WOMAN WITH BROWN HAIR --
OBVIOUSLY NOT CALLIOPE -- POSSIBLY WEARING GLASSES.
THEY'RE WEARING LIGHT CLOTHES -- SHE'S IN A SILKY SORT OF
EVENING DRESS. THEY'RE WALKING AWAY FROM US. HE'S
RESTING ONE HAND ON HER BOTTOM, POSSESSIVELY AND JUST A
LITTLE OFFENSIVELY. SHE'S OBVIOUSLY HERO-WORSHIPPING HIM.

Cap:July 1987.

Her:When they said in the TLS that you could be considered the
greatest epic poet since Byron--

Rick:It surprised the hell out of me. I saw The Spirit Who Had Half of
Everything as a lightweight project between real books...

I was honestly surprised when my publisher agreed to take it.

An oblique James Branch Cabell reference. "The Spir[it] Who Had Half of [Every]thing" was a [cha]pter he never go[t] around to writing in "Figures of Earth".

Page 12 panel 4

WE'RE IN RICK'S STUDY. HE'S TALKING ON A MOBILE PHONE NOW,
NOT THE OLD PHONE HE WAS ON BEFORE, POSSIBLY SITTING IN A
LARGE LEATHER CHAIR. BUT KEEP A COUPLE OF THINGS THE SAME
-- A LITTLE STONE SCULPTURE OF ATHENE, OR SOMETHING. HE'S
GOT A NEW HAIRCUT, NOW, AND LOOKS A LOT SLICKER.

Cap:October 1988.

Rick:Look, Harry, it's nothing that you've done. It's just that the
William Morris agency can look after my interests better. They've got
contacts you haven't.

But you've still got the first three novels and the poetry collection to
handle...

Rick:Don't be like that, Harry.

Page 13 panel 1

OKAY -- STRAIGHT SIX-PANEL GRID, THREE ON TOP, THREE BELOW.
FIRST PANEL -- WE'RE ON A STAGE -- AND UNDER THE SPOTLIGHT
STANDS RICK IN HIS TUXEDO, HOLDING A BIG BOUQUET OF
FLOWERS. HE'S TALKING INTO THE MICROPHONE; WE CAN SEE A
THEATRE SET BEHIND HIM. POSSIBLY DO THIS AS A FAIRLY LONG
SHOT, SO WE CAN SEE THE HEADS OF THE THEATRE-GOING
AUDIENCE.

Cap:February 1989

Rick:Thank you, all of you, so much. You know, when I first told my agent I was planning to write a play, he said Ric, you're crazy.

Rick:So I got a new agent. Ha ha ha.

Page 13 panel 2

SAME CHARACTER AS PAGE 12 PANEL 2: THE PRODUCER, IN AN OFFICE, WITH A DIFFERENT CIGAR. RICK (ALL RIGHT, WE'LL CALL HIM RIC, SINCE THAT'S WHAT HE CALLS HIMSELF), RIC IS WEARING SOMETHING LARGE AND WHITE AND SHARP. HE'S FAR MORE COMFORTABLE THAN HE LOOKED ON THE PREVIOUS PAGE, WHILE THE PRODUCER IS BEING FAR LESS CONDESCENDING.

Caption:April 1989.
Producer:...we've been actively discussing your original offer to write a screenplay, if we let you direct. I'm pleased to tell you that--

Ric:Harvey, it's too late. I've already signed a three-film deal in the US. But thanks, y'know.

Page 13 panel 3

A LARGE HOUSE. SOMEWHERE PRETTY OLD AND IMPRESSIVE. EXTERNAL SHOT. DAYLIGHT. WE CAN SEE AN ATTIC WINDOW AT THE TOP, BARRED, BUT NO-ONE IN THERE.

Caption:May 1989.

Caption:Ric Madoc buys a new house, in Chelsea. He's busy on pre-production for the film, and most of the moving is done for him.

Caption:He moves his most valuable possession himself, though, late one spring night.

Page 13 panel 4

RIC, COOL AND COLLECTED ON A US TV SHOW -- WHATEVER YOUR LOCAL EARLY MORNING TV SHOW IS, CHATTING TO SOMEONE ON A SOFA. WAKE UP AMERICA TYPE LOGO BEHIND THEM. THE ANNOUNCER IS LOOKING AT THE CAMERA, NOT AT RIC.

Cap:September 1989

Ric:No. No, I like Hollywood well enough, but I'm really pleased to be going home. Two months away is enough for me.

Announcer:Hi! In case you've just tuned in, I'm talking to Ric Madoc, writer, poet and soon-to-be film director, about his new epic novel Eagle Stones...

Eagle Stones are stones with magical properties, once said to have been found in eagles' nests. Without the stones the eggs would not hatch.

-22-

Page 13 panel 5

NOW WE'RE LOOKING AT A TV SET, AT A SLICK PRESENTER OF U.S. TV SHOW
THE TRAILER, WHICH SHOWS TRAILERS OF UPCOMING MOVIES. HE'S SOME
SLICK IDIOT, WITH 'THE TRAILER' IN THE BACKGROUND. YOU CAN SET THE TV
WHEREVER YOU LIKE, AS LONG AS THE LOCATION'S IN THE US OF A.

Cap:October 1989

Announcer:...Writer of the best-selling novel 'Eagle Stones' talks to us about his
extraordinary new film, "...And the Madness of Crowds," and we'll be showing
some exclusive footage!
That's all... after this short break.

Ric took the title from a Victorian book called "Extraordinary Popular Delusions and the Madness of Crowds", by Charles Mackay.

Page 13 panel 6

WE'RE LOOKING AT A MOVIE POSTER -- BASICALLY HAVE FUN DESIGNING IT. I
IMAGINE THAT IT'S A NUMBER OF FACES STARING BLANKLY OUT AT US.
LARGE ON IT IS THE TITLE RIC MADOC'S '...AND THE MADNESS OF CROWDS,'
AND THERE'S A FLASH ACROSS THE BOTTOM RIGHT HAND CORNER, READING
NOMINATED FOR 3 OSCARS. BEST ORIGINAL SCREENPLAY, BEST DIRECTOR, AND
BEST PICTURE.

TODD -- YOU'LL PROBABLY WANT TO DO THE LETTERING FOR THIS. DO IT LIKE
A FAIRLY CLASSY MOVIE POSTER. THINK WOODY ALLEN, I SUPPOSE.

Caption:March 1990.

ON A FENCE - NOT BRICK.

Page 14 panel 1

I'LL STICK TO THE SAME KIND OF GRID STRUCTURE HERE, BUT FEEL FREE TO
LOOSEN IT UP NOW, SINCE WE'RE IN REAL TIME. WE'RE NOW IN THE ATTIC OF
THE NEW HOUSE. WE'RE LOOKING AT CALLIOPE. SHE'S NOW SORT OF DRESSED -
- A LIGHT BLOUSE, AND A SKIRT, ALTHOUGH SHE'S BAREFOOT. THE WALLS ARE
BARE, AND, BEHIND HER, WE CAN SEE THE WINDOW, BARRED. IT'S NOT AS
TACKY AS THE ROOM WE SAW BEFORE, IN WHICH SHE WAS IMPRISONED, BUT
NEITHER IS IT FURNISHED IN ANY WAY. SHE'S LOOKING STRAIGHT TOWARD US.
SHE LOOKS A LITTLE SURPRISED. A LITTLE STARTLED. ALSO A LITTLE
NERVOUS. THIS IS FROM THE SANDMAN'S VIEWPOINT, SO WE CAN'T ACTUALLY
SEE THE SANDMAN.

Calliope:Oh. It's you.

Page 14 panel 2

I always refer to him in scripts as The Sandman, that's though not me ...

SANDMAN'S VIEWPOINT AGAIN. SHE'S LOOKING DOWN, NOW, A LITTLE
EMBARRASSED PERHAPS. IT'S BEEN FOUR THOUSAND YEARS SINCE SHE'S HAD
ANYTHING TO DO WITH HIM, AND THEY DIDN'T PART ON THE BEST OF TERMS.

Calliope:They... they told me that you had been imprisoned. Just like me.

-23-

Sandman caption:They spoke the truth. I was imprisoned. But, as you can see, I am free now.

Page 14 panel 3

RIGHT -- SAME VIEWPOINT, BUT SHE'S TAKEN A STEP TOWARD US, NERVOUSLY, BUT URGENTLY.

calliope:Then please -- by the love I once had for you. By -- whatever you felt for me. Please.

Make him give me my freedom. Make him let me go.

Page 14 panel 4

WE'RE IN A TV STUDIO, AND THE LOGO BEHIND US READS "THE BOOK NOOK." AN INTERVIEWER SITS IN A CHAIR, WEARING A HAT, WITH A HANDLEBAR MOUSTACHE. ON THE TABLE BETWEEN THEM ARE GLASSES OF WATER, AND PERHAPS A COUPLE OF BOOKS. HE'S EXPOUNDING. RIC SITS ON A CHAIR NEXT TO HIM. WE MAY BE ABLE TO SEE A FEW CAMERAMEN WITH CAMERAS AROUND.

Interviewer:Although you've been compared to the multi-talented Jean Cocteau, and to a lesser extent to writer-directors like Clive Barker, it seems to me that the creator who perhaps you most resemble is the late 1940s cult figure, Erasmus Fry...

The interviewer bears an uncanny resemblance to my friend and sometime collaborator, Kim Newman.

Page 14 panel 5

CLOSE IN ON RIC. HE LOOKS A LITTLE PERTURBED. HE'S LEANING FORWARD, ONE FINGER RAISED. BY NOW RIC HAS A TOTALLY NEW IMAGE THAT HE'S COMFORTABLE WITH -- ONE EARRING PERHAPS, HIS RED HAIR CUT VERY SHORT AT THE SIDES, LONGER AT THE BACK.

Ric:Excuse me -- you said 'the late.' He's dead?

Interviewer:Last summer. Did you know him?

Big Shot
Lotsa Shadow
FROM here ON - ALL shots of RICK close or CROPPED, MORE ANXIETY in Atmosphere

Page 14 panel 6

PULL BACK AGAIN INTO A TWO SHOT. RIC'S SITTING BACK IN HIS CHAIR, A LITTLE STUNNED.

Ric:I didn't know him. We met... on a couple of occasions. He was... interested in my work.

Interviewer:Ah. Anyway, like you, Fry was above all a creator of epics, of huge, towering romances...

Page 15 panel 1

AFTER THE TAPING'S OVER, THE INTERVIEWER IS TALKING WITH RIC IN THE BBC BAR, AND SINCE I'M NOT GOING TO GET YOU PHOTOREF OF THE BBC BAR, JUST IMAGINE ANY SMALL BAR, VERY HIGH CLASS WITHOUT BEING POSH, AND YOU'LL DO FINE. THEY'RE STANDING TOGETHER, BOTH WITH DRINKS IN THEIR HANDS.

Interviewer:...went very well, I thought. It'll be broadcast in June -- we'll let you know the exact date.

Ric:Thanks.

I suppose Fry must have died when I was shooting in the US. Old age, I suppose. He must've been almost ninety.

Page 15 panel 2

CLOSE IN ON THE INTERVIEWER. HE'S JUST TALKING CASUALLY -- AS FAR AS HE'S CONCERNED THIS IS JUST A GOOD ANECDOTE.

Interviewer:Oh no. He poisoned himself.

It's quite funny. Apparently the last thing he did was write a letter to his old publishers, begging them to bring one of his books back into print...

Page 15 panel 3

PULL BACK AGAIN FOR A TWO SHOT, OR CLOSE IN ON RIC. HE LOOKS A LITTLE GUILTY, A LITTLE HURT.

Again Lotsa shadow— almost sillouette.

Ric:'Here Comes A Candle,' I suppose.

Interviewer:I think that was it. How did you guess?

Ric:It was a good book. Perhaps my favourite book, when I was growing up.

Very moving, and honest, and strange.

Ric:Poor old sod.

Page 15 panel 4

OUTSIDE THE HOUSE WE SAW ON PAGE 13 PANEL 3. A CAR IS PARKED IN FRONT OF THE HOUSE, AND RIC IS GETTING OUT AND SHUTTING THE DOOR.

No dialogue.

After this story wa published, my friend Pete Atkins told me that "Here comes A Candle" was the title of his first-published short story. I had to confess I hadn't known that before. But Pete's mind and mine often run* in similar directions...

*or hop. Or shuffle.

Page 15 panel 5

RIC, OPENING THE FRONT DOOR, WITH HIS FRONT DOOR KEY. UP TO YOU
REALLY HOW YOU DO THIS PANEL, AND THE TWO ON EITHER SIDE -- BASICALLY
WE'RE JUST SPENDING THREE SILENT PANELS WATCHING HIM GO INTO HIS
HOUSE. WE'RE ALSO BUILDING UP THE SUSPENSE A BIT, BECAUSE DEEP IN
THEIR GUTS, THE READER KNOWS THAT WHEN WE TURN THE PAGE, THE
SANDMAN'S GOING TO BE THERE, AND INDEED HE IS. SO MAKE THESE THREE
PANELS AS PROSAIC AS POSSIBLE. IT'S LIKE THE MOMENT IN A MOVIE WHEN
YOU SUDDENLY NOTICE THAT THE MUSICAL SOUNDTRACK HAS STOPPED, AND
ALL WE CAN HEAR ARE HIS FEET CRUNCHING ON THE GRAVEL, THE KEYS IN
THE LOCK, HIS FOOTSTEPS ECHOING MUFFLED DOWN THE HALL.

No dialogue.

Page 15 panel 6

RIC, PROBABLY FROM BEHIND, WALKING DOWN A CORRIDOR.
No dialogue.

Page 16. Panel 1

OKAY. OVER THE PAGE. WE'RE LOOKING AT THE SANDMAN. NOW, LOOKING AT
SANDMAN 13, WITH ALL THE VARIANT CLOTHES THROUGH THE YEARS,
SHOWED ME THAT THE CHARACTER LOOKS PRETTY GOOD HOWEVER HE'S
DRESSED, AND I'VE WANTED TO EXPERIMENT A LITTLE, FOR A WHILE. SO, HOW
HE'S DRESSED: HE'S DRESSED IN BLACK. YOU'LL PROBABLY WANT TO
ACTUALLY BLACK IN AS MUCH AS POSSIBLE OF THIS, AND NOTE ON THE
ARTWORK THAT THE REST OF IT'S IN K-TONE GREYS, OTHERWISE ROBBIE WILL
PROBABLY DO HIM IN PURPLE, WHICH THE SEPARATORS WILL PRINT PINK FOR
NO IMMEDIATELY OBVIOUS REASON... ANYWAY, THIS IS WHAT HE LOOKS LIKE.
FACIALLY, AND HAIR-WISE, NOTHING MUCH HAS CHANGED -- STILL A SHOCK
MOP OF BLACK HAIR, AND A LONG, THIN, SLIGHTLY ANDROGYNOUS FACE WITH
GOOD CHEEKBONES AND NO EYES -- JUST BLACK SHADOWS WHERE THE EYES
SHOULD BE WITH, OCCASIONALLY, LONE AND DISTANT SINGLE STARS GLINTING
IN THE SOCKETS. BUT INSTEAD OF WEARING A BLACK COAT, PUT HIM IN A
LARGE BLACK LEATHER JACKET, WITH A HIGH COLLAR IN THE BACK, THIN
BLACK JEANS, AND A JET-BLACK TEE SHIRT. HE DOMINATES ANY ROOM HE'S
IN: HE'S REGAL, ARISTOCRATIC; ALTHOUGH IN A LEATHER JACKET HE LOOKS
MORE LIKE THE SKINNY, UNDEAD KING OF THE STYLE BIKER PUNKS FROM
HELL. HE'S SITTING ON A CHAIR, WITH HIS ARMS CROSSED, AND LEGS
CROSSED, LOOKING FAIRLY COMFORTABLE. HAVING SAID THAT, HE IS NOT
PLEASED -- THE IMPRISONMENT ASPECT REMINDS HIM TOO MUCH OF HIS OWN
IMPRISONMENT. IMAGINE A PARENT, OR A COP, WAITING FOR YOU TO COME
HOME. IF HE'S NEXT TO A TABLE ONE OF HIS ARMS COULD BE ON THE TABLE,
PERHAPS. HE'S LOOKING UP AT RIC, EITHER ON THE EXTREME LEFT OR OFF
PANEL TO THE LEFT. OH -- THE LOUNGE -- GO FOR THAT LARGE, SPACIOUS,
UNLIVED-IN SORT OF LOOK YOU GET IN MAGAZINES, BUT ONLY EVER REALLY
GET BY NOT LIVING SOMEWHERE. POSSIBLY A FEW HUGE PAINTINGS ON THE
WALL, DEPICTING CLASSICAL SCENES -- PERSEUS CUTTING OFF THE GORGON'S
HEAD, FOR EXAMPLE.   SANDMAN IS NIGHT'S FACE

Ric (off, left):Christ! What are you doing in my house?

Who let you in?

Sandman:Nobody let me in, Richard Madoc.

Page 16 panel 2

WE'RE LOOKING AT RICK, IN MEDIUM CLOSE UP -- HE'S ANGRY, IS GESTURING TOWARDS US, WHITE WITH ANGER AND THE SHOCK YOU GET WHEN YOU FIND A STRANGER IN YOUR HOME. TIGHT-LIPPED.

Like me, Knows the deal and is Guilt Ridden

Ric:I don't know who you are, but I want you out of here, now, or I'm calling the police.

Page 16 panel 3

BOTTOM TIER. LONG, THIN PANEL; AN EXTREME CLOSE-UP ON THE SANDMAN'S FACE. DARK SHADOWY EYES, WITH SINGLE STAR GLINTING IN ONE EYE. HE'S REASONABLY ANGRY AS WELL, BUT THE SANDMAN GETS QUIETLY ANGRY, NOT LOUDLY ANGRY.

Sandman:Be quiet.

Page 16 panel 4

OKAY -- THE SANDMAN HAS STOOD UP, NOW. WE'VE GOT A TWO SHOT -- THE SANDMAN'S STOOD UP, NOW. HE'S ON LEFT OF PANEL, HIS BACK SLIGHTLY TO US, FACING THE SANDMAN, IS ON THE RIGHT. THE SANDMAN IS ABOUT 6'4" AT THIS POINT, RIC IS ABOUT 5'11", SO THAT RIC IS LOOKING UP AT THE SANDMAN. IF THE SANDMAN'S ARMS WEREN'T FOLDED BEFORE, THEY ARE NOW.

Sandman:You are keeping a woman imprisoned here, Richard Madoc. Keeping her against her will.

I have come to request that you set her free.

Page 17 panel 1

FOUR PANELS ON THE TOP TIER. SMALL PANEL -- RIC, TRYING TO BLUSTER IT OUT. HEAD SHOT.

Ric:Are you out of your mind? There's no woman here. Now get out of here. Do you know who I am? There -- there's a law against people like you.

Page 17 panel 2

SAME SIZED PANEL. THE SANDMAN, HEAD AND SHOULDERS, STARING AT US. HE'S NOT SAYING ANYTHING. HIS EXPRESSION IS BLANK. HE KNOWS MADOC IS

LYING.

No dialogue.

Page 17 panel 3

SAME SHOT AS PANEL 1. RIC, LOOKING DOWN; HE'S REALLY WORRIED. HE'S
REALLY FRIGHTENED. HE KNOWS HE CAN'T BLUFF THIS ONE OUT.

Ric:Are you going to call the police? Is that it?

Page 17 panel 4
THE SANDMAN -- LOOKING STRAIGHT AT US, HEAD SHOT AGAIN. HE'S JUST
STATING THE FACTS.

SM:No. I will not call any human agency.

SM:Just let her go.

page 17 panel 5

PANEL ALONG THE MIDDLE OF THE PAGE. LONG PANEL -- ON THE LEFT IS RIC,
LOOKING DOWN, LOOKING SHAKEN, AND BROKEN. HE'S ABOUT TEN FEET AWAY
FROM US. ON THE EXTREME RIGHT, FAIRLY CLOSE TO US, WE CAN SEE THE
SANDMAN'S FACE IN PROFILE.

Ric:But you don't understand -- I need her. If I didn't have her, I wouldn't be able
to write. I wouldn't have ideas.

I can't free her yet. Not now. Maybe in a year or so.

Look, I have money -- an awful lot of money -- and ...

SM:Hold your tongue.

Page 17 panel 6

TWO PANELS ON THE BOTTOM TIER. HEAD SHOT OF THE SANDMAN, STARING
STRAIGHT AT US: HE SEEMS HALF AMUSED, HALF DISGUSTED, HALF HURT.
(YES, I KNOW IT MAKES THREE HALVES.) IT's okay -I FAILed math ir

SM:She has been held captive for more than sixty years. Stripped of all
posessions. Demeaned, abused, and hurt.

I... know how she must feel.

SM:And you will not free her, because 'you need the ideas'?

Page 17 panel 7
OK -- NOW GO IN FOR THE FINAL PANEL FOR A REALLY CLOSE-CLOSE UP: ONE
EYE, STARING AT US, WITH A LITTLE WHITE SKIN AROUND IT.

SM:You disgust me, Richard Madoc.

SM:You want ideas? You want dreams? You want stories?
Then ideas you will have.

Ideas in abundance.

Page 18 panel 1

WE'RE OPPOSITE AN AD PAGE HERE, AND THE FIRST PANEL'S A SMALLISH
PANEL, SHOWING RIC. HE'S RAISED HIS HAND TO HIS FACE. HE'S WAKING UP --
HE WAS ASLEEP. SITTING IN A LARGE ARMCHAIR, IF WE CAN SEE IT. THIS IS A
CLOSE-UP ON HIS FACE. THIS PAGE IS ROUGHLY A NINE-PANEL GRID.

Ric:Uhhhnn.

Page 18 panel 2

LARGER PANEL. IT WOULD COVER TWO PANELS OF A NINE PANEL GRID. THE
ROOM -- THE SAME ROOM WE WERE IN ON THE PAGE BEFORE. RIC'S GETTING
UP FROM HIS CHAIR, WIPING HIS EYES. THE SIZE OF THE ROOM, THE
CLEANLINESS AND CLEAN LINES, EMPHASISE THE EMPTINESS OF THE ROOM,
AND THE FACT THE ONLY PERSON IN IT IS RIC HIMSELF. HE'S POSSIBLY
RUBBING HIS EYES, POSSIBLY LOOKIING AROUND THE ROOM. VERY CLEAN
LINES -- ALMOST MOEBIUS-LIKE.

No dialogue.

Page 18 panel 3

NEXT TIER. OKAY -- NOW WE'RE UPSTAIRS IN THE ROOM WHERE SHE'S BEING
KEPT PRISONER. WE'RE LOOKING STRAIGHT AT RIC. NOW FOR THE FIRST TIME
IN A WHILE WE CAST SHADOWS UP HIS FACE, PROBABLY LIGHTING HIM FROM
BELOW. REAL BRIDE OF FRANKENSTEIN STUFF. HE LOOKS A LITTLE HAUNTED.

Ric:I just had this weird dream....

What do you know about it? Huh? Are you doing that? Giving me nightmares?

Are you doing it?

Page 18 panel 4

WE'RE LOOKING AT CALLIOPE, WHO'S JUST STARING UP AT US SULLENLY.

No dialogue.

Page 18 panel 5

POSSIBLY DO THIS FROM CALLIOPE'S VIEWPOINT. RIC HAS RAISED HIS FIST. HE
LOOKS A LITTLE CRAZY. HIS EYES ARE WIDE, HIS NOSTRILS FLARED. HE'S

REALLY READY TO BEAT THE SHIT OUT OF HER.

Ric:Tell me.

Ric:Tell me, or so help me, I'll, I'll...

Page 18 panel 6

CALLIOPE, IN CLOSE UP, TALKING, LOOKING TOWARD US, OR SLIGHTLY TO THE LEFT. SHE LOOKS PROUD, LIKE SHE'S PULLED WHATEVER REMNANTS OF DIGNITY SHE HAS AROUND HER, BECAUSE SHE KNOWS THAT RIC'S TIME HAS COME.

Calliope:No, I am not doing it, Richard Madoc.

You have met Oneiros, whom the Romans called the Shaper of Form.

A possible etymology of "Morpheus" is "He who shapes"...

Calliope:He was once my lover, and he was the father of my son.
Ric (off, small):I didn't know you'd ever had a son.

Page 18 panel 7

PULL BACK -- REALLY LONG SHOT. OF THE TWO OF THEM. TWO TINY FIGURES -- HE'S NEARER TO US, SHE'S TURNED TO THE WINDOW.

SHE should BE LOOKING out of THE WINDOW LIKE SHE'S WAITING FOR SOMETHING

Calliope:You know nothing about me, Richard Madoc.

I am alive in my own right. I am more than a receptacle for your seed, or an inspiration for your tales.

A line I changed on the second draft of the script, but that has been left as it was originally in the lettered version.

Page 18 panel 8

ANOTHER LONG SHOT. HE'S WALKING TOWARD US, SEEMING PUZZLED AND WEIRDED OUT. SHE'S IN THE BACKGROUND, STARING OUT OF THE WINDOW, SADLY. SHE'S NOT LOOKING AT HIM.

Calliope:Still, it is too late now to let that concern you.

Calliope:Goodbye, Richard Madoc. Enjoy your party.

Page 19, panel 1

OKAY -- OVER THE PAGE, NOW: I TEND TO IMAGINE THE NEXT TWO PAGES AS BEING LAID OUT BY EARLY SWAMP THING BISSETTE AND TOTLEBEN, ALL PANEL ANGLES JAGGED AND ANGULAR, AS IF THE PAGE IS A HUGE SHATTERED MIRROR. DON'T DO PANELS 19 AND 20 AS A DOUBLE PAGE SPREAD, COS WHEN OR IF IT'S EVER COLLECTED UP, 19 IS OPPOSITE 18, WHICH ISN'T TRUE HERE.
WE'RE LOOKING AT A SMALLISH PANEL. RICK IS CLOSE TO US, AND IN FRONT OF HIM, FURTHER AWAY FROM US, IS A NEWSPAPER-

SELLER, ON A PAPER STALL. RIC'S DRESSED AS HE WAS BEFORE -- IT'S NOW LATE AFTERNOON, EARLY AFTERNOON. HE'S TAKING A MAGAZINE AND A NEWSPAPER.

Ric:A Time Out, please. And a Standard.

Paperman:Right-ho. Saw you on the telly the other night. I said to my wife, he buys papers from me, she said, He never, I said, he does. One twenty, please.

RIc: Ah... I'm going to a party...

Page 19 panel 2

OKAY -- BEGIN TO DISTORT THINGS. RIC'S LOOKING TOWARDS US, INTENTLY, POSSIBLY IN REAL CLOSE-UP. HE'S CRACKING UP -- IS EXCITED AND OBSESSED.

Ric:You know, I could write a whole story set at a party. Possibly something could have happened to the world outside -- a holocaust of some kind...
These people are partying against the darkness.

Page 19 panel 3

RIC IS STUMBLING TOWARDS US DOWN THE PAVEMENT, TOWARDS OUR TILTED CAMERA, ACROSS A JAGGED PANEL BORDER -- POSSIBLY WE CAN SEE THE NEWSPAPERSELLER IN THE BACKGROUND, WAVING, WORRIEDLY.

Newspaperman (smallish):Here! Mister Madoc! That's one pound twenty you owe me!

Ric:The fraternity of critics. In reality a dark brethren, linked by profane rites and blood vows. To destroy an author they sacrifice a child and perform a critical mass...

Page 19 panel 4

OKAY -- RIC'S NOW GRABBED SOMEONE, POSSIBLY A LITTLE OLD LADY, BY THE LAPELS, AND, OBSESSED AND CRAZED, IS PULLING HER UP OFF THE GROUND, SHOUTING IN HER FACE. SHE'S TERRIFIED, NOT SAYING ANYTHING.

Ric:A city in which the streets are paved with time.

Ric:A train full of silent women, plunging forever through the twilight.

Ric:Heads made of light. A small piece of blue cardboard. A plum, sweet and tart and cold. A were-goldfish who transforms into a wolf at full moon.

I may write this story one day!

Page 19 panel 5

LONG PANEL. HALF AN HOUR LATER. OKAY -- A CROWDED SIDEWALK, AND RIC'S CRAWLING ON THE GROUND TOWARD US. PEOPLE AROUND ARE STANDING AND LOOKING AT HIM -- NO-ONE'S DOING ANYTHING TO HELP HIM. HIS CLOTHES

ARE LOOKING FRAYED AND DIRTY AS IF HE'S BEEN CLIMBING AROUND ON THE
SIDEWALK FOR HALF AN HOUR. HIS FINGERNAILS HAVE BEEN WORN DOWN
AND THE TIPS OF HIS FINGERS ARE BLEEDING. EITHER IN THIS PANEL OR ONE
OF THE NEXT FEW, YOU COULD SHOW A WALL WITH, OVER IT, ON A RED
OVERLAY, SOME KIND OF WEIRD IMPRESSIONISTIC DRAWING, LOOKING LIKE IT
WAS EXECUTED WITH RED PAINT.

TODD-- THE LETTERING'S GRADUALLY GETTING WAVIER, AS RIC LOSES HIS
GRIP ON EVERYTHING. WAVERY ALL THROUGH.

Ric:Two old women taking a weasel on holiday.

Ric: Gryphons shouldn't marry. Vampires don't dance.

Ric:A man who inherits a library card to the library at Alexandria.

Ric:A rose bush, a nightingale, and a black rubber dog- collar.

Page 20 panel 1

OKAY, STILL REALLY JAGGEDY PANELS. AND WE CAN SEE THE PREVIOUS
SCENE FROM A BIT OF A DISTANCE NOW. A MAN -- FELIX GARRISON -- FOUR
YEARS OLDER, IS WALKING WITH HIS BACK TO US, ATTRACTED BY A KNOT OF
PEOPLE STANDING AROUND THE FALLEN MAN.

Ric: (small and wavery):A man who falls in love with a paper doll.

The sun setting over the Parthenon. Shark's teeth soup.

*People should do nothing
But watch-- Look
EERIE R*

Felix:Is something wrong? I'm a doctor. Stand back, please.

Page 20 panel 2

FELIX LEANING OVER RIC, WHO'S NOW LYING ON HIS BACK ON THE SIDEWALK,
STILL TOTALLY HYPER AND OBSESSED. FELIX, WHO WE CAN NOW RECOGNISE,
IS SHOCKED, BUT, BEING A GOOD DOCTOR, SIMPLY LOOKS CONCERNED, NOT
UPSET.

Felix:Good grief -- Richard Madoc!

What's the matter, old fellow?

Ric: (wavery)I'm just having ideas. So many...

Ric:(wavery)An old man in Sunderland who owned the universe, and who kept it
in a jam-jar in the dusty cupboard under his stairs...

Page 20 panel 3

OKAY -- RIC IS NOW SORT OF STANDING UP, LEANING HEAVILY ON FELIX,

WHO'S THROWN RIC'S ARM OVER HIS SHOULDER. HE'S STAGGERING DOWN THE PAVEMENT, SUPPORTING MUCH OF RIC'S WEIGHT, WHILE AROUND THEM (IF YOU CAN GET THEM IN) SPECTATORS JUST STAND AND STARE, MAKING NO EFFORT TO DO ANYTHING AT ALL. IF YOU CAN'T GET THE SPECTATORS IN THEN DON'T WORRY AND DON'T PUSH IT.

Felix:My home is just around the corner. Lean on me. Do you remember me -- Felix Garrison?

Ric:(wavery)It's the ideas. Where we get them from. A sestina about silence, using the key words Dark, Ragged, Never, Screaming, Fire, Kiss.

Strangely enough, people actually did write sestinas using these key words and sent them in. I think if I'd known anyone was actually going to attempt it, I'd've made it a triolet or a villanelle. Sestinas take ages, and are a bitch to do well.

Page 20 panel 4

FELIX IS PUSHING OPEN HIS FRONT DOOR, WITH RIC JUST SORT OF CLUTCHING HIM. RIC HAS ONE ARM OVER FELIX'S SHOULDER -- FELIX IS TAKING ALL HIS WEIGHT. RIC OBVIOUSLY JUST DOESN'T HAVE MUCH FREE ATTENTION, HE'S STARING OFF IN SOME OTHER DIMENSION, TALKING TO HIMSELF, TALKING. FELIX GARRISON F.R.C.S. ON A BRONZE PLATE ON THE DOOR.

Felix:Come on inside. You'll have to tell me what's the matter. Soon have you feeling better...

Ric: (wavery) A biography of Keats, from the Lamia's viewpoint...

Page 20 panel 5

OKAY -- INSIDE FELIX'S HOUSE. RIC IS NOW SITTING IN A LARGE LEATHER CHAIR, STARING HOPELESSLY IN FRONT OF HIM -- HE'S NOT FOCUSING ON ANYTHING, STARING OFF BLANKLY. HE'S RAISED HIS HANDS TO HIS FACE, AND WE CAN SEE THAT THE ENDS OF THE FINGERS ARE REALLY DISGUSTING -- HE'S ALMOST WORN THEM DOWN -- THEY'RE ALMOST JUST NUBS OF BLOODY MEAT, CRACKED FINGERNAILS. FELIX HAS REACHED DOWN AND IS TOUCHING ONE OF THE HANDS, ALTHOUGH I SUSPECT HE'S STANDING UP, AND GOES OFF ABOVE THE TOP OF THE PANEL, SO IT'S PROBABLY JUST HIS ONE ARM, COMING FROM OFF PANEL. TODD -- NOT WAVERY ANY MORE.

Felix:God -- what did you do to your hands?

Ric:All the pictures in my head. I had to get them down, but I didn't have any paper, or paints. So I used a wall.

And my fingertips.

Page 21 panel 1

ANOTHER STANDALONE PAGE OPPOSITE AN ADVERT. OKAY -- NOW REGULARISE THE PANELS. WE'RE IN FELIX'S HOUSE. LONG SHOT OF THE TWO MEN -- RIC IS SITTING DOWN, FELIX IS STANDING UP, GETTING A BOTTLE OF PILLS OUT OF A CABINET OR SOMETHING.

Ric:All the ideas, inside. All the pictures and poems and tales and songs and plays and speeches and fragments...

They're all coming out. You must help me.

Felix:I'll give you a sedative. And I'll bandage those fingers.

Ric:No! No... I'm sorry. Nothing like that.

Page 21 panel 2

GO IN FOR AN EXTREME CLOSE-UP OF RIC'S FACE, TORTURED AND UNHAPPY.

Ric:It's her revenge, you see. Or his revenge. I said I needed the ideas -- but they're coming so fast, swamping me, overwhelming me...

You have to make them stop.

Page 21 panel 3

WE CAN SEE FELIX'S OUTSTRETCHED HAND, WITH THREE PILLS IN THE PALM.

Felix:Here -- this will calm your nerves.

Concentrate on Ric's Hands

Ric:No! I told you.

Look -- go to my house. The keys are in my pocket if - if you can take them out for me. I don't think I can use my hands any more.

Page 21 panel 4

RIC IN MEDIUM CLOSE-UP, OR A TWO-SHOT OF THE BOTH OF THEM. HE'S PLEADING WITH FELIX. FELIX COULD BE HOLDING THE DOOR KEYS.

Ric:Go upstairs. At the top of the house there's a room. There's a woman in there.

Let her out. She's locked up in there, you see.

Page 21 panel 5

FELIX IS PUTTING ON HIS COAT. NEARER TO US, RIC SITS IN THE CHAIR, IN HIS OWN LITTLE UNIVERSE, STARING AT US AS WELL. HIS EYES ARE LARGE AND WHITE AND ROUND, HIS PUPILS ALMOST PINPRICKS; HE'S HALF TALKING TO HIMSELF, HALF TO FELIX. FELIX IS READY TO GO. HE LOOKS CONCERNED.

Ric:Tell her -- tell her that she can go. That I free her. Make her leave. Make her go away.

Ric:I signed a book for you once, didn't I?

Oh god. Please.

Page 21 panel 6

FELIX IS OVER BY THE DOOR, IN THE BACKGROUND, FACING US. RIC IS STILL IN
THE CHAIR, STARING OFF INTO THE UNFOCUSED DISTANCE. FACE SCRATCHED,
CLOTHES TORN, HANDS RUINED.

Felix:All right. Stay there. I'll be back soon.

Ric:Make it stop. Tell her I'm sorry.

Ric:Magical and alchemical traditions seen as a cargo cult; Aureolus Theophrastus
Bombastes Paracelsus and Raymond Lulli were the same man.

page 22 panel 1

OK -- OUTSIDE SHOT OF RIC'S HOUSE. IT'S NOW EVENING -- ABOUT THREE OR
FOUR HOURS LATER THAN OUR LAST GLIMPSE OF THE HOUSE. NOT A BIG
PANEL. WE CAN SEE FELIX GOING IN.

No dialogue.

Page 22 panel 2

OK -- NOW DO AN ANGLE SHOT, SO WE CAN SEE UPWARDS, UP A SPIRAL
STAIRCASE, AND, AT THE TOP OF THE STAIRS, IS FELIX, OPENING A DOOR --
THE ROOM WHERE CALLIOPE HAS BEEN KEPT PRISONER. HE'S UNDOING A
PADLOCK.

Felix:Um. Hello?

Felix:Is there, um, anyone here? He says -- Ric, uh, says you're free to go. Hello?

Page 22 panel 3

OKAY -- NOW, WE'RE IN A ROOM, WHICH IS HER CELL. IT'S EMPTY: THERE ARE
BARE WALLS, BARE FLOORBOARDS, A BARRED WINDOW, AND, ON THE FLOOR,
A LARGE, OLD LEATHERBOUND BOOK, WITH A PAPERJACKET. BY OLD, I MEAN
PROBABLY ABOUT FIFTY YEARS OLD. WE CAN EITHER SEE FELIX IN THE ROOM,
OR WE CAN SEE HIS SHADOW COMING IN FROM OUTSIDE. WE SHOULD FEEL
WE'RE ABLE TO SEE ALL THE ROOM, POSSIBLY SLIGHTLY FISH-EYE, AND WE
CAN TELL IT'S EMPTY.

No dialogue.

Page 22 panel 4

WE'RE LOOKING, FROM FELIX'S VIEWPOINT, AT THE BOOK ON THE FLOOR.
IT'S CALLED HERE COMES A CANDLE BY ERASMUS FRY, AND IT'S GOT AN
ILLUSTRATION ON THE FRAYED PAPER JACKET -- AN OLD-FASHIONED,

SLIGHTLY STYLISED ILLUSTRATION SHOWING A YOUNG WOMAN, NAKED BUT ALWAYS DISCREETLY COVERED BY HAIR. THERE'S A BLURB ON THE BOOK-COVER AS WELL, WHICH READS SHE WAS HIS MUSE -- AND THE SLAVE OF HIS LUST!

No dialogue.

Page 22 panel 5

WE CAN SEE FELIX NOW, IN THE ROOM. HE'S PICKED UP THE BOOK, AND HE'S RAISED HIS HAND TO HIS FOREHEAD, LOWERED HIS HEAD; IT'S OBVIOUS TO HIM THAT RIC'S CRACKED UP COMPLETELY BY NOW.

No dialogue.

Page 22 panel 6

WE CAN SEE HIM WALKING AWAY, LOOKING DEJECTED -- HE'S ON HIS WAY TOWARD THE FRONT DOOR. WE'RE LOOKING FROM A SECOND FLOOR STAIRCASE DOWN AT HIM BELOW US. HE'S STILL GOT THE BOOK.

No dialogue.

Page 23 panel 1

OKAY -- NOW, GO FROM A LOT OF SHADING TO VERY STARK WHITES AND BLACKS. NO MORE WEIRD ANGLE SHOTS ON THIS PAGE, EITHER. VERY REGULAR PANEL GRID -- THREE ON THE TOP, THREE ON THE BOTTOM. WE'RE LOOKING AT, ON THE LEFT, CALLIOPE, AND ON THE RIGHT, THE SANDMAN. THEY'RE BOTH LEANING ON THE BANISTER, LOOKING DOWNWARDS, INTERESTED. SHE'S NOW WEARING A LIGHT TUNIC -- A CHITON, I SEEM TO REMEMBER IT'S CALLED, UNLESS THAT'S SOMETHING ELSE, BUT A STANDARD CLASSICAL GREEK TUNIC-SKIRT, AND HER HAIR IS PILED UP ON HER HEAD, BEHIND HER. SHE LOOKS A LOT MORE IN CONTROL. CLEAN AND PERFECT. HE'S WEARING HIS BLACK ROBE, COVERING ALL OF HIM, FROM HEAD TO TOE.

SANDMANS CAPE IS ALIVE, FOLDS ARE LIKE INTESTINES.

Calliope:So. It's over. Thank you.

Sandman:What will you do now, Calliope?

Calliope:I don't know. Return to the minds of humanity, I suspect. My time is over, and this age of the world is not my age.

Page 23 panel 2

SHE'S NOW LOOKING UP AT HIM, WHILE HE'S STILL STARING STRAIGHT AHEAD OF HIMSELF. SHE'S LOOKING AT HIM WITH WONDER, OR WITH DEEP THOUGHT.

Calliope:You have changed, Oneiros. In the old days, you would have left me to rot forever, without turning a hair...

Calliope:Do you still hate me? For what I did?

...Morpheus? ...Orpheus? ...One of those...

Page 24 panel 6

SAME AS PANELS 2 AND 4, ONLY THE SANDMAN FIGURE IS TINY NOW.

no dialogue.

Page 24 panel 7

PULL BACK A BIT -- FELIX IS HOLDING OUT THE BOOK TO RIC, WHO'S STILL
SITTING, SLIGHTLY HUNCHED, STARING INTO SPACE, AND DOESN'T REGISTER
IT.

Felix:You can take it with you to the hospital, Richard.
Ric:She's gone, you see. And it's all gone with her. Everything. All of them, all the
dreams...

Ric:No... I can't remember. I've lost it...

Page 24 panel 8

WHITE PANEL.

No dialogue.

Page 24 panel 9

OKAY -- FINAL SHOT IS OF RIC, LOOKING AT US, UNFOCUSED. TRY TO ECHO --
THOUGH NOT COPY -- THE FIRST SHOT WE SAW, PAGE 1 PANEL 1, AT LEAST IN
TERMS OF THE SIZE OF THE FACE, AND THE DIRECTION IT'S LOOKING. HE
LOOKS HURT, WOUNDED, DESTROYED, MESSED UP. ZOMBIE.

Ric:It's gone.

Ric:I've got no idea any more.

No idea at all.

Then either END or,
NEXT: A Dream of a Thousand Cats -- whichever you think works best.

CAT-EYES

Okay -- that's it; a bit delayed due to power cuts, caused by hurricane winds
(remember the last time that happened, Karen?) --anyway, if anyone has a
question, ring me. Hope you all like it; enjoy.
best

n.

Dedication:

Four stories for four good people:
CLIVE BARKER,
JILL KARLA SCHWARTZ,
AIMEE HORSTING, and
MIKAL GILMORE.

Hi guys.
Neil.

For **Mom**, who rationalized my early, odd drawings as normal; for **Dad**, who watched FRANKENSTEIN and KOLCHAK, THE NIGHT STALKER with me; for **Jeff**, who let his little brother be his friend, as well as **Lynn**, **Bill**, **Ed**, **Steve** and **Carol**; also **Robert Pickman**, the best artist ever, Roger Corman, James Whale, Boris Karloff and Peter Cushing; and Gustav Quadrangle for endless inspiration; and finally, Knuckles, the very patient and orange model of the "Sandcat".
Kelley.

This one's for "Mr. Sandman" himself, Michael Wm Kaluta, who taught me a lot about making dreams come true.
Charles.

For my mother and father.
Colleen

To Inell Jones.
Malcolm

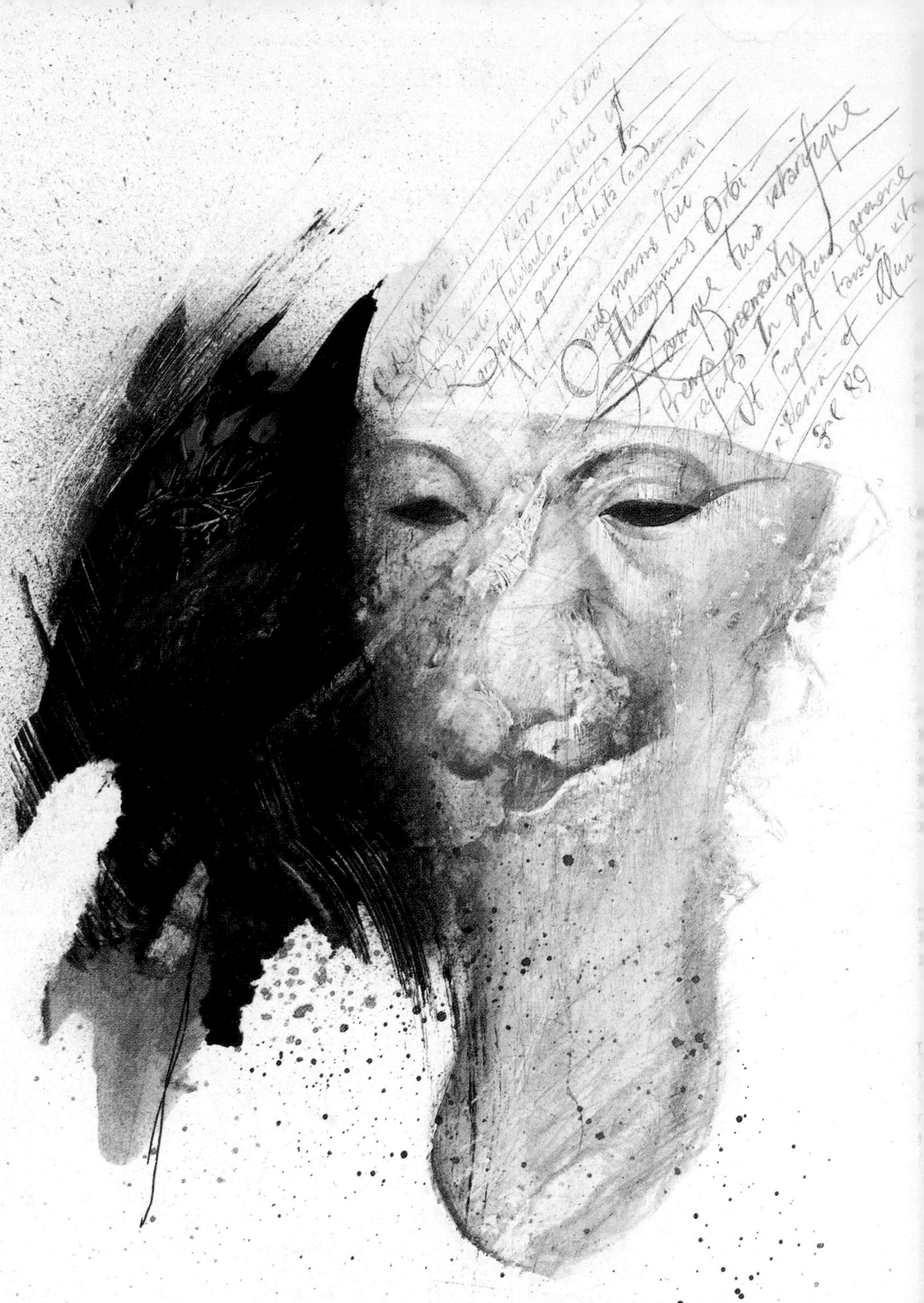

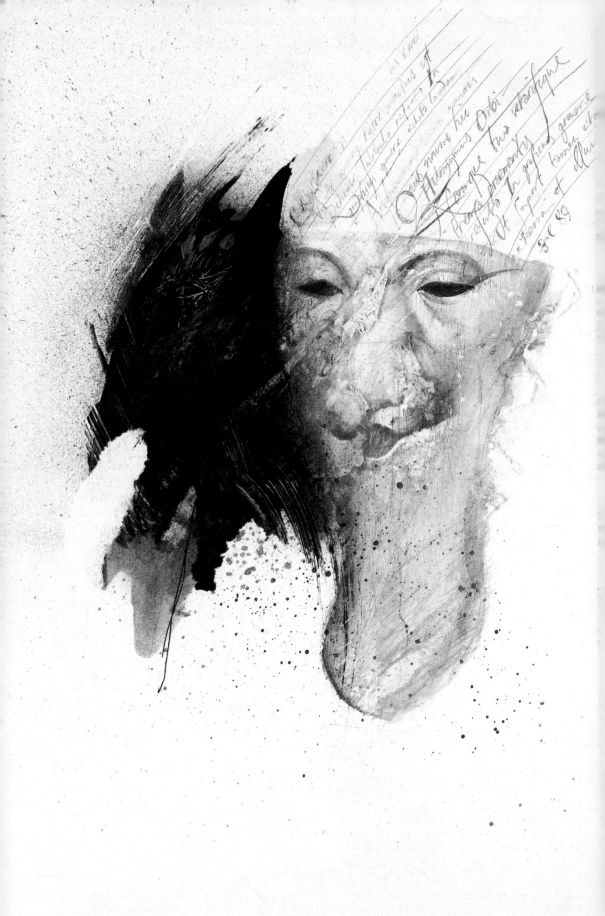

BIOGRAPHIES

NEIL GAIMAN

Neil Gaiman is currently living in a big, dark house in America with two cats, two white dogs and a number of awards from all over the world. He still does not understand how he came to be responsible for the feeding and domestic arrangements of these animals, nor, for that matter, what he is doing living in America. He has eight beehives and many bees. He has written novels and comics and movies and TV and poems and an opera and he keeps an enormous blog, which is nothing like keeping bees at all. He enjoys old fountain pens and sushi.

KELLEY JONES

Born in 1962, Kelley Jones would have been an all-star baseball player except that he could not hit a curve ball with any consistency. Now an artist of some renown, Jones has lent his unique gothic style to a wide selection of comic book titles, including THE SANDMAN, DEADMAN, BATMAN, *Moon Knight*, *Aliens* and *Grendel*, to name just a few. A resident of the Golden State, Jones continues to enjoy drawing comics because it remains one of the only jobs where you can listen to a ball game and not get into trouble.

CHARLES VESS

The award-winning work of Charles Vess has graced both covers and pages for numerous comics and mainstream publishers, including DC, Marvel, Dark Horse, Viking, Tor and HarperCollins. His work has been featured in numerous gallery and museum exhibitions in the U.S. and abroad, and his awards include an Ink Pot, two World Fantasies, the Mythopoeic, a Gold and Silver Spectrum Annual, two Chesleys, a Locus for Best Artist and two Will Eisner Comic Industry Awards. He also shared the prestigious World Fantasy Award for Best Short Story with Neil Gaiman in 1991 for their collaboration on THE SANDMAN #19, "A Midsummer Night's Dream." The two reunited to produce the illustrated fantasy novel NEIL GAIMAN AND CHARLES VESS' STARDUST, which was adapted in 2007 into an acclaimed motion picture.

COLLEEN DORAN

A professional illustrator since the age of fifteen, Colleen Doran has contributed to hundreds of comic book titles, including THE SANDMAN, LUCIFER, WONDER WOMAN, *The Amazing Spider-Man* and *Captain America*, as well as *The Book of Lost Souls* by *Babylon 5* creator J. Michael Straczynski and the graphic novel adaptations of Anne Rice's *The Master of Rampling Gate* and Disney's *Beauty and the Beast*. Following a successful collaboration with writer Warren Ellis on the Vertigo graphic novel ORBITER, she is currently working on the upcoming STEALTH TRIBES with Ellis and GONE TO AMERIKAY with Derek McCulloch. Doran also continues to write and illustrate her creator-owned series *A Distant Soil*, an epic science fiction/fantasy tale that now spans some 40 issues (or four trade paperback collections).

MALCOLM JONES III

Malcolm Jones III attended the High School of Art and Design and the Pratt Institute in New York City before making his comics debut in the pages of DC's YOUNG ALL-STARS. In addition to his celebrated work on THE SANDMAN, Jones contributed work to many other titles from both DC and Marvel, including BATMAN, THE QUESTION QUARTERLY, *Dracula* and *Spider-Man*. He died in 1995.

DAVE McKEAN

Dave McKean has illustrated many comics and books, including BATMAN: ARKHAM ASYLUM (written by Grant Morrison), MR. PUNCH, *Signal to Noise*, *Coraline* and the Newbery/Carnegie Medal-winning *The Graveyard Book* (all written by Neil Gaiman), *What's Welsh For Zen* (John Cale), *The Fat Duck Cookbook* (Heston Blumenthal) and the self-penned Harvey/Alph Arte-winning *Cages*. He is currently working with Richard Dawkins on *The Magic of Reality*. He has also created hundreds of CD covers and contributed production designs to two Harry Potter films, as well as writing and directing five short films and two features: *MirrorMask* (with Neil Gaiman) and *Luna*. He lives in England's Kent countryside.

DANIEL VOZZO

Daniel Vozzo was born and raised in Brooklyn, New York. After spending most of the 1980s drumming for several rock-and-roll bands, he landed a job working in DC Comics' production department, where he helped develop a computer coloring department in 1989. He soon began to work freelance, coloring a number of titles for DC's Vertigo line. Currently living in northern New Jersey, Vozzo continues to color comics and is once again playing music. He has also been working on fine-tuning his writing skills. When asked if he thinks he's good at writing, he insists that he has always had very good penmanship.

STEVE OLIFF

A professional colorist for more than 25 years, Steve Oliff has also been a pioneer in bringing comics into the digital age. Beginning in 1989 with his Harvey Award-winning computer coloring work on Katsuhiro Otomo's *Akira* for Marvel, Oliff and his coloring house Olyoptics have revolutionized the field of comic book coloring as well as winning over a dozen industry awards for color excellence on such titles as *Spawn*, BATMAN, THE SANDMAN and THE MAXX.

TODD KLEIN

One of the industry's most versatile and accomplished letterers, Todd Klein has been lettering comics since 1977 and has won numerous Eisner and Harvey Awards for his work. A highlight of his career has been working with Neil Gaiman on nearly all the original issues of THE SANDMAN, as well as BLACK ORCHID, DEATH: THE HIGH COST OF LIVING, DEATH: THE TIME OF YOUR LIFE and THE BOOKS OF MAGIC.

SANDMAN
DREAM COUNTRY:
Afterword

Thank you:

To **Kelley Jones**, for dark shadows and pussycats.

To **Charles Vess**, for Puck.

To **Colleen Doran**, for an empty room full of faces.

To **Malcolm Jones**, for wonderful work – always above and always beyond.

To **Todd Klein**, for great lettering and for spotting the most obscure of references.

To **Steve Oliff**, for all the colors of night.

To **Kim Newman**, for telling me when the Oscar Nominations were announced.

To **Guy Lawley** for finding me a bezoar.

To **Terry Pratchett**, because we've been through Hell together, not to mention America.

To **Tom Peyer**, and **Karen Berger**, for encouragement and help.

To **Dave** and **Clare**, as always.

To **Michael McGarvey** and **Michael Houseknecht**, who never read SANDMAN. Rest in peace, guys.

To the late **Reverend E. Cobham Brewer**, author of, amongst other things, BREWER'S DICTIONARY OF PHRASE AND FABLE. I always keep meaning to dedicate a book to him and I'll probably never get round to it, so this'll have to do.

To the people who've publicly supported SANDMAN, particularly **Mikal Gilmore**, **Tom Whitmore**, **Ed Bryant**, **Steve Erikson** and **Dave Sim**. Thanks guys.

To everyone who's made my life easier and left me alone to write. And to the kids, who don't.

And to you – whatever your dreams may be.

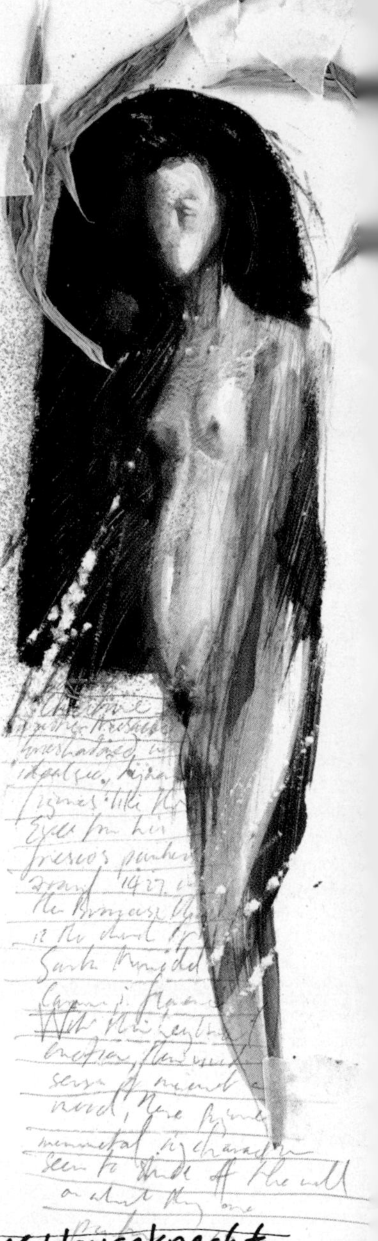

Neil Gaiman. 21 June 1991 Sussex, England